COBBETT'S
ENGLAND

COBBETT'S ENGLAND

A SELECTION FROM THE WRITINGS
OF WILLIAM COBBETT

ILLUSTRATIONS BY JAMES GILLRAY
EDITED WITH AN INTRODUCTION
BY JOHN DERRY

PARKGATE
BOOKS

First published by The Folio Society, 1968
This edition published in 1997 by

Parkgate Books Ltd
London House
Great Eastern Wharf
Parkgate Road
London SW11 4NQ
Great Britain

9 8 7 6 5 4 3 2 1

© for this edition Parkgate Books Ltd, 1997

ISBN 1 85585 535 6

Cover design by Book Creation Services, London

Printed and bound in Finland by WSOY

CONTENTS

ILLUSTRATIONS

This series of eight caricatures by James Gillray entitled 'The Life of William Cobbett,—written by himself' was first published by H. Humphrey, St James's Street, London, on 29 September 1809, and was occasioned by the long article that Cobbett wrote in his own defence in the Political Register *for 17 June, 1809.*

No. 1 Cobbett as a sturdy but ragged boy enticing a dog to maul a cat to the approval of his father and the disapproval of his mother. The caption is based on Cobbett's own account of his youth in *The Life and Adventures of Peter Porcupine*, but is totally different from it.

No. 2 Cobbett as a clumsy recruit marching away from his plough and oxen. His first attempt to join the navy in 1782 failed, but he later succeeded in enlisting in the army after a period as a copyist in Gray's Inn. Fitzgerald was the Colonel of his regiment (the 54th not the 51st) and gave him his discharge in 1791.

No. 3 Cobbett as a young corporal reading the riot act to two officers appreciably older—and smaller—than himself. In the *Political Register*, Cobbett had given an extremely boastful account of his service including the statement that his superiors 'were in every thing excepting mere authority, by inferiors, and ought to have been commanded by me'.

No. 4 Cobbett as Sergeant-Major furtively copying regimental documents behind a bolted door, and being watched apprehensively by Corporal Bestland, 'with the sole exception of myself, the only sober man in the *whole regiment*'. Cobbett had explained how he had secretly gone about collecting material with a view to exposing abuses.

No. 5 Cobbett as accuser, his words taken from a letter he wrote to the Judge-Advocate on 11 March, 1792. In the *Political Register*, Cobbett told how, after his discharge, he had pressed for the court martial of three of his officers, and had also tried to justify himself for leaving England rather than appear before a court to substantiate his charges.

No. 6 The sequel to No. 5 showing an usher summoning Cobbett to appear before the court, while Cobbett himself is sailing away across the river. After three days of waiting, the accused were honourably acquitted, and consideration was given to the possibility of prosecuting Cobbett who 'has availed himself of a judicial process for the conveyance of the most gross slanders'

No. 7 Cobbett in America—the one caricature in the series that does not spring from his apologia in the *Political Register*. Cobbett had been fined $5,000 for a libel on Dr Rush, and although his writings in America were strongly anti-Jacobin, he wrote in the *Political Register* that Napoleon 'has nothing in his dominions that is not manly and dignified, compared to our gang'.

No. 8 Cobbett and the day of reckoning. Some of Cobbett's more virulent attacks had been made against the Peninsular War, in particular the Talavera campaign. Paper money was another of his favourite targets.

INTRODUCTION

William Cobbett is best remembered as the greatest of English political journalists. He was no political thinker, for his mind was too warped by prejudice and too easily moved by emotion for him to attain any real depth or consistency as a theorist. And although for the last few years of his life he represented Oldham in the reformed House of Commons, he was singularly ineffective as a practising politician. It is as a journalist and traveller that he is familiar to posterity. *Rural Rides* is a legendary book, though it is more difficult and less rewarding, especially if read at a sitting, than its reputation suggests. Cobbett's highly personal impression of life in rural England just when the impact of the industrial and agricultural revolutions was being felt has helped to perpetuate the myth that industrialization destroyed a society which was harmonious, happy, and prosperous. The truth was infinitely more complex and far less simple than Cobbett's dramatic fondness for broad contrasts of vivid colour allowed it to appear, but men are fond of romanticizing the past, and his mixture of personal reminiscence and partisan comment still exercises a potent influence over those who, while basking in the affluence which industrialization has made possible, nevertheless hanker for a merry England, a land of robust villagers and noble yeomen, in the days before the dark, satanic mills were reared in England's green and pleasant land.

But *Rural Rides* is only a fragment of Cobbett's literary output. From the time that he found his vocation as a journalist in America during the turbulent 1790s publications poured from his pen. He wrote compulsively and prolixly, never worrying over relevance or repetitiveness. Articles on politics and finance, pieces of autobiography and reminiscence, compendiums of instruction and advice, even textbooks for those wishing to find a wife or improve their command of the English language: this was the myriad jumble of miscellaneous publications which made up Cobbett's lifework. He participated vigorously in most of the major controversies of his time. Parliamentary reform, the evils of paper-money, the problems of the Poor Law, the consequences of enclosing the open fields and building new factories, the abolition of slavery and the plight of English urban workers: all of these received their due share of attention. Often Cobbett was inconsistent. The foe of Parliamentary reform became its doughtiest exponent, the scourge of the Jacobins and the French Revolution became the opponent of the war against Napoleonic France, and the man who had jeered at the Peace of Amiens eventually saw the war as engineered by capitalists and Jews. Cobbett was in the thick of controversy, and he never shrank from using the vilest abuse or appealing to men's baser instincts if he thought it advantageous to do so. To ignore this aspect of Cobbett's career is to misinterpret what he meant in his own time. England was a country in turmoil. Industrial change at home was going ahead at the same period as the greatest war in the country's history was being waged abroad. Political controversy was marked by ferocious extravagance: charges of corruption on the one hand were answered by allegations of treason on the other. Any notion of Cobbett which underplays the vindictive, even cruel, streak in his personality and in his writings is false. The brutality, the indifference to the gentler side of human nature, the unrelenting coarseness, and the determination to win no matter how high the cost, these were as much part of the England of the age as they were of Cobbett's own character. And because he had a journalist's sense of what made good reading, of what was good news, he reflected all the twists and changes of mind and fortune which moulded the contemporary English scene.

Usually described as a Radical, he was a traditionalist above everything else. He looked back, not forward. He even constructed his own fanciful version of English history to give his prejudices a show of learning. Throughout his career he claimed that he was seeking to restore not innovate. He wished merely to remove the pollutions and corruptions which were warping the country's institutions and debasing its manners. Until the end of his life he was preoccupied with restoring traditional values, with winning back for the people of England the rights which they had once enjoyed, but which had been falsely and dishonestly taken from them by unscrupulous men –

usually, according to Cobbett, immigrants, Scotsmen, or Jews – who were seeking to advance their own fortunes at the expense of the common weal. This is the only vestige of consistency which can be discerned in Cobbett's public career. It helps to explain some of the more obvious contradictions in his political development.

He was born in Farnham, Surrey, the son of a farm labourer. The date of his birth is uncertain – he himself usually underestimated his age – but probably he was born in 1763. He had little formal education, and despite his fondness in later life for the delights of rural England, he soon showed a desire to escape from the plough. A visit to Portsmouth gave him the idea of going to sea, but his attempt to join the navy was thwarted. For a time he tried to make a living as a clerk in London, but the longing for adventure and excitement was too great. He joined the army, was shipped off to Canada, and proceeded to make himself a model soldier. He was hard-working, while his superiors were lazy. He made up for his lack of knowledge by reading for himself. He always prided himself on his own initiative, and he never lost a disdain for the formalities of the classroom. He became a sergeant-major, and while he was undeniably also something of a barrack-room lawyer no one could ever claim that he was less than a conscientious, honest, and thoroughly reliable soldier. Hints to the contrary by his enemies always stirred Cobbett's wrath.

But the inefficiencies and prevalent corruption of the army, as well as his own desire to marry and found a home of his own, made him leave the service. He attempted to bring the embezzlement and dishonesty of his officers to the attention of superior authority, naïvely thinking that his efforts to clean up army administration would be welcomed. Instead he found himself unpopular and rejected. He went to France, together with his wife, but, because of the troubles there as a result of the Revolution, he sailed to America. There he made his name as a journalist, under the pseudonym of Peter Porcupine. His chief task was the defence of English honour and the justification of the English Government in the war against Revolutionary France. Cobbett bitterly resented the corruptions of the order, but the French Revolution seemed to him to be a compound of atheism, republicanism, immorality, and shameless robbery. His pamphlets delighted the pro-English faction in the United States and enraged the pro-French. Cobbett never minced words and he found himself involved in a suit for libel. He left America and returned to England. In his own way he was something of a hero. He was fortunate enough to dine with William Pitt on one occasion, and he was taken up by Windham, Burke's old disciple, and a distinguished exponent of the thesis that the war against France had to be fought relentlessly to a finish. When peace was signed at Amiens, Cobbett indignantly denounced the Government for weakness. He claimed that the war would soon be resumed and that the peace merely gave the French the opportunity to prepare for the inevitable second stage. He could finally claim that the re-opening of hostilities against France in 1803 proved him right, but his disillusionment with the English Government was beginning.

He hated the French because their ideas were new, revolutionary, and destructive of customary ways. But the English Government had also flirted with dangerously novel ideas. Chief among these was paper-money. The suspension of cash payments by Pitt during the darkest period of the struggle against the French Republic seemed to Cobbett to be too reminiscent of the reliance which the French themselves had placed on paper-money – the notorious *assignats* – only a few years earlier. He had a peasant's suspicion of paper-money and a countryman's fondness for gold and silver. Gradually he became convinced that most of the ills afflicting the country stemmed from the artificial system of printing paper notes, and behind the reliance upon paper he detected an ominous con-spiracy. He never understood high finance; speculation was another word for robbery; and soon as the conduct of the war languished, and as food shortages, inflation, and spasmodic outbreaks of indust-rial unrest dominated the situation at home, Cobbett saw the war as a contest shot through with duplicity and fraud. The crusade for morality and religion was transformed into a trick by which financiers were growing rich. He read Tom Paine's *Decline and Fall of the English System of Finance*, and his worst fears were confirmed. For the rest of his life he never lost his obsession with paper-money. It became the most obvious and most terrible symptom of the disease which was affecting the whole country. It proved how supine the rulers of the country were, as they allowed themselves to be manipulated by sinister intriguers.

Since the Government was so enmeshed in the toils of speculation and fraud, the only explanation was that it was itself corrupt. Parliament was polluted by the same unhealthy lust for wealth. At first Cobbett contented himself with reviving remedies which had been put forward as long ago as the reign of Queen Anne, and which had often been propounded during the eighteenth century. If Parliament was corrupt, this was because there were too many placemen – that is to say men who held an office of profit under the Crown – in the House of Commons. If the Commons were subservient to the Cabinet, this was because Cabinet ministers sat in the House, and prevented it from carrying out its traditional function of checking the activities of the Government, especially where finance was concerned, and subjecting the actions of the King's ministers to a thorough and genuinely independent scrutiny. If M.P.s accepted favours from the King and his ministers, this was explained by the fact that for seven years they escaped from the necessity of answering for their actions to their constituents. Cobbett therefore urged that all ministers and placemen should be excluded from the Commons, and that there should be a reversion to shorter Parliaments, with elections being held triennially if not annually. All this was familiar to anyone who was acquainted with the demands of English reformers as various as Wilkes, Cartwright, and Wyvill in the 1770s and 1780s. Cobbett had initially denounced parliamentary reform as irrelevant to the key questions of the day, and even when he came to embrace it he did so without any great concern for the extension of the franchise. The elimination of corruption was his first preoccupation, and the purification of public life, in that it meant abolishing paper-money and bringing speculators to account, was his ultimate objective.

But as the years wore on, and as the politicians in power seemed more oblivious of the rightful demands of the people, Cobbett accepted the need for a wider and more uniform franchise. At first he wanted to limit it to all who paid direct taxes; then he came to see that this was itself inadequate. But although by the 1830s he was among the more radical reformers in theory, he always maintained that a moderate measure of reform should be accepted, whoever put it into operation, because it would make it easier for further steps to be taken along the road towards a House of Commons which would be truly representative of the people. For this reason Cobbett threw himself into the agitation on behalf of the Great Reform Bill of 1832, not because he was satisfied with the measure in itself, but because he believed that tactically speaking some reform was better than none. Despite the frequent violence of his language he was eager for reform to take place peacefully, without any disturbance of the country's social life and without threatening the security of property. The caution with which Cobbett became a reformer, the gradualness with which he abjured his former opinions while advocating remedies which he had once denounced as inappropriate, and his evolution as a Radical, are mirrored in the extracts on parliamentary reform printed in this selection. They give a valuable picture of the way many Englishmen, who had once opposed the reform of Parliament as dangerous and revolutionary, came to accept it as necessary and just. The very traditionalism which marked so much of Cobbett's thinking was the best of all arguments for reform in the eyes of many of his contemporaries. When Bentham demonstrated that reform was, above all else, useful, the eventual conversion of enough of the upper and middle classes to carry at least a moderate instalment of cautious reform was certain.

It is, however, worth noting that Cobbett had little notion of what democracy would mean in practice. He did not anticipate the development of party as the answer to the perennial problem of how an executive was to control the legislature, nor did he perceive that politics would become more highly organized and more professional. He had no notion of how a mass electorate could be swayed as surely as a minority one. He believed in the old-fashioned idea of the balance of the Constitution, with King, Lords, and Commons each checking the others, and in the virtues of mixed government. He thought that the Commons should be independent of the Cabinet, and that this was the greatest security for the traditional liberties of the country. He did not understand that any democratic theory of government was bound to elevate the House of Commons at the expense of the other branches of the legislature. He believed that once Parliament was purified taxes would fall. He could not appreciate that a society which was becoming more and more urban would see the growth, not the extinction, of government departments and the extension of governmental activity, and that governments would find themselves assuming new responsibilities over a wide range of human concerns. Cobbett hated the new Poor Law, not only because it deprived the poor of their traditional right to outdoor relief, but because it represented a new form of government action and a more systematic type of bureaucratic organization. He hated Edwin Chadwick and the administrators, but while they typified the future he represented the past.

Yet, despite his limitations, Cobbett bridged the gulf between the old-fashioned Radicalism of the eighteenth century – typified by John Wilkes, the shrewd rake, and Christopher Wyvill, the absentee clergyman – which was preoccupied with a concern for property and low taxation, and the new Radicalism which sought to win new privileges for the mass of the people: not yet all of the people, but at least the more responsible and reliable of the skilled artisans. Cobbett's *Political Register* carried on where Tom Paine had left off, but whereas the *Rights of Man* became the Bible of English Radicalism, Cobbett's 'twopenny trash' came out week by week, month by month, year by year, humiliating established authority by its constant flow of savage vilification, shrewd criticism, and mordant satire. Cobbett defied attempts to destroy the Radical Press by levying high stamp duties. Finally, in order to escape what he believed was imminent imprisonment, he fled to America, where he stayed for two years, continuing his career as a journalist all the while. He boasted of resorting to a long arm to combat corruption, but many of his fellow Radicals, who remembered his imprisonment in 1810 after being found guilty of publishing a treasonable libel in denouncing a case of flogging in the militia, were unconvinced by his pretence of self-justification. They thought him a coward, and though he gained some merit in their eyes when he returned to England in 1819, bringing with him the bones of Tom Paine as signs of his sincere contrition towards the old enemy of his Tory days, he was always sensitive towards charges that he had lost his nerve. It was much easier to defy Liverpool and Sidmouth in the remote security and comfort of the United States than to challenge them at home, where the laws of libel, sedition, and blasphemy often trapped the unsuspecting or overhasty publicist of known Radical views.

Cobbett did not like the new England, of towns and factories and high finance, which was destroying the England he knew, the old England of villages and farms and domestic industries and honest money. He hated towns and London above all others. To him London was not a glittering metropolis, the gay and splendid centre of the nation's political and commercial life. It was 'the Great Wen', a vile and nauseating sore which was disfiguring the face of the country with its ugliness. More and more Englishmen were going to live in towns, and to Cobbett this implied a deterioration in the national character. In towns men became depraved and degenerate. As their bodies became tainted with disease, so their minds became perverted and corrupt. Their children languished far from the countryside and the healthy life of the open air. This was all part of the great speculators' plot, for while honesty withered and died in the anonymity of great towns, fraud and greed flourished. Even the railways were damned by Cobbett, for they made it easier for men to live in towns, assisting the tendency for the population to be piled up in great heaps. Cobbett never asked why country labourers preferred to go off to work in the mills and factories of the new towns. He forgot how dreary and wearisome their lives already were in the villages and on the farms. The factory meant long hours, but it usually meant higher pay. If the old habits of casual labour had provided a greater measure of freedom, they had also brought days of intense and poorly remunerated toil and a nagging fear of what the future might bring. Life in the towns was inferior to life in the country, in so far as freedom and the benefits of a received social order were concerned, but Cobbett forgot that there was gain as well as loss. The skilled craftsman was threatened by new inventions and the achievements of the factories, but Cobbett could only lament what was happening. He had no answer to the problems of industry. Because he did not understand what was happening to the England of his youth he could only fall back on dark allegations of conspiracy as the explanation of the drift to the towns.

Cobbett despised men like Malthus, Ricardo, and Robert Owen, who, in their different ways, were trying to grapple with the facts of economic life. He hated economists and Scotch 'feelosophers', who produced theories to justify everything that his soul revolted against. He dismissed suggestions that there were dangers in the over-rapid growth of population, and he was too willing to content himself with the accusation that unpleasant theories about birth-rates and wage-rates merely demonstrated the wickedness of their exponents. He had little sympathy with contemporary attempts to understand the nature of industrial society. But even here he was hardly consistent. He once confessed that he did not like to see machines lest this should help him to understand them, yet it would be misleading to suggest that he was by temperament a machine-breaker. He sensed that the machines themselves were potentially valuable, and he doubted whether a bout of destruction would restore the good old days. But he nevertheless easily slipped into offering paper-money and what he called the Pitt System of Finance as the explanation for every ill which was harming the nation.

His attitudes towards schemes of education were as baffling. He had no doubt that the best sort of education was that which he himself had enjoyed and which he strove to give to his sons. He distrusted mere 'book-learning' and he was suspicious of plans for the education of the urban poor. Teaching people to read and write could do them harm. Much of what they would read would be vapid and useless, possibly even corrupting. A measure of education would make them discontented with their lot. It was no good educating people who would then be useless for all forms of employment, despising what was available for them to do, and yet utterly unfitted for anything else. Cobbett did not exclude the utility of schools altogether, but at best they were concessions to the evil conditions which existed in towns. Education was more than the process of acquiring a certain amount of book-learning. It ought to prepare people for life, and here a knowledge of the skills which would be of practical help to the individual was of more value and more relevance than an acquaintance with literary affectations. Ignorance was as common among intellectuals as among ploughmen, and the ability to do a job well and without fuss was more important than having one's head filled with pretentious nonsense. Much of what Cobbett said was true, in so far as a mere ability to read and write was not as significant educationally as many of his contemporaries made out. But he was deficient in indicating what the positive content of education should be, and what he would put in the place of the schools he so disliked. All he could do was to say that book-learning was of some value, but he preferred to pride himself on the way in which he taught his own sons rather than to get to grips with the complicated problems of mass education in an urban society.

He was bitterly conscious of the horrors of the factories and he was eager to denounce the regulations with which employers sought to discipline their employees. He became impatient with men whose sense of priorities was different from his own. When William Wilberforce campaigned for the abolition of slavery in the British colonies Cobbett was indignant. He contrasted Wilberforce's indifference to the fate of the English factory workers with his sensitivity towards the welfare of negroes in the West Indies. Here Cobbett's anger led him to exaggerate the alleged comforts enjoyed by African slaves on the West Indian plantations, and his contempt for the negro added a raw, cruel edge to his attack on Wilberforce. He could not appreciate the virtues or significance of Wilberforce's concern for the emancipation of the slaves, and, as always, Cobbett compensated for weaknesses in argument by heaping abuse upon the head of his antagonist.

He loathed Evangelicals, Methodists, Quakers, Dissenters, and Jews. No picture of Cobbett would be complete which did not reflect his racial and religious prejudices. Most of these are repugnant to modern taste, but, however reprehensible, they added colour and vigour to Cobbett's denunciation of the evils, real or imagined, of his time. His own religious position comprised a formal and non-doctrinaire Anglicanism. His attitude towards the Catholic Church was mixed. He detested dogma and pomp, was dubious about ritualistic ceremony, and distrusted the Pope as a foreigner, but he had a regard for the Catholic faith because it had been the faith of all Englishmen before the Reformation. He idealized the Middle Ages, and in his willingness to glamorize the period before Henry VIII broke with Rome Cobbett shared an unlikely affinity with the Anglo-Catholics of the 1840s and with political novelists like the young Disraeli. His *History of the Protestant Reformation* gave his assorted prejudices ample expression, but his religious predilections recur throughout his work, as the extracts I have chosen to print demonstrate.

Cobbett was incapable of discriminating between the important and the trivial. Often he denounced venial sins with as much energy as major errors. His detestation of contemporary fashions, his dislike of men who shaved with hot water and a mirror, or who stayed in bed in the morning, and his assertion that tea and coffee were corrupting the morals of the young, are only the more ludicrous instances of his tendency to bewail the age as one which was especially debauched. He was something of a prig, and in his own way rather a prude. He prided himself on his education, his career in the army, the way in which he had chosen a wife, and the style in which he brought up his family. He made no secret of the fact that if all men had been like himself the world would have been a better and a happier place. His *Advice to Young Men* is a richly entertaining collection of his prudential warnings on a variety of topics. The sections I have chosen will, I hope, convey something of Cobbett's bluff charm, as well as his self-righteousness. Much of what he said to young people is typical of the attitude of the middle-aged towards those who are younger than themselves. It may not be without interest to note the parallels between the way in which Cobbett shook his head over the sins of youth, and the jeremiads which are so commonly recited over the younger generation in our own day. In moments like these the years fall away, and we recognize in Cobbett a man very much like ourselves, however different our circumstances and however much we differ from him in upbringing and attitude.

Cobbett's writings abound in autobiographical references. Many of these passages constitute some of his best writing, and I have therefore followed the example of the anonymous *Life* of 1835, and, more recently, of W. Reitzel, in his *Autobiography of William Cobbett*, first published under the title *Progress of a Ploughboy to a Seat in Parliament*, in assembling many of these passages so as to form something like a consecutive whole. I have felt that it is better to allow Cobbett to speak for himself whenever possible, and in doing so I believe that the reader will find it easier to form his own impression of the man and of his age. I have printed several of Cobbett's attacks on eminent contemporaries, so that the flavour of his invective can be appreciated at first hand. At the same time, I have thought it right to conclude this selection with a fairly extensive series of extracts from *Rural Rides*. I have sought to give Cobbett's reactions to a diverse number of towns and counties in England, over a number of years, but throughout I have tried to avoid printing too many short snippets. Though Cobbett can be irritatingly repetitive and exasperatingly discursive, his unique style is best appreciated in something like a coherent sequence.

Of course, the reader must be on his guard. Cobbett was never objective. The French were never as bad as he originally painted them in his days as Peter Porcupine, just as Pitt was never a dupe of the Jewish financiers in the way that Cobbett suggests. As for the people of England, the age was a hard age, judged by the standards which we take for granted. But the general movement, nevertheless, was upwards, so far as the standard of living was concerned. Englishmen were eating better and living longer. More of their children were surviving the hazards of childhood. Even the enclosures, conventionally regarded as the cause of unemployment and depopulation, assisted the agriculturalist to farm more efficiently, and so far as those labourers who remained on the land were concerned the enclosures probably provided them with more secure jobs than previously. There was no period when agricultural labourers were universally happy or contented and the sins which Cobbett identified with the new era were often the same as those which had existed in the allegedly good old days. Child labour and the exploitation of women, long hours and low wages, the fear of an old age lived out in destitution, were familiar evils. Perhaps the factories made them more obvious and less tolerable. Before men could tackle these problems, before they could humanize society, they had to subject their own attitudes of mind to a fundamental re-examination. They had to seek for new solutions to problems which had reached a new scale. This Cobbett was incapable of doing. He was no prophet for a new England. He was, rather, the apologist for old England, and, like most men who sing the praises of the past, the England he loved so dearly was as much the creation of his own imagination as it was part of historical reality. Cobbett's England was a subjective entity, the product of his own experience of life, his own psychology, and his own inner compulsions. Cobbett tells us something about the England of his time, of how it was peopled and with what sort of men; but Cobbett, the restless controversialist, tells us even more about himself. He is the epitome of those who take refuge in the past when they find the present difficult and perplexing and impossible to comprehend, believing as they do that only their own limited experience of life has a lasting validity and an abiding worth.

COBBETT'S
ENGLAND

COBBETT THE MAN

All that I can boast of in my birth is that I was born in old England. With respect to my ancestors, I shall go no further back than my grandfather, and for this very plain reason, that I never heard talk of any prior to him. He was a day-labourer, and I have heard my father say, that he worked for one farmer from the day of his marriage to that of his death, upwards of forty years. He died before I was born, but I have often slept beneath the same roof that had sheltered him, and where his widow dwelt for seven years after his death. It was a little thatched cottage with a garden before the door. It had but two windows: a damson tree shaded one, and a clump of filberts the other. Here I and my brothers went every Christmas and Whitsuntide, to spend a week or two, and torment the poor old woman with our noise and dilapidations. She used to give us milk and bread for breakfast, an apple pudding for our dinner, and a piece of bread and cheese for supper. Her fire was made of turf cut from the neighbouring heath and her evening light was a rush dipped in grease.

My father, from the poverty of his parents, had received no very brilliant education; he was, however, learned for a man in his rank of life. When a little boy, he drove the plough for two pence a day and these his earnings were appropriated to the expenses of an evening school. What a village schoolmaster could be expected to teach he had learnt, and had besides considerably improved himself in several branches of the mathematics. He understood land-surveying well, and was often chosen to draw the plans of disputed territory; in short, he had the reputation of possessing experience and understanding, which never fails in England to give a man in a country place some little weight with his neighbours. He was honest, industrious, and frugal; it was not, therefore, wonderful that he should be situated in a good farm, and happy in a wife of his own rank, like him, beloved and respected.

I was born in the month of March, 1766 [1763]: the exact age of my brothers I have forgotten, but I remember having heard my mother say, that there was but three years and three-quarters difference between the age of the eldest and that of the youngest.

I do not remember the time when I did not earn my living. My first occupation was driving the small birds from the turnip seed and the rooks from the peas. When I trudged afield, with my wooden bottle and my satchel over my shoulders, I was hardly able to climb the gates and stiles, and, at the close of day, to reach home was a task of infinite labour. My next employment was weeding wheat, and leading a single horse at harrowing barley. Hoeing peas followed, and hence I arrived at the honour of joining the reapers in harvest, driving the team and holding the plough. We were all of us strong and laborious, and my father used to boast, that he had four boys, the eldest of whom was but fifteen years old, who did as much work as any three men in the parish of Farnham. Honest pride and happy days!

I have some faint recollection of going to school to an old woman who, I believe, did not succeed in teaching me my letters. In the winter evenings my father taught me to read and write, and gave me a pretty tolerable knowledge of arithmetic. Grammar he did not perfectly understand himself, and therefore his endeavours to teach that necessarily failed; for, though he thought he understood it, and though he made us get the rules by heart, we learnt nothing at all of the principles.

As to politics, we were like the rest of the country people in England; that is to say we neither knew nor thought anything about the matter. The shouts of victory or the murmur at a defeat would now and then break in upon our tranquillity for a moment; but I do not remember ever having seen a newspaper in the house, and most certainly that privation did not render us less free, happy or industrious.

After, however, the American War had continued for some time, and the cause and nature of it began to be understood, or rather misunderstood, by the lower classes of people in England, we became a little better acquainted with subjects of this kind. My father was a partisan of the Americans: he used frequently to dispute on the subject with the gardener of a nobleman who lived near us. This was generally done with good humour, over a pot of our best ale; yet the disputants sometimes grew warm, and gave way to language that could not fail to attract our attention. My father was worsted without a doubt, as he had for antagonist, a shrewd and sensible old Scotchman, far his superior in political knowledge; but he pleaded before a partial audience: we thought there was but one wise man in the world, and that one was our father.

[*Life and Adventures of Peter Porcupine*, PHILADELPHIA, 1796]

At eleven years of age* my employment was clipping of box-edgings and weeding beds of flowers in the garden of the Bishop of Winchester, at the Castle of Farnham. I had always been fond of beautiful gardens; and a gardener who had just come from the King's gardens at Kew gave me such a description of them as made me instantly resolve to work in these gardens. The next morning, without saying a word to anybody, off I set, with no clothes, except those upon my back, and thirteen halfpence in my pocket. I found that I must go to Richmond, and I accordingly went on, from place to place, inquiring my way thither. A long day (it was in June) brought me to Richmond in the afternoon. Two pennyworth of bread and cheese and a pennyworth of small beer, which I had on the road, and one halfpenny that I had lost somehow or other, left three pence in my pocket. With this for my whole fortune, I was trudging through Richmond in my blue smock-frock and my red garters tied under my knees, when, staring about me, my eye fell upon a little book in a bookseller's window: *Tale of a Tub*; price 3d. The title was so odd that my curiosity was excited. I had the 3d., but, then, I could have no supper. In I went and got the little book, which I was so impatient to read that I got over into a field, at the upper corner of Kew Gardens, where there stood a haystack. On the shady side of this I sat down to read. The book was so different from anything that I had ever read before: it was something so new to my mind, that, though I could not at all understand some of it, it delighted me beyond description; and it produced what I have always considered a sort of birth of intellect. I read on till it was dark, without any thought about supper or bed. When I could see no longer, I put my little book in my pocket, and tumbled down by the side of the stack, where I slept till the birds in Kew Garden awaked me in the morning; when off I started

* Since Cobbett habitually underestimated his age, he was probably about fourteen years old at the time of this incident.

to Kew, reading my little book. The singularity of my dress, the simplicity of my manner, my confident and lively air, induced the gardener, who was a Scotchman, I remember, to give me victuals, find me lodging, and set me to work . . . The gardener, seeing me fond of books, lent me some gardening books to read but these I could not relish after my Tale of a Tub, which I carried about with me wherever I went, and when I, at about twenty years old, lost it in a box that fell overboard in the Bay of Funday in North America, the loss gave me greater pain than I have ever felt at losing thousands of pounds.

[*Political Register* XXXVI, 19 FEBRUARY 1820]

Towards the autumn of 1782 I went to visit a relation who lived in the neighbourhood of Portsmouth. From the top of Portsmouth I, for the first time, beheld the sea, and no sooner did I behold it than I wished to be a sailor. I could never account for this sudden impulse, nor can I now. Almost all English boys feel the same inclination: it would seem that, like ducks, instinct leads them to rush on the bosom of the water.

But it was not the sea alone that I saw: the grand fleet was riding at anchor at Spithead. I had heard of the wooden walls of Old England: I had formed my idea of a ship and of a fleet; but what I now beheld so far surpassed what I had been able to form a conception of that I stood lost between astonishment and admiration. I had heard talk of the glorious deeds of our admirals and sailors, of the defeat of the Spanish Armada, and of those memorable combats that good and true Englishmen never fail to relate to their children about a hundred times a year. The brave Rodney's victories over our natural enemies, the French and the Spaniards, had long been the theme of our praise and the burden of our songs. The sight of the fleet brought all these into my mind; in confused order, it is true, but with irresistible force. My heart was inflated with national pride. The sailors were my countrymen, the fleet belonged to my country, and surely I had my part in it, and in all its honours; yet these honours I had not earned; I took to myself a sort of reproach for possessing what I had no right to, and resolved to have a just claim by sharing in the hardships and dangers.

I arrived at my uncle's late in the evening, with my mind full of my seafaring project. Though I had walked thirty miles during the day, and consequently was well wearied, I slept not a moment. It was no sooner daylight than I arose and walked down toward the old castle on the beach at Spithead. For a sixpence given to an invalid I got permission to go upon the battlements; here I had a closer view of the fleet, and at every look my impatience to be on board increased. In short I went from the castle to Portsmouth, got into a boat, and was in a few minutes on board the *Pegasus* man-of-war, commanded by the Right Honourable George Berkley, brother to the Earl of Berkley.

The Captain had more compassion than is generally met with in a man of his profession: he represented to me the toils I must undergo, and the punishment that the least disobedience or neglect would subject me to. He persuaded me to return home, and I remember he concluded his advice with telling me that it was better to be led to church in a halter to be tied to a girl that I did not like, than to be tied to the gang-way, or, as the sailors call it, married to Miss Roper. From the conclusion of this wholesome counsel I perceived that the Captain thought I had eloped on account of a bastard. I blushed, and that confirmed him in his opinion.

I in vain attempted to convince Captain Berkley, that choice alone led me to the sea; he sent me on shore, and I at last quitted Portsmouth; but not before I had applied to the Port Admiral, Evans, to get my name enrolled among those who were destined for the service. I was, in some sort, obliged to acquaint the Admiral with what had passed on board the *Pegasus*, in consequence of which my request was refused, and I happily escaped, sorely against my will, from the most toilsome and perilous profession in the world.

I returned once more to the plough, but I was spoiled for a farmer. I had, before my Portsmouth adventure, never known any other ambition than that of surpassing my brothers in the different labours of the field; but it was quite otherwise now; I sighed for a sight of the world; the little island of Britain seemed too small a compass for me. The things in which I had taken the most delight were neglected; the singing of the birds grew insipid, and the heart-cheering cry of the hounds, after which I formerly used to fly from my work, was heard with the most torpid indifference. Still, however, I remained at home till the following spring, when I quitted it for-ever.

It was on the sixth of May, 1783, that I, like Don Quixote, sallied forth to seek adventures. I was dressed in my holiday clothes, in order to accompany two or three lasses to Guildford Fair. They were to assemble at a house about three miles from my home, where I was to attend them; but unfortunately for me I had to cross the London turnpike road. The stage-coach had just turned the summit of a hill, and was rattling down towards me at a merry rate. The notion of going to London never entered my mind till this very moment, yet the step was completely determined on, before the coach came to the spot where I stood.

It was by mere accident that I had money enough to defray the expenses of this day. Being rigged out for the fair, I had three or four crown and half-crown pieces (which most certainly I did not intend to spend) besides a few shillings and halfpence. This my little all, which I had been years in amassing, wilted away like snow before the sun, when touched by the fingers of the inn-keepers and their waiters. In short, when I arrived at Ludgate Hill, and had paid my fare, I had but about half a crown in my pocket.

By a commencement of that good luck, which has attended me in all the situations in which fortune has placed me, I was preserved from ruin. A gentleman, who was one of the passengers in the stage, fell into conversation with me at dinner, and he soon learnt that I was going I knew not whither nor for what. This gentleman was a hop-merchant in the borough of Southwark, and, upon closer inquiry, it appeared that he had often dealt with my father at Weyhill. He knew the danger I was in; he was himself a parent, and he felt for my parents. His house became my home, he wrote to my father, and endeavoured to prevail upon me to obey his orders, which were to return immediately home. I am ashamed to say that I was disobedient. Willingly would I have returned, but pride would not suffer me to do it. I feared the scoffs of my acquaintances more than the real evils that threatened me.

My generous preserver, finding my obstinacy not to be overcome, began to look out for an employment for me, when an acquaintance of his, an attorney, called in to see him. He related my adventure to this gentleman, whose name was Holland, and how, happening to want an understrapping quill driver, did me the honour to take me into his service, and the next day saw me perched upon a great high stool, in an obscure chamber in Gray's Inn, endeavouring to decipher the crabbed thoughts of my employer . . .

No part of my life has been totally unattended with pleasure, except the eight or nine months I passed in Gray's Inn. The office (for so the dungeon where I wrote was called) was so dark, that, on cloudy days, we were obliged to burn candle. I worked like a galley-slave from five in the morning till eight or nine at night, and sometimes all night long. I never quitted this gloomy recess except on Sundays, when I usually took a walk to St James's Park, to feast my eyes with the sight of the trees, the grass, and the water. In one of these walks I happened to cast my eye on an advertisement, inviting all loyal young men, who had a mind to gain riches and glory, to repair to a certain rendezvous, where they might enter into His Majesty's Marine Service, and have the peculiar happiness and honour of being enrolled in the Chatham division. I was not ignorant enough to be the dupe of this morsel of military bombast; but a change was what I wanted; besides, I knew that marines went to sea, and my desire to be on that element had rather increased than diminished by my being penned up in London. In short, I resolved to join this glorious corps; and, to avoid all possibility of being discovered by my friends, I went down to Chatham, and enlisted in the marines as I thought, but the next morning I found myself before a Captain of a marching regiment. There was no retreating: I had taken a shilling to drink His Majesty's health, and his further bounty was ready for my reception.

When I told the Captain that I thought myself engaged in the marines 'By Jasas, my lad,' said he, 'and you have had a narrow escape.' He told me that the regiment into which I had been so happy as to enlist was one of the oldest and boldest in the whole army, and that it was at that time serving in that fine, flourishing and plentiful country, Nova Scotia. He dwelt long on the beauties and riches of this terrestrial paradise, and dismissed me, perfectly enchanted with the prospect of a voyage thither. I enlisted in 1784, and, as peace had then taken place, no great haste was made to send recruits off to their regiments.

My leisure time was spent, not in the dissipations common to such a way of life, but in reading and study. In the course of this year I learnt more than I had ever done before. I subscribed to a circulating library at Brompton, the greatest part of the books in which I read more than once over. The library was not very considerable, it is true, nor in my reading was I directed by any degree of taste or choice. Novels, plays, history, poetry, all were read, and nearly with equal avidity.

Such a course of reading could be attended with but little profit: it was skimming over the surface of everything. One branch of learning, however, I went to the bottom with, and that the most essential, too, the grammar of my mother tongue. I had experienced the want of knowledge of grammar during my stay with Mr Holland; but it is very probable that I never should have thought of encountering the study of it, had not accident placed me under a man whose friendship extended beyond his interest. Writing a fair hand procured me the honour of being copyist to Colonel Debieg, the commandant of the garrison . . . The Colonel saw my deficiency, and strongly recommended study. He enforced his advice with a sort of injunction, and with a promise of reward in case of success . . .

[*Life and Adventures of Peter Porcupine*, 1796]

I learned grammar when I was a private soldier on the pay of six-pence a day. The edge of my berth, or that of the guard-bed, was my seat to study in; my knapsack was my book-case; a bit of board, lying in my lap, was my writing-table; and the task did not demand anything like a year of my life. I had no money to purchase candle or oil; in winter-time it was rarely that I could get any evening-light but that of the fire, and only my turn even of that. And if I, under such circumstances, and without parent or friend to advise or encourage me, accomplished this undertaking, what excuse can there be for any youth, however poor, however pressed with business, or however circumstanced as to room or other conveniences? To buy a pen or a sheet of paper I was compelled to forgo some portion of food, though in a state of half-starvation; I had no moment of time that I could call my own; and I had to read and to write amidst the talking, laughing, singing, whistling and brawling of at least half a score of the most thoughtless of men, and that, too, in the hours of their freedom from all control. Think not lightly of the farthing that I had to give, now and then, for ink, pen, and paper! That farthing was, alas! a great sum to me! I was as tall as I am now; I had great health and great exercise. The whole of the money, not expended for us at market, was two-pence a week for each man. I remember, and well I may! that upon one occasion I, after all absolutely necessary expenses, had, on a Friday, made shift to have a halfpenny in reserve, which I had destined for the purchase of a red herring in the morning; but, when I pulled off my clothes at night, so hungry then as to be hardly able to endure life, I found that I had lost my half-penny! I buried my head under the miserable sheet and rug, and cried like a child!

[*Advice to Young Men*, 1829]

Though it was a considerable time before I fully comprehended all that I read, still I read and studied with such unremitted attention, that, at last, I could write without falling into any very gross errors. The pains I took cannot be described: I wrote the whole grammar out two or three times; I got it by heart. I repeated it every morning and every evening, and, when on guard, I imposed on myself the task of saying it all over once every time I was posted sentinel. To this exercise of my memory I ascribe the retentiveness of which I have since found it capable, and to the success with which it was attended, I ascribe the perseverance that has led to the acquirement of the little learning of which I am master.

I was soon raised to the rank of Corporal, a rank, which, however contemptible it may appear in some people's eyes, brought me in a clear twopence per diem, and put a very clever worsted knot upon my shoulder, too. As promotion began to dawn, I grew impatient to get to my regiment, where I expected soon to bask under the rays of royal favour. The happy days of departure at last came: we set sail from Gravesend, and, after a short and pleasant passage, arrived at Halifax in Nova Scotia.

When I first beheld the barren, not to say hideous, rocks at the entrance of the harbour, I began to fear that the master of the vessel had mistaken his way; for I could perceive nothing of that fertility that my good recruiting captain had dwelt on with so much delight. Nova Scotia had no other charm for me than that of novelty. Everything I saw was new: bogs, rocks, and mosquitoes and bull-frogs . . . We staid but a few weeks in Nova Scotia, being ordered to St Johns in the Province of New Brunswick. Here, and at other places in the same province, we remained till the month of September, 1791, when the regiment was relieved and sent home.

[*Life and Adventures of Peter Porcupine*, 1796]

While I was corporal I was made clerk to the regiment. In a very short time, the whole of the business in that way fell into my hands; and, at the end of about a year, neither adjutant, paymaster, or quarter-master, could move an inch without my assistance. The accounts and letters of the paymaster went through my hands; or, rather, I was the maker of them. All the returns, reports, and other official papers were of my drawing up. Then I became Sergeant-Major to the regiment, which brought me in close contact at every hour with the whole of the epaulet gentry, whose profound and surprising ignorance I discovered in a twinkling.

[*Political Register* XV, 17 JUNE 1809, also ibid. XXXII, 6 DECEMBER 1817]

In early life I contracted the blessed habit of husbanding well my time. To this, more than to any other thing, I owed my very extraordinary promotion in the army. I was always ready: if I had to mount guard at ten, I was ready at nine: never did any man, or any thing, wait one moment for me. Being, at an age under twenty years,* raised from Corporal to Sergeant Major at once, over the heads of thirty sergeants, I naturally should have been an object of envy and hatred; but this habit of early rising and of rigid adherence to the precepts I have given you† really subdued these passions; because every one felt that what I did he had never done, and never could do. Before my promotion, a clerk was wanted to make out the morning report of the regiment. I rendered the clerk unnecessary; and, long before any other man was dressed for the parade, my work for the morning was all done, and I myself was on the parade, walking, in fine weather, for an hour perhaps. My custom was this: to get up, in summer, at day-light, and in winter at four o'clock; shave, dress, even to the putting of my sword-belt over my shoulder, and having my sword lying on the table before me, ready to hang by my side. Then I ate a bit of cheese, or pork, and bread. Then I prepared my report, which was filled up as fast as the companies brought me in the materials. After this I had an hour or two to read, before the time came for any duty out of doors, unless when the regiment or part of it went out to exercise in the morning. When this was the case, and the matter was left to me, I always had it on the ground in such time as that the bayonets glistened in the rising sun, a sight which gave me delight, of which I often think, but which I should in vain endeavour to describe. If the officers were to go out, eight or ten o'clock was the hour, sweating the men in the heat of the day, breaking in upon the time for cooking their dinner, putting all things out of order and all men out of humour. When I was commander, the men had a long day of leisure before them: they could ramble into the town or into the

---

* Again it was worth remembering that Cobbett usually underestimated his age: he was about twenty-two at this period.

† i.e. simplicity in dress, temperance in food and drink, the avoidance of gambling, civility without servility, and husbanding one's time.

woods; go to get raspberries, to catch birds, to catch fish, or to pursue any other recreation, and such of them as chose, and were qualified, to work at their trades. So that here, arising solely from the early habits of one very young man, were pleasant and happy days given to hundreds.

[*Advice to Young Men*, 1829]

It is the custom in regiments to give out orders every day from the officer commanding. These are written by the Adjutant, to whom the Sergeant-Major is a sort of deputy. The man whom I had to do with was a keen fellow, but wholly illiterate. The orders, which he wrote, most cruelly murdered our mother-tongue. But, in his absence, or during a severe drunken fit, it fell to my lot to write orders. As we both wrote in the same book he used to look at these. He saw commas, semi-colons, colons, full points, and paragraphs. The questions he used to put to me, in an obscure sort of way, in order to know why I made these divisions, and yet, at the same time, his attempts to disguise his object, have made me laugh a thousand times. He, at last, fell upon this device: he made me write, while he pretended to dictate! Imagine to yourself, me sitting, pen in hand, to put upon paper the precious offspring of the mind of this stupid curmudgeon! But here a greater difficulty than any former arose. He that could not write good grammar could not, of course, dictate good grammar. Out would come some gross error, such as I was ashamed to see in my handwriting. I would stop; suggest another arrangement; but, this I was at first obliged to do in a very indirect and delicate manner. But this course could not continue long; and he put an end to it in this way; he used to tell me his story, and leave me to put it upon paper; and this we continued to the end of our connection.

[*Political Register* XXXII, 6 DECEMBER 1817]

When I first saw my wife, she was thirteen years old, and I was within a month of twenty-one. She was the daughter of a Sergeant of artillery, and I was the Sergeant-Major of a regiment of foot, both stationed in forts near the city of St John, in the Province of New Brunswick. I sat in the same room with her for about an hour, in company with others, and I made up my mind that she was the very girl for me. That I thought her beautiful is certain, for that I had always said should be an indispensable qualification; but I saw in her what I deemed marks of that sobriety of conduct . . . which has been by far the greatest blessing of my life. It was now dead of winter, and, of course the snow several feet deep on the ground, and the weather piercing cold. It was my habit, when I had done my morning's writing, to go out at break of day to take a walk on a hill at the foot of which our barracks lay. In about three mornings after I had first seen her, I had, by an invitation to breakfast with me, got up two young men to join me in my walk; and our road lay by the house of her father and mother. It was hardly light, but she was out on the snow, scrubbing out a washing-tub. 'That's the girl for me,' said I, when we had got out of her hearing. One of these young men came to England soon afterwards; and he, who keeps an inn at Yorkshire, came over to Preston at the time of the election, to verify whether I were the same man. When he found that I was he appeared surprised; but what was his surprise, when I told him that those tall young men, whom he saw around me, were the sons of that pretty little girl that he and I saw scrubbing out the washing-tub on the snow in New Brunswick at day-break in the morning!

From the day that I first spoke to her, I never had a thought of her ever being the wife of any other man, more than I had a thought of her being transformed into a chest of drawers; and I formed my resolution at once, to marry her as soon as we could get permission, and to get out of the army as soon as I could. So that this matter was, at once, settled as firmly as if written in the book of fate. At the end of about six months, my regiment, and I along with it, were removed to Frederickton, a distance of a hundred miles, up the river of St John; and, which was worse, the artillery were expected to go off to England a year or two before our regiment! The artillery went, and she along with them; and now it was that I acted a part becoming a real and sensible lover. I was aware that, when she got to that gay place Woolwich, the house of her father and mother, necessarily visited by numerous persons not the most select, might become unpleasant to her, and I did not like, besides, that she should continue to work hard. I had saved a hundred and fifty guineas, the earnings of my early hours, in writing for the paymaster, the quartermaster, and others, in addition to the savings of my own pay. I sent her all my money, before she sailed; and wrote to her to beg of her, if she found her home uncomfortable, to hire a lodging with respectable people; and, at any rate, not to spare the money, by any means, but to buy herself good clothes, and to live without hard work, until I arrived in England; and I, in order to induce her to lay out the money, told her that I should get plenty more before I came home.

As the malignity of the devil would have it, we were kept abroad two years longer than our time, Mr Pitt (England not being so tame then as she is now) having knocked up a dust with Spain about Nootka Sound.* Oh, how I cursed Nootka Sound, and poor bawling Pitt, too, I am afraid! At the end of four years, however, home I came; landed at Portsmouth, and got my discharge from the army by the great kindness of poor Lord Edward Fitzgerald, who was then the Major of my regiment. I found my little girl a servant of all work (and hard work it was), at five pounds a year, in the house of a Captain Brisac; and, without hardly saying a word about the matter, she put into my hands the whole of my hundred and fifty guineas unbroken!

Need I tell the reader what my feelings were? Need I tell kind-hearted English parents what effect this anecdote must have produced on the minds of our children? Need I attempt to describe what effect this example ought to have on every young woman who shall do me the honour to read this book? Admiration of her conduct, and self-gratulation on this indubitable proof of the soundness of my own judgement, were now added to my love of her beautiful person.

[*Advice to Young Men*, 1829]

The object of my quitting the army, to which I was attached, was to bring certain officers to justice for having, in various ways, wronged both the public and the soldier. If my officers had been men of manifest superiority of mind, I should, perhaps, not have soon conceived the project of bringing them, or some of them at least, to shame and punishment for the divers flagrant breaches of the law, committed by them. The circumstances which first disgusted me, and that finally made me resolve to tear myself from a service, to which my whole mind and heart were devoted, was, the abuses, the shocking abuses as to money matters, the peculation, in short, which I witnessed, and which I had, in vain, endeavoured to correct. The project was conceived so early as the year 1787, when an affair happened, that first gave me a full insight into regimental justice. It was shortly this: that the Quarter-Master, who had the issuing of the men's provisions to them, kept about a fourth part of it to himself. This, the old sergeants told me, had been the case for many years;

* In 1790 Pitt successfully asserted the right of English tradesmen to settle and do business in Nootka Sound, Vancouver Island, in defiance of the obsolete Spanish claim to the Pacific coastline of Canada.

and they were quite astonished and terrified at the idea of my complaining of it. This I did, however; but the reception I met with convinced me that I must never make another complaint, till I got safe to
England, and safe out of the reach of that most curious of courts, a
court-martial.

From this time forward I began to collect materials for an exposure, upon my return to England. I had ample opportunities for
this, being the keeper of all the books of every sort, in the regiment,
and knowing the whole of its affairs better than any other man. But,
the winter previous to our return to England, I thought it necessary
to make extracts from the books, lest the books themselves should
be destroyed. In order to be able to prove that these extracts were
correct it was necessary that I should have a witness as to their being
true copies. This was a very ticklish point. One foolish step here
could have sent me down to the ranks with a pair of bloody shoulders.
I hesitated many months. At one time I had given the thing up. I
dreamt twenty times, I dare say, of my papers being discovered, and
of my being tried and flogged half to death. At last, however, some
fresh act of injustice towards us made me set all danger at defiance. I
opened my project to a corporal, whose name was William Bestland,
who wrote in the office under me, and who was very much bound to
me for my goodness to him. To work we went, and during a long
winter, while the rest were boozing and snoring we gutted no small
part of the regimental books, rolls and other documents. Our way was
this: to take a copy, sign it with our names, and clap the regimental
seal on it, so that we might be able to swear to it, when produced in
court.

All these papers were put into a little box, which I myself had
made for the purpose. When we came to Portsmouth there was talk
of searching all the boxes, etc., which gave us great alarm; and
induced us to take all the papers, put them in a bag, and trust them
to a custom-house officer, who conveyed them on shore to his own
house, whence I removed them a few days after.

Thus prepared I went to London, and on 14 January 1792 I
wrote to the then Secretary of War, Sir George Yonge, stating my
situation, my business with him, and my intentions; enclosing him
a letter or petition from myself to the King. I waited from the 14th
to the 24th of January without receiving any answer at all, and all I
then heard was that he wished to see me at the War Office. At the
War Office I was shown into an ante-chamber amongst numerous

anxious-looking men, who, every time the door which led to the great man was opened, turned their heads that way with a motion as regular and as uniform as if they had been drilled to it . . . Sir George Yonge heard my story; and that was apparently all he wanted of me. I was to hear from him again in a day or two; and after waiting for fifteen days, without hearing from him, or any one else upon the subject, I wrote to him again, reminding him that I had, from the first, told him that I had no other business in London; that my stock of money was necessarily scanty; and that to detain me in London was ruin to me. I therefore began to be very impatient, and, indeed, to be very suspicious, that military justice in England was pretty nearly akin to military justice in Nova Scotia and New Brunswick. The letter I now wrote was dated the 10th of February, to which I got an answer on the 15th, though the answer might have been written in a moment. I was informed that it was the intention to try the accused upon only a part of the charges which I had preferred, and even on those charges that were suffered to remain, the parts most material were omitted. But this was not all. I had all along insisted that unless the court-martial were held in London I could not think of appearing at it; because if held in a quarrelsome place like Portsmouth the thing must be a mere mockery. In spite of this, the Judge-Advocate's letter of the 23rd of February informed me, that the court was to be held at Portsmouth or Hilsea. I remonstrated against this, and demanded that my remonstrance should be laid before the King, which, on the 29th, the Judge-Advocate promised should be done by himself; but on the 5th of March he informed me that he had laid my remonstrance before – whom, think you? Not the King, but the accused parties; who, of course, thought the court ought to assemble at Portsmouth.

Plainly seeing what was going forward, I, on the 7th of March, made, in a letter to Mr Pitt, a representation of the whole case. This letter had the effect of changing the place of the court-martial, which was now to be held in London; but, as to my other great ground of complaint, the leaving of the regimental books unsecured, it had no effect at all; and it will be recollected that without those books, there could be no proof adduced, without bringing forward Corporal Bestland, and the danger of doing that will presently be seen. Without these written documents nothing of importance could be proved, unless the non-commissioned officers and men of the regiment could get the better of their dread of the lash; and even then they could only speak from memory. As the court-martial was to assemble on the

24th of March I went down to Portsmouth on the 20th, in order to know for certain what was become of the books; and, I found, that they had never been secured at all; that they had been left in the hands of the accused from the 14th of January to the very hour of the trial.

There remained, then, nothing to rest upon with safety but our extracts, confirmed by the evidence of Bestland, and this I had solemnly engaged with him not to have recourse to, unless he was first out of the army; that is to say, out of the reach of the vindictive and bloody lash . . . I resolved not to appear at the court-martial, unless the discharge of Bestland was first granted. Accordingly on the 20th of March I wrote . . . to the Judge-Advocate, stating over again all the obstacles that had been thrown in my way, and concluding by demanding the discharge of a man, whom I should name, as the only condition upon which I would attend the court-martial. I requested him to send me an answer by the next day . . . No answer came, and, as I had learned in the meanwhile that there was a design to prosecute me for sedition, that was an additional motive to be quick in my movements.

[*Political Register* xv, 17 JUNE 1809]

By way of episode I had now married.* I had, in the whole world, but about 200 guineas, which was a very great deal for a person in my situation. From the moment that I had resolved to quit the army, I had also resolved to go to the United States of America, the fascinating and delusive description of which I had read in the works of Raynal. To France I went for the purpose of learning to speak the French language, having, because it was the language of the military art, studied it by book in America . . . I went to France in the spring of 1792.

[*Political Register* xv, 17 JUNE 1809; also ibid. VIII, 5 OCTOBER 1805]

I arrived in France in March 1792, and continued there till the beginning of September following, the six happiest months of my life. I went to that country full of all those prejudices that Englishmen suck in with their mother's milk, against the French and against their religion: a few weeks convinced me that I had been deceived with

* Cobbett married his wife, Anne, on 5 February 1792 at Woolwich Parish Church.

respect to both. I met everywhere with civility, and even hospitality, in a degree that I had never been accustomed to.

I did intend to stay in France till the Spring of 1793, as well to perfect myself in the language as to pass the winter at Paris; but I perceived the storm gathering; I saw that a war with England was inevitable, and it was not difficult to foresee what would be the fate of Englishmen in that country. I wished, however, to see Paris and had actually hired a coach to go thither. I was even on the way, when I heard at Abbeville that the King was dethroned and his guards murdered. This intelligence made me turn off towards Havre de Grace, whence I embarked to America.

[*Life and Adventures of Peter Porcupine*, 1796]

When I first came to Philadelphia I was charmed with the liberty which its inhabitants seemed to enjoy. I saw pamphlets in every window, and newspapers in every hand. I was, indeed, rather surprised to find that these pamphlets and these newspapers were all on one side: but, I said to myself, this must be the fault of the authors and editors. Long did I hope and expect to see something like a manly and effectual opposition, but I hoped and expected in vain. At last it was my fate to enter the field. It is now a long time since I first took up the pen with an intention to write for the press on political subjects; and the occasion of my doing so is too curious in itself, as well as of too much importance as to the sequel, not to be described somewhat in detail.

It was at the memorable epoch of Dr Priestley's emigration to America.* Newspapers were a luxury for which I had little relish, and which, if I had been ever so fond of, I had not time to enjoy. The manifestos, therefore, of the Doctor, upon his landing in that country, and the malicious attacks upon the monarchy and the monarch of England which certain societies in America thereupon issued from the press, would, had it not been for a circumstance purely accidental, have escaped, probably forever, not only my animadversions, but my knowledge of their existence.

One of my scholars, who was that we call in England a Coffee-House Politician, chose, for once, to read his newspaper by way of lesson; and it happened to be the very paper which contained the

* In 1794 Dr Joseph Priestley, the eminent Unitarian minister and scientist, emigrated from England to the United States because of the unpopularity of his Radical opinions. In 1791 his house had been sacked by the Birmingham mob.

addresses presented to Dr Priestley at New York, together with his replies. My scholar, who was a sort of republican, or at best but half a monarchist, appeared delighted with the invectives against England, to which he was very much disposed to add. Those Englishmen who have been abroad, particularly if they have had time to make a comparison between the country they are in and that which they have left, well know how difficult it is, upon occasions such as I have been describing, to refrain from expressing their indignation and resentment; and there is not, I trust, much reason to suppose, that I should, in this respect, experience less difficulty than another. The dispute was as warm as might reasonably be expected between a Frenchman, uncommonly violent even for a Frenchman, and an Englishman not remarkable for *sang-froid*; and the result was a declared resolution on my part to write and publish a pamphlet in defence of my country, which pamphlet he pledged himself to answer: his pledge was forfeited: it is known that mine was not. Thus it was that, whether for good or otherwise, I entered on the career of political writing; and, without adverting to the circumstances under which others have entered on it, I think it will not be believed that the pen was ever taken up from a motive more pure and laudable.

From that time (the summer of 1794) to the year 1800 my labours were without intermission. During that space there were published from my pen about twenty different pamphlets, the whole number of which amounted to more than half a million copies. During the three last years a daily paper, surpassing in extent of numbers any ever known in America, was the vehicle of my efforts; and by the year 1800 I might safely have asserted that there was not, in the whole country, one single family in which some part or other of my writings had not been read; and in which, generally speaking, they had not produced some degree of effect favourable to the interests of my country.

[Political Register VI, 29 SEPTEMBER 1804]

In the Spring of the year 1796 I took a house in Second Street, Philadelphia, for the purpose of carrying on the book-selling business, which I looked upon as being at once a means of getting money, and of propagating writings against the French. I went into my house in May, but the shop could not be gotten ready for some time; and, from one delay to another, I was prevented from opening until the second week in July.

Till I took this house I had remained almost unknown as a writer. A few persons did, indeed, know that I was the person who had assumed the name of Peter Porcupine; but the fact was by no means a matter of notoriety. The moment, however, that I had taken the lease of a large house the transaction became a topic of public conversation, and the eyes of the Democrats and the French, who still lorded it over the city, and who owed me a mutual grudge, were fixed on me.

I thought my situation somewhat perilous. Such truth as I had published no man had dared to utter, in the United States, since the rebellion. I knew that these truths had mortally offended the leading men amongst the Democrats, who could, at any time, muster a mob quite sufficient to destroy my house and to murder me . . . There were in Philadelphia about ten thousand persons, all of whom would have rejoiced to see me murdered; there might, probably, be two thousand, who would have been very sorry for it; but not above fifty of whom would have stirred an inch to save me.

As the time approached for opening my shop my friends grew more anxious for my safety. It was recommended to me, to be cautious how I exposed, at my windows, anything that might provoke the people; and, above all, not to put up any aristocratical portraits, which would certainly cause my windows to be demolished.

I saw the danger; but also saw that I must at once set all danger at defiance, or live in everlasting subjection to the prejudices and caprices of the democratical mob. I resolved on the former; and, as my shop was to open on a Monday morning, I employed myself all day on Sunday in preparing an exhibition, that I thought would put the courage and powers of my enemies to the test. I put up in my windows, which were very large, all the portraits that I had in my possession of kings, queens, and nobles. I had all the English ministry; several of the Bishops and Judges; the most famous Admirals; and, in short, every picture that I thought likely to excite rage in the enemies of Great Britain. In order to make the test as worthy as possible I had put up some of the worthies of the Revolution . . . Early on Monday morning I took down my shutters. Such a sight had not been seen in Philadelphia for twenty years. Never since the beginning of the rebellion had anyone dared to hoist at his windows the portrait of George III.

[*Porcupine's Works*, 1801]

From my very first outset in politics I formed the resolution of keeping myself perfectly independent. In adherence to this resolution I rejected, in America, many offers of great pecuniary advantage. Had I been willing to become what they call a citizen of the United States in how many ways might I have profited from it! There were no reasonable bounds to which I might not confidently have looked forward to see my fortune extended! My perseverance in a contrary line of conduct appeared as unaccountable, upon any common principle, that the people in America, friends as well as foes, regarded me as being in the pay of the British government. I always denied the fact; but my zeal, my efforts, my sacrifices of every sort, were such that it was impossible to make men believe that I was not regularly and amply supplied with 'the gold of Pitt'!

[*Political Register* VIII, 12 OCTOBER 1805]

I began my editorial career with the presidency of Mr Adams, and my principal object was to render his administration all the assistance in my power. I flattered myself with the hope of accompanying him through his voyage, and of partaking in a trifling degree of the glory of the enterprise; but he suddenly tacked about and I could follow him no longer. I therefore waited for the first opportunity to haul down my sails. My Gazette, instead of being a mine of gold to me, never yielded me a farthing. Gain was never a primary object with me. The other branches of my business enabled me to support the loss. It was my intention to continue it till the month of March 1801; but as this intention was founded entirely upon my persuasion of the public utility of the continuation, it fell, of course, the moment that persuasion was removed from my mind. I addressed a Farewell Number of 'Porcupine's Gazette' from New York City in January of the year 1800 and I congratulated myself on having established a paper, carried it to a circulation unparalleled in extent, and preserved the circulation to the last number; on having, in the progress of this paper, uniformly supported with all my feeble powers, the cause of true religion, sound morality, good government, and real liberty.

When I determined to discontinue the publication of 'Porcupine's Gazette' I intended to remain for the future, if not an unconcerned, at least a silent spectator of public transactions and political points; but the unexpected and sweeping result of a lawsuit decided against me induced me to abandon my lounging intention. The suit to which I allude was an action of slander, commenced against me in the autumn of 1797 by Dr Benjamin Rush,* the noted bleeding physician of Philadelphia. It was tried on the 14th of December 1799, when 'the upright, enlightened, and impartial republican jury' assessed, as damages, five thousand dollars; a sum surpassing the aggregate amount of all the damages assessed for all the torts of this kind ever sued for in the United States from their first settlement to the time of the trial. To the five thousand dollars must be added the costs of the suit, the loss incurred by the interruption in collecting debts in Pennsylvania, and by the sacrifice of property taken in execution and sold by the Sheriff in public auction in Philadelphia, where a great number of books in sheets (among which was a part of a new edition of 'Porcupine's Works') were sold, or rather given away as waste paper; so that the total of what was wrested away from me by Rush fell little short of eight thousand dollars.

To say that I did not feel this stroke, and very sensibly too, would be a great affectation; but to repine at it would have been folly, and to have sunk under it cowardice. I knew an Englishman in the Royal Province of New Brunswick, who had a very valuable house which was, I believe, at that time nearly his all, burnt to the ground. He was out of town when the fire broke out, and happened to come home just after it had exhausted itself. He came very leisurely up to the spot, stood about five minutes looking steadily at the rubbish, and then, stripping off his coat, 'Here goes,' said he, 'to earn another!' and immediately went to work, raking the spikes and bits of iron out of the ashes. This noble-spirited man I had the honour to call my friend; and if ever this page meet his eye, he will have the satisfaction to see that, though it was not possible for me to follow, I at least remembered his example.

[*The Rushlight*, 15 FEBRUARY 1800]

We came home to England from New York, I, my wife, and two little children, in the post office packet, for which I paid very highly . . . Arrived at Falmouth I was most kindly lodged and entertained by the

* Dr Benjamin Rush advocated severe bleedings accompanied by harsh purgatives as a method of treating yellow fever. Cobbett denounced Rush's treatment in *Porcupine's Gazette*, and the consequent libel suit was complicated by the activities of Cobbett's political opponents (principally of the pro-French and anti-British party), who sought to exploit the case as a means of discrediting Cobbett as a journalist. Cobbett believed that he had suffered chiefly because of his political attitudes, rather than for his criticisms of Rush as a physician.

collector of customs. For my fame had, even then, spread very widely amongst all persons connected with the Government. Arrived in London (July 1800) I took a hired lodging and deliberated what I should do with my slender means, amounting to only about £500, the proceeds of the sale of goods and books at New York.

[*Political Register* LXIX, 10 APRIL 1830]

Arrived in London all who knew the history of my exploits in America supposed as a matter of course that showers of gold were about to fall upon me. Many persons will recollect that, in 1803, the late Mr Windham said in the House of Commons that I, for my services in America, 'merited a statue of gold'. In a few days after my arrival I was, by him, who was then Secretary of War, invited to dine at his house, with a party of whom Pitt and Canning were two. I was, of course, very proud of this invitation: and I felt more than ever disposed to use my talents in support of the system as it was then going on; which stood in real need of support, for Bonaparte was making fearful progress; and I resolved in my mind to set up a daily paper.

While I was thinking about this Mr George Hammond, the Under Secretary of State for Foreign Affairs (Lord Grenville being the Secretary) sent for me to his office, and made me an offer of a Government paper. The Government had two, *The True Briton* and *The Sun*, the former a morning, the latter an evening paper. They were their property, office, types, lease of houses, and all; and the former was offered to me as a gift with all belonging to it . . . I refused the offer, though worth several thousand pounds. From that moment all belonging to the Government looked on me with great suspicion.

[*Political Register*, LXIX, 10 APRIL 1830]

When I returned to England in 1800, after an absence from the country part of it of sixteen years, the trees, the hedges, even the parks and the woods, seemed so small! It made me laugh to hear little gutters that I could jump over called Rivers! The Thames was but a 'Creek'! But when, in about a month after my arrival in London, I went to Farnham, the place of my birth, what was my surprise! Everything was so pitifully small! I had to cross, in my post-chaise, the long and dreary heath of Bagshot. Then, at the end of it, to mount a hill, called Hungry Hill; and from that hill I knew that I should look down into the beautiful and fertile vale of Farnham. My heart fluttered with impatience mixed with a sort of fear, to see all the scenes of my childhood; for I had learnt before, the death of my father and mother. There is a hill, not far from the town, called Crooksbury Hill, which rises up out of a flat, in the form of a cone, and is planted with Scotch fir trees. Here I used to take the eggs and young ones of crows and magpies. This hill was a famous object in the neighbourhood. It served as a superlative degree of height. 'As high as Crooksbury Hill' meant, with us, the utmost degree of height. Therefore, the first object that my eyes sought was this hill. I could not believe my eyes! Literally speaking, I for a moment thought the famous hill removed, and a little heap put in its stead; for I had seen in New Brunswick a single rock, or hill of solid rock, ten times as big, and four or five times as high! The post-boy, going downhill, and not a bad road, whisked me, in a few minutes to the Bush Inn, from the garden of which I could see the prodigious sand hill, where I had begun my gardening works. What a nothing! But now came rushing into my mind, all at once, my pretty little garden, my little blue smock-frock, my little nailed shoes, my pretty pigeons that I used to feed out of my hands, the last kind words and tears of my gentle and tenderhearted and affectionate mother! I hastened back into the room. If I had looked a moment longer I should have dropped. When I came to reflect, what a change! I looked down at my dress. What a change! What scenes I had gone through! How altered my state! I had dined the day before at a Secretary of State's with Mr Pitt, and had been waited upon by men in gaudy liveries! I had had nobody to assist me in the world. No teachers of any sort. Nobody to shelter me from the consequence of bad, and no one to counsel me to good behaviour. I felt proud. The distinctions of rank, birth, and wealth, all became nothing in my eyes; and from that moment (less than a month after my arrival in England) I resolved never to bend before them.

[*A Year's Residence in the United States of America*, 1819]

I set out as a sort of self-dependent politician. My opinions were my own. I dashed at all prejudices. I scorned to follow anybody in matter of opinion. Before my time, every writer of talent enlisted himself under the banners of one party, or one minister or other. I stood free from all such connections; and therefore, though admired by many, I was looked upon with an evil eye by all. All had been used to see men of no rank glad to receive the approbation of men of rank. All had been used to see talent crouch to power. All were, therefore, offended at my presumption, as they deemed it. My great success as a writer; the great admiration which my writings frequently excited; the effect on the public mind which they frequently produced: these were much more than sufficient to draw down on me the mortal hatred of the 'race that write'.

[*Political Register* XXXV, 2 OCTOBER 1819]

I had no intention to range myself in a systematic opposition to His Majesty's Ministers or to their measures. The first object was to contribute my mite toward the support of the authority of that Sovereign whom God had commanded me to honour and obey. The uniform intention of my writings was and is to counteract the effects of the enemies of monarchy in general, and of the monarchy of England in particular, under whatever guise those enemies have appeared; to check the spirit and oppose the progress of levelling innovation, whether proceeding from clubs of Jacobins, companies of traders, synagogues of saints, or boards of government; to cherish an adherence to long-tried principles, an affection for ancient families and ancient establishments.

[*Political Register* VI, 6 OCTOBER 1804]

But many things led me into opposition. The ancient nobility and gentry of the kingdom had been thrown out of public employment: a race of merchants and manufacturers, and bankers and loan-jobbers and contractors had usurped their place. Good honest men, plain men, men in middle classes of life, as Mr Wilberforce said, may be excellent judges of public measures; but, unfortunately, in searching after these men, we went too far, and took them out of the lower classes of life. Who was it that stirred up these lees? Mr Pitt himself . . . Generally speaking, the great evil of a national debt, of a great accumulation of personal property of any sort, is that the holders of such property are ever upon the rack to increase its immediate value. Hence the subserviency of statesmen to the views of the money lenders. The funding system* was eating the heart out of the nobility; stifling every high and honourable feeling. It was engaged in a desperate contest against the aristocracy and monarchy of England, and this contest

---

* Cobbett always detested high finance. In particular he thought the national debt an unnecessary burden upon posterity. He strongly disapproved of Pitt's attempt to pay off the national debt by the establishment of a sinking fund. Together with the introduction of paper-money in 1797 this would make it easier for speculators to make huge profits at the expense of the taxpayer.

must finally terminate in the destruction of one or the other.
[*Autobiography of William Cobbett* (ed. WILLIAM REITZEL), 1947]

I naturally opposed the Preliminaries of the Peace of Amiens in 1801. From the scenes of violence and outrage, which had taken place in some parts of the town, not far from my shop in Pall Mall, I had reason to expect that, on the arrival of the Ratification of the Preliminaries, my dwelling house there, as well as my printing-office in Southampton Street, would be attacked, because my sentiments respecting these Preliminaries were publicly known. It happened precisely as I had expected: about eight o'clock in the evening my dwelling-house was attacked by an innumerable mob, all my windows were broken, and when this was done the villains were preparing to break into my shop. The attack continued at intervals, till past one o'clock. During the whole of this time not a constable nor peace officer of any description made his appearance; nor was the smallest interruption given to the proceedings of this ignorant and brutal mob, who were thus celebrating the Peace. The 'Porcupine' office experienced a similar fate.

With the signing of the Peace in a few months' time this scene was repeated . . . My wife's removal had not taken place many hours before I had reason to congratulate myself upon it. A numerous and boisterous rabble, coming from Cockspur Street, began to assault the house, at about half-past nine o'clock. The Bow Street Magistrate with his men used their utmost exertions to prevent violence, but in vain. The attack continued, with more or less fury, for about an hour and half, during which time a party of horse-guards were called in to the aid of the civil power. Great part of the windows were broken; the sash frames of the ground floor almost entirely demolished; the panels of the window shutters were dashed in; the door nearly forced open; and much other damage done to several parts of the house.

With such troubles, and since I knew nothing of business which demanded thousands in place of a few hundreds of pounds my daily paper was soon gone, and with it more than all that I possessed in the money way. I lost about £450, which was enough, in all conscience, to reward me for all my exertions, dangers, and losses in America . . . I had not the means . . . of establishing a new work . . . If I had not been aided by a private subscription . . . the now famous 'Register' never could have been begun.

[*The Autobiography of William Cobbett* throughout, 1947]

In 1806 I announced my intention to stand for the borough of Honiton. My expressed principles were the necessity for a strong front against bribery; never to touch the public money by my own hands, or by those of relatives. All professions short of this I accounted as nothing.

[*Political Register* X, 20 SEPTEMBER 1806]

Before I set off from London . . . I met Mr Johnstone (Lord Cochrane's uncle), and asked him if he had any news of his nephew, of whose recent gallant conduct the newspapers had just informed us. Mr Johnstone said that he was then going to the Admiralty, in order to get him leave of absence to come part of the way from Plymouth to London to meet him upon some business; whereupon I observed that as I was going to Honiton he might as well go with me. Mr Johnstone accepted of my offer . . . We arrived at Honiton on Saturday* and on the same day Mr Johnstone received a letter from Lord Cochrane informing him that his Lordship could not leave Plymouth just then. But on Sunday, while we were at dinner, there came an express from Lord Cochrane, bearing a letter for me, informing me that his Lordship, having read my address to the people of Honiton in the London newspapers, and having perceived that I had resolved to stand myself merely because I could find no other independent man, he had determined to accept of my general invitation, and that he was actually on his way . . . to put his purpose in execution. In an hour afterward, having stopped at Exeter to provide lawyers, his Lordship arrived. I declined proceeding to the poll.

Now, as to the state of this borough, who shall describe it? Who shall describe the gulf wherein have been swallowed the fortunes of so many ancient and respectable families? There was, the electors would tell you, no bribery. They took a certain sum of money each, according to their consequence; 'but this', they said, 'came in the shape of a reward after the election, and, therefore, the oath might be safely taken'. Considered as a question of morality, how contemptible this subterfuge was need hardly be noticed; but, to say the truth, they did not deceive themselves, and I must do them the justice to say that they were not very anxious to deceive anybody else. They told you, flatly and plainly, that the money which they obtained for their votes was absolutely necessary to enable them to live; that without it they could not pay their rents; and that, from election to election,

* 7 June 1806.

poor men ran up scores at the shops, and were trusted by the shop-keepers, expressly upon the credit of the ensuing election; and that, thus, the whole of the inhabitants of the borough, the whole of the persons who returned two of the members of every Parliament, were bound together in an indissoluble chain of venality . . . In quitting this scene, looking back from one of the many hills that surrounded the fertile and beautiful valley in which Honiton lay, with its houses spreading down the side of an inferior eminence crowned by its ancient and venerable church; in surveying the fields, the crops, the cattle, all the blessings that nature could bestow, all the sources of plenty and all the means of comfort and happiness, it was impossible to divest myself of a feeling of horror at reflecting upon the deeds which the sun witnessed upon this one of his most favoured spots.

[*Political Register* IX, 28 JUNE 1806]

For the next three years Cobbett continued his journalistic activities, while moving further over into the Radical camp. But his old concern for the correction of abuses within the army eventually brought him into conflict with the authorities.

In 1809 some young men at Ely, in what was called the 'local militia', had refused to march without the 'marching guinea', which the Act of Parliament awarded them. This was called Mutiny; and a body of Hanoverian horse were brought from Bury St Edmunds to compel these young Englishmen to submit to be flogged! They were flogged, while surrounded by these Hanoverians; and the transaction was recorded in 'The Courier' ministerial paper. I, in my 'Register', expressed my indignation at this, and to express it too strongly was not in the power of man. The Attorney-General, Gibbs, was set upon me; he harassed me for nearly a year, then brought me to trial. This took place on the 15th of June 1810, when I was found guilty of treasonous libel by a Special Jury. On the 20th, I was compelled to give bail for my appearance in court to receive judgement, and as I came from Botley (to which place I had returned on the evening of the 15th) a Tip-Staff went down in order to seize me personally, and to bring me up to London to give bail . . . I was brought up to receive judgement on the 5th of July, when, after the Attorney-General had made the speech, I was sent to the King's Bench Prison, and ordered to be brought up again on the 9th of July. On this day I was . . . sentenced to be imprisoned two years in Newgate amongst felons, to pay a fine to the King of a thousand pounds, and to be held in heavy bail for seven years after the expiration of the imprisonment! . . . Everyone regarded it as a sentence of death, and it was intended to be a sentence of death. I lived in the country, seventy miles from London; I had a farm on my hands; I had a family of small children, amongst whom I constantly lived; I had a most anxious and devoted wife, who was, too, in that state which rendered the separation more painful tenfold . . .

I . . . bought myself out of the company of felons. By great favour I finally obtained leave to occupy two rooms in the jailer's house, paying for them twelve guineas a week, and it required eight more to fee the various persons, and to get leave to walk an hour in the leads of the prison in the morning: so that here were £2,080 during the two years besides the £1,000 to the good old King. These direct losses were, however, trifling compared with the indirect. I was engaged in the publication of two works, called 'The State Trials' and 'The Parliamentary History'. There had been a great outlay for these works; several thousands of pounds were due to the paper-maker and the printer. These works were, as far as regarded me, ruined . . . Almost exactly ten years after landing in England, having lost a fortune in America, solely for the sake of England, I was sent to prison in that same England! It was quite impossible for me to banish reflections of this sort from my mind.

Many gentlemen, by letter as well as verbally, proposed to me the putting forward a subscription, for the purpose of indemnifying me and my family against the heavy expense and loss which had been incurred in consequences of the prosecution. I was, however, happy to say that I had been not only able to withstand all pressure; but that without any extraordinary aid, from any quarter, I felt confident of my ability to proceed, and, with the blessing of continued health, make a suitable provision for all my children. My health, thank God, was as good as ever it was. But I had no security for either health or life, any more than other men; and, if I had attempted an insurance upon my life, Newgate would have told pretty strongly against me. It was, therefore, impossible for me not to feel an anxious desire to see my family at least guarded against certain expense and loss.

Everyone will easily imagine that every debt I owed, of every description, came pouring in for payment . . . The sons and daughters of corruption openly chuckled at what they thought my extinguishment. Almost everyone stood aloof, except my creditors (never the last to visit you in such a season) who pressed on amain; so that I really forgot that I was in prison, so great and so numerous were the torrents arising. I was looked upon as a man given over by the doctors; and everyone to whom I owed a shilling, brought me sighs of sorrow indeed; but, along with these, brought me his bill. Why, the truth is that had it not been for one thing I should not have been able to bear up under this accumulation of evil; and, that one thing was that I had a friend, to whom, on the third day after I entered the accursed jail, I wrote, requesting him, in case of my death, to send for, and take care of, my wife and children, and from whom I received an answer, containing, amongst others, these words: 'Give thyself no trouble about Nancy and the children. If thee should die, which I hope thee will not for years to come, thy dear family shall find a home under my roof, and shall be to me and all of us as our own kindred' . . . It was James Paull, a Quaker farmer, of Lower Dublin Township, in the state of Pennsylvania; a native American; a man on whom I had never conferred a favour to the amount of the value of a pin.

[*The Autobiography of William Cobbett*, 1947]

The sentence, though it proved not to be one of death, was, in effect, one of ruin, as far as then-possessed property went. But this really appeared as nothing, compared with the circumstance, that I must now have a child born in a felons' jail, or be absent from the scene at the time of the birth. My wife, who had come to see me for the last time previous to her lying-in, perceiving my deep dejection at the approach of her departure for Botley, resolved not to go; and actually went and took a lodging as near to Newgate as she could find one, in order that the communication between us might be as speedy as possible; and in order that I might see the doctor, and receive assurances from him relative to her state. The nearest lodging that she could find was in Skinner-street, at the corner of a street leading to Smithfield. So that there she was, amidst the incessant rattle of coaches and butchers' carts, and the noise of cattle, dogs, and bawling men; instead of being in a quiet and commodious country-house, with neighbours and servants and everything necessary about her. Yet, so great is the power of the mind in such cases, she, though the circumstances proved uncommonly perilous, and were attended with the loss of the child, bore her sufferings with the greatest composure, because, at any minute she could send a message to, and hear from, me. If she had gone to Botley, leaving me in that state of anxiety in which she saw me, I am satisfied that she would have died; and that event taking place at such a distance from me, how was I to contemplate her corpse, surrounded by her distracted children, and to have escaped death or madness myself? If such was not the effect of this merciless act of the government towards me, that amiable body may be well assured that I have taken and recorded the will for the deed, and that as such it will live in my memory as long as that memory shall last.

[*Advice to Young Men*, 1829]

During my imprisonment I wrote and published 364 Essays and Letters upon political subjects; during the same time I was visited by persons from 197 cities and towns, many of them as a sort of deputies from Societies and Clubs; and, at the expiration of my imprisonment, on the 19th of July 1812, a great dinner was given in London for the sake of receiving me, at which dinner upwards of 600 persons were present, and at which Sir Francis Burdett presided. Dinners and other parties were held on the same occasion in many other places in England. On my way home I was received at Alton, the first town in Hampshire, with the ringing of the church bells. A respectable company met me and gave me dinner at Winchester. I was drawn for more than the distance of a mile into Botley by the people; upon my arrival in the village I found all the people assembled to receive me. I concluded the day by explaining to them the cause of my imprisonment.

[*Political Register* XXII, 1 AUGUST 1812]

When I left prison in 1812 I thought it prudent to quit so large a house as my own at Botley was, and to lessen all my expenses I therefore took the place of a Mr Kempt, which had a neat little gentlemen's house on it, and the best gardens in the country, having nearly three quarters of a mile of high walls, for fruit trees. I laid out more than £150 in purchasing and planting the walls and gardens with all the finest sort of peaches, nectarines, apricots, plums, cherries, pears and apples. The vines against the walls, which bore nothing scarcely before I went to the place, I made by my management bear half a ton of grapes . . . I mention these things to show what pains I took with these gardens, where I grew as great a weight of melons as was grown in any 20 gentlemen's gardens round the country; where I had very large watermelons, which I never saw in England except in my gardens. In short, I never set myself down in any spot in my whole life, without causing fruits and flowers and trees (if there was time) and all the beauties of vegetation to rise up around me.

[*Political Register* XXXII, 12 JULY 1817]

My imprisonment gave me, as to money matters, a blow not easily recovered. The Peace came, too, in about twenty months afterward, which was greatly injurious to me as a farmer, and at the same time as a writer; for, in its fit of drunken joy, the nation in general laughed at me.

[*Political Register* LXIX, 10 APRIL 1830]

The intelligence of this grand event reached me in the following manner. I had been out very early in the morning, and in returning home to breakfast I met a populous gang of gypsies. At the first view of them, I thought of nothing but the robberies which they constantly committed upon us, and I began to plan my measures of defence. But, upon a nearer approach to them, I perceived the whole caravan decorated with laurel. The blackguard ruffians of men had laurel boughs in their hats; the nasty ferocious-looking women, with pipes in their jaws, and straddling along like German trulls, had laurel leaves pinned against their sides. The poor asses that went bending along beneath their burdens laid on them by their merciless masters, and that were quivering their skins to get the swarms of flies from those parts of their bodies which the wretched drivers had beaten raw, had their bridles and halters and pads stuck over with laurel. Somewhat staggered by this symbol of victory, I hesitated what to do, passed the gang in silence, until I met an extraordinarily ill-looking fellow, who, with two half-starved dogs, performed the office of rear-guard. I asked him the meaning of the laurel boughs, and he informed me that they were hoisted on account of the 'glorious victory obtained by the Duke of Wellington over Boney'; that they were furnished them by a good gentleman, whose house they had passed the day before, between Andover and Botley, and who had given them several pots of ale, wherein to drink the Duke's health. 'And to be sure,' added he, 'it is glorious news, and we may now hope to see the gallon loaf at a groat again, as 'twas in my old father's time.' I left this political economist, this 'loyal man and friend of social order', to overtake his companions; I went homeward with a mind far from being as completely made up as that of the Gipsey and his black-coated and white-wigged benefactor.

[*Political Register* XXVII, 1 JULY 1815]

By the beginning of 1816, my pecuniary affairs became so desperate as to make me determined on selling my land and everything else, and on beginning the world afresh . . . I was aware that the high price of 'The Register', though it had not prevented it from being more read than any other publication, still it prevented it from being so generally read as would be necessary to put the people right . . . Hence came the observation from one of us, I forget which, that if, for this one time, for this particular purpose,* the price could be, by some means or other, reduced to two pence, then the desired effect would be produced at once. I said, before we parted, that this should be done.

But as it was impossible for me to prove to the people what was *not* the cause of their misery, without proving to them what was the cause of their misery; as the remedy, at last, came to a Reform of Parliament; and, as I feared, that the best time was not come for urging on this grand question, I delayed, from time to time, the fulfilment of my promise . . . As . . . topics had long been passing through my mind, they came very naturally and easily into their place upon paper; and, as I most sincerely felt the truth and justice of all that I wrote, I wrote with as much force both of language and argument as I had at my command. The arrangements had been made the week before for the manner and price of publication; and I felt quite confident not only of a great sale, but of a very great effect. I changed the price of 'The Register' from 1s. to 2d., publishing it without a stamp, and keeping myself sheltered from the law by not being the legal proprietor.

After the manuscript had gone off, my fears of premature effect returned; and after two days resolving and re-resolving and misgiving I sent off my son John by the night coach to prevent the Cheap Edition being published for a short time at any rate. But, instead of informing me that he had obeyed my orders, he informed me that six thousand of the Cheap Edition had been sold before his arrival. It was too late to balance. I put myself before the wind, which I well

* i.e. to inform people of the true causes of agricultural distress.

knew would prove too strong to suffer me to stop or to slacken my pace. It was impossible now, in this new scene, to remain at Botley. I went off to London in a few days, and remained there until my final departure for Liverpool; and, of the eventful days of my wonderful life, these were certainly the most eventful.

The effects of No. 18* were prodigious. It occupied the conversation of three-fourths of all the acting men in the kingdom. The whole town was in a buzz. The labouring classes of people seemed as if they had never heard a word on politics before. The effect on their minds was like what might be expected to be produced on the eyes of one bred up in the dark, and brought out, all of a sudden, into broad daylight. In town and country, there were, in two months, more than two hundred thousand of this one Number printed and sold; and this, too, in spite of all the means which the Government, the Church, the Military, the Naval Half-Pay, and all the innumerable swarms of Tax-Gatherers and Tax-Eaters, were able to do to check the circulation. The 'Paper Against Gold' was selling in weekly numbers at the rate of twenty to thirty thousand a week. In short, clear of all expenses, there was a profit of £200 a week; so that, if I had been let alone, if no law had been passed to stop and ruin me, my estate would have been clear at the end of two years, and I should have been as rich as I ever wanted to be.

Among the striking and instantaneous effects of this Cheap 'Register' was the unlocking of the jaws of the London Press with regard to me and my writings. For nearly five years I had been unable to extort a word from this Press. Upon the appearance, however, of No. 18, away went all the *chuchutements*, and all the pretendings of ignorance; and the corrupt part of the Press, instead of its apparently sworn silence, treated the public with volleys of lies and execrations against me that never had a parallel in the world . . .

Early in December, Mr Becket, the Under Secretary of State to Lord Sidmouth, said, in answer to a proposition for silencing me in some very atrocious manner, 'No: he must be written down.' Accordingly, up sprang little pamphlets at Norwich, at Romsey, at Oxford, and at many other places, while in London there were several, one of which would not cost less than two thousand guineas in advertising and in large and expensive placards, which were pulled down, or effaced, the hour they were put up, and which were replaced the next hour as one wave succeeds another in the sea. At last, after all

* The first cheap issue of *The Register*.

other efforts of this kind, came 'Anti-Cobbett', written 'by a Society of Gentlemen', amongst whom, I was told, were Canning, Mr Gifford, and Southey. Not content with advertisements in three hundred newspapers; not content with endless reams of placards, the managers of this concern actually sent out two hundred thousand circular letters, addressed to persons by name, urging them to circulate this work amongst all their tradesmen, farmers, work people, and to give it their strong recommendation; and this they were told was absolutely necessary to prevent bloody revolution.

By the beginning of January 1817 or thereabouts, the Government had discovered that it was quite useless to carry on any longer this contest with the pen. But, though open force appears now to have been resolved on, it was very hard to make out any pretext for employing such force. Sidmouth and Castlereagh were authorized to shut up in prison every one 'suspected of treasonable practices'; and when Sidmouth brought in the Bill he distinctly stated, as a reason for it, that the publications then going on were such that the law-officers of the crown could find nothing in them to prosecute with any chance of success! Lord Holland asked Sidmouth, why, if there were such seditious works going forth from the press, he did not cause them to be prosecuted; to which the latter answered, that he had laid them all before the law-officers, and that they could find nothing to prosecute, such was the art and malignity of the writers! Therefore the Power of Imprisonment Bill was passed!* a law to enable some of themselves to shut me up in prison at their pleasure; to keep me in a dungeon as long as they pleased; and this too without even telling me what I was accused of; and all this they did, as expressly stated by Sidmouth, because I had committed no offence against the laws; because the law-officers could find nothing to prosecute in my publications . . .

Nothing could have induced me to quit my country while there remained the smallest chance of my being able, by remaining, to continue to aid her cause. The laws which had just been passed forbade me to entertain the idea that it would be possible to write on political subjects according to the dictates of truth and reason, without drawing down upon my head certain and swift destruction. If I removed to a country where I could write with perfect freedom, it was not only possible, but very probable, that I should, sooner or later, be able to render that cause important and lasting service.

* Seditious Meetings Bill and Suspension of Habeas Corpus, 1817.

Upon this conclusion it was that I made my determination: for though life would have been scarcely worth preserving, with the consciousness that I walked about my fields, or slept in my bed, merely at the mercy of a Secretary of State; though, under such circumstances, neither the song of the birds in spring, nor the well-thatched homestead in winter, could make me forget that I and my family were slaves, still there was something so powerful in the thought of country, and neighbourhood, and home, and friends, there was something so strong in the numerous and united ties with which these and endless other objects fastened the mind to a long-inhabited spot, that to tear oneself away nearly approached to the separating of the soul from the body.

A few years before, being at Barnett Fair, I saw a battle going on, arising out of some sudden quarrel, between a Butcher, and the servant of a West-country Grazier. The Butcher, though vastly superior in point of size, finding that he was getting the worst of it, recoiled a step or two, and drew out his knife. Upon the sight of this weapon, the Grazier turned about and ran off till he came up to a Scotchman who was guarding his herd, and out of whose hand the former snatched a good ash stick about four feet long. Having thus got what he called a long arm, he returned to the combat, and, in a very short time, he gave the Butcher a blow upon the wrist which brought his knife to the ground. The Grazier then fell to work with his stick in such a style as I never before witnessed. The Butcher fell down and rolled and kicked; but, he seemed only to change his position in order to insure to every part of his carcase a due share of the penalty of his baseness. After the Grazier had, apparently, tired himself, he was coming away, when, happening to cast his eye upon the knife, he ran back and renewed his basting, exclaiming every now and then, as he caught his breath: 'dra they knife wo't!' till at last the Butcher was so bruised that he was actually unable to stand, or even to get up; and yet, such amongst Englishmen was the abhorrence of foul fighting, that not a soul attempted to interfere, and nobody seemed to pity a man thus unmercifully beaten. It was my intention to imitate the conduct of this Grazier; to resort to a long arm, by going to America, and to combat Corruption while I kept myself out of the reach of her knife. Nobody called the Grazier a coward because he did not stay to oppose his fists to a pointed and cutting instrument.

I and my two sons, William and John, set off from London early in the morning of Saturday, the 22nd of March 1817. We reached Litchfield that night, and Liverpool the next night about ten o'clock . . . On Wednesday evening, the 27th of March, we embarked on board the ship 'Importer' . . . bound to New York. When we went on board it was nearly dark. The boat was so full that some of the passengers were obliged to quit and go to another boat . . . Every morning of my passage I was up, shaved and dressed, before any other person was stirring. Then I called up my sons. Our place was swept out or washed out, aired and beds made by ourselves before breakfast. While others were lolling in their berths we were out on deck. During the time of sea-sickness, which I had none of, I took care of my sons, attended them on deck, brought them down, waited on them like a nurse, gave no trouble to anybody; and when that was over, our room was, at all times, night as well as day, fair weather or foul, as clear from all annoyances as one of our fields at Botley. We were stinted to one tumbler of fresh water a day to wash in. We never complained of this, and we kept ourselves perfectly clean. The consequence was we landed at New York as fresh as we were when we went on board the ship. We arrived on the 5th of May. In all respects that can be named our passage was disagreeable; and, upon one occasion, very perilous from lightning which struck the ship twice, shivered two of the masts, killed a man, struck several people slightly, between two of whom I was sitting without at all feeling the blow.

[Autobiography of William Cobbett, 1947]

We went to an inn, 13 miles from New York, in Long Island. It was on the main road to the city. We lodged and boarded in this inn, had each a bedroom and a good bed, had a room to sit in to ourselves, ate by ourselves; and it really was eating. We had smoked fish, chops, butter and eggs for breakfast, with bread, crackers, sweet cakes; and, when I say that we had such and such things, I do not mean that we had them for show, or just enough to smell to; but in loads. Not an egg, but a dish full of eggs. Not a snip of meat or of fish, but a plate full. Lump sugar for our tea and coffee; not broke into little bits the size of a hazelnut, but in good thumping pieces. For dinner we had the finest of fish, bass, mackerel, lobsters; of meat, lamb, veal, ham, etc. Asparagus in plenty, apple pies (though in the middle of May). And for all this an excellent cider to drink, with the kindest and most obliging treatment, on the part of the Landlord and Landlady and their sons and daughters, we paid no more than twenty-two shillings and sixpence a week.

But there were two things which no money could purchase anywhere. The first was, no grumbling on the part of the Landlady, except on account of our eating and drinking too little, and the other was, that Mr Wiggins had no fastening but a bit of chip run in over the latch of the door to a house which was full of valuable things of all sorts. All this was the effect of good government, of just and mild government, which took so little from the people in taxes that they had the means of happiness fully left in their hands.

We soon, however, took a place, pleasant and agreeable, a beautiful place, called Hyde Park; a fine park, orchards, gardens ,and fields and woods. It was at North Hempstead in Long Island. A fine house, too, but out of repair. Everybody was kind and obliging. If this untaxed, beautiful, fertile and salubrious island had been inhabited by Englishmen it would very far have surpassed the Garden of Eden; for here the trees produced golden fruit and we were forbidden to eat none of them. I had good servants in my man Churcher and his Wife, and I heard their Hampshire tongues so often, that I almost conceited myself at home; only the fine sun, the fine roads, the fine fruits, and the happy labourers told me that I was not. Tranquillity I enjoyed unalloyed by one bitter reflection as to any act of my whole life. Simply to preserve life and health was all that reason, or common sense, permitted me to go to the expense of.

[*The Autobiography of William Cobbett*, 1947]

Cobbett's sojourn in the United States did not interrupt his career as a publicist, but despite the hospitality of his friends he never settled in America. He was always conscious that many English Radicals suspected that he had gone to America because he was afraid to face his enemies at home. He therefore determined to return to England.

After twenty-one days' sailing over a sea almost as smooth as the beautiful Long Island Lake , I arrived at Liverpool, on a Sunday evening, in November 1819. We were not permitted to land until Monday about two o'clock. There had been a great multitude assembled on the wharf the whole of the day; and, when I landed, I was received with cheers and with shakings of the hand, which made me feel that I was once again in England . . . On Sunday, the 28th of November, I, accompanied by my sons William and John, left

Liverpool, on my road to Manchester, which I had been invited to visit, and where I had been invited to partake of a dinner on the Monday. We proceeded on our way to an Inn at a little hamlet called Irlam, which was within ten miles of Manchester. There we slept, and the next morning prepared to get into our coach and to go to receive the welcome intended for us. A deputation had arrived to accompany us on the way, when, not to my surprise at all, arrived a messenger on horseback with a notification from the Borough-reeves and Constables of Manchester and Salford, interdicting any further advance toward the Town! . . . We went back to Warrington and took the road to London; not, however, before I took an opportunity to make a short address to about two hundred persons who had assembled round the Inn, some of whom had come on foot all the way from Manchester. I shall never forget the looks of these men, and, indeed, of these women, for there were some of both sexes. My hand yet reminds me of the hard squeezes I had from them; and how great a favourite of mine a hard squeeze of the hand is!

We arrived at Coventry late on the evening of the 30th November. When I came down into a front room of the house to breakfast I found a great number of persons assembled in the street opposite the house; and finding that they were there for the purpose of seeing me, I informed them that I should set off in precisely an hour. When we started a great number followed us to a distance of about a mile out of the city, where there was an open space on the side of the road, surrounded by some high banks. Having drawn the chaise up in a suitable position, and having placed myself upon the outside of the chaise on the foot-board, I found myself surrounded by several thousands of persons of both sexes, the females forming a very beautiful battalion, many of them with children in their arms, in one part of the circle, not mixed among the men, while other persons were running towards us, not only along the track of the chaise from the city, but in all directions over the fields and meadows. This was not a meeting. There had been nothing done to call it together. It was spontaneous, it was collected of itself, by the mere sound of my name. Never did I behold any spectacle in my whole life that gave me so much pleasure as this.

[*Political Register* xxxv, 4 DECEMBER 1819]

My son William and I went down from London to Botley in December. The people of the village, notwithstanding the threats of the Parson, came to meet us upon the hill on the Winchester Road. They took out the horses and drew us into the village, whence, after I had shortly addressed them, they took us to my house. The farm was in very neat order, the turnpike perfectly good, the trees monstrously grown; the American trees of finer growth than any that I ever saw in America of the same age.

[*Political Register* XXXV, 24 DECEMBER 1819]

After my return, though my heart was always at home, I had to have my mind and hand in London. We started a daily paper.* It was a trying time and fortitude was required. My boys were wonders of activity and sense and spirit. And then, the opportunity coming, I resolved to stand for Parliament again.

I set off for Coventry with my eldest daughter on the 28th of February. We went all the night (the coldest of the winter) in a post-chaise; breakfasted at Daventry, and then proceeded on towards Dunchurch, which is eleven miles from Coventry. Here we were met by messengers who brought accounts that I should certainly be murdered if I attempted to enter the city. A band of rich ruffians had leagued together against me. They had got together a parcel of men, whom they made partly drunk, and whom they gave orders to go out, meet me at a bridge about a mile from the city, and if I refused to return to London, to fling me over the bridge.

While we were deliberating on what course to pursue a gentleman arrived with intelligence, that the enemy had drawn up, rank and file, in the city; that they were marching off with fourteen banners waving over their heads, and with drum and music in their front; and that they had not reached the outside of the city, when our friends sallied forth upon them, took away their banners, staved in their drums, dispersed them in all directions, and set off to meet me.

At about four miles from Coventry, we met with small advanced parties of young men, with leaves of laurel in their hats and boughs in their hands. The groups grew more frequent and larger as we approached the city. The curiosity to see me was so strongly expressed that I was obliged to get out of the chaise and stand upon the footboard with my hat off . . . My friends, satisfied with the victory of the day, had retired to their houses, when the savages sallied forth, dashed in the windows of the house of Mr Serjeant, at which

* The *Evening Post*, edited by William Cobbett, jun., commenced publication on 29 January 1820, but survived for only two months.

Cobbett's England

I was, and made many brutal attacks upon individuals, whom they took unawares in the street or at public-houses. Even at this early period they cut several persons with knives. On Monday, the 6th of March, Moore and Ellice, my opponents, arrived, and as a signal of their arrival their hired savages again dashed in the windows of Mr Serjeant. Upon this occasion they made an attempt to enter the house; but they, after getting into the passage, were beaten back into the street.

On Wednesday morning the election began; and the poll closed in the afternoon, leaving me at the head of it.* On Thursday the savages came well fed and well supplied, all the day long, with gin and brandy, brought out to them in glass bottles, and handed about from one to another. I, that day, saw about twenty of my voters actually torn away from the polling-place, and ripped up behind, and stripped of their coats. During the afternoon, several fresh bands of savages arrived from the country; so that, by the hours of closing the poll, an immense multitude of these wretches, roaring like wolves, and foaming with rage and drink, were collected round the Booth.

As I went out of the Booth I had to pass through bands of savages; and I was scarcely among them, when they began an endeavour to press me down. I got many blows in the sides, and, if I had been either a short or a weak man, I would have been pressed under foot and inevitably killed. However, the crowd took a sway toward a row of houses, standing on a pavement above the level of the area of the open street. With a good deal of difficulty I reached the pavement keeping my feet. I had to fight with my right hand. I had to strike back-handed. One of the sharp corners of my snuff-box, which stuck out beyond the bottom of my little finger, did good service. It cut noses and eyes at a famous rate, and assisted mainly in securing my safe arrival on the raised pavement. Just at this time one of the savages exclaimed: 'Damn him! I'll rip him up!' He was running his hand into his breeches pocket, apparently to take out his knife, but I drew up my right leg, armed with a new and sharp gallashe† over my boot, and dealt the ripping savage so delightful a blow, just between his two eyes, that he fell back upon his followers. For this I should certainly have been killed in a few moments, had not Mr

* Under the traditional election arrangements the poll could be spread over as many as forty days.
† Cobbett is here referring not to a rubber overshoe, but to a stout piece of leather round the lower part of his boot's uppers.

Frank Serjeant made shift to get along, by the side of the houses, to the spot where I was. Getting to me, he turned round, saying, 'Follow me, sir!' and, beating back three or four so as to make them press upon others behind them, the whole body turned about, while he with thumps on some, with kicks bestowed on others, set the body on a sway toward the house, at which we arrived safely.

The next day we were informed that the bands had been greatly augmented from the country; that they were now divided into regular bodies, fed and drenched at different houses, regularly paid, and ready to be brought out in succession, in order to relieve each other. When the poll opened, we had between three and four hundred men, all ready to poll; all was quiet. The Booth had no railway, or any other protection for the voters. The ground, too, was sloping, and the slope ran longways of the Booth. So that, though my men might be ready to poll, it was by no means difficult to force them away.

The Ruffians came, not less than five hundred in number, in regular order, about eight or ten deep, with drums and banners at their head. They made their approach by the higher part of the ground, and began the attack upon my voters. All attempts to resist were in vain. And, in five minutes, three hundred of my voters were as completely driven away as if an army had made an attack upon them. After this, not a man dared to show his face to vote for me.

The way I managed these brutes was well calculated to sting them and their employers to madness. My way was to stand and look upon the yelling beasts with a most good-humoured smile, turning my head now and then, as it were to take different views. Now and then, I would put my mouth close to the ear of some friend, and then point to some beast, giving him at the same time a laughing look, such as we bestow on a dog that is chained up and barking at us. I never had so good an opportunity to philosophize before. The scene was far more horrible than anything of which any man not actually present could have formed an idea. The bottles of gin and brandy continually passed from mouth to mouth; and, from the mass of heads which were closely jammed together, there arose a reek, or steam, just like the reek that rises, in a morning, from a heating dung-hill. What was still more shocking and disgusting than all the rest, was the sight of the wives and daughters of the Rich Ruffians, who were seated on the balconies and at the windows, looking directly down upon this scene, and discovering every symptom of satisfaction and delight, at hearing what would have made a bevy of common prostitutes hang their heads with shame. I remember seeing crowds of prostitutes on the Point at Portsmouth; and, I once saw three hundred on board of a Seventy-Four at Spithead; but I never before saw anything in the shape of woman that would have remained and listened to what appeared to give delight to those wives and daughters.

The savages finally conceived the idea of driving me out of the city. They made a regular attack upon Mr Serjeant's house. They first dashed in the upper-room windows; next they pulled down the shutters of the ground-floor room. Then they broke into the house passage by forcing the door; and while the main body were entering in front, others were (as we could see from the window of our room) scaling a wall to get into the house in the rear. I, who was very ill with a cold, was sitting in my bedroom with my daughter Nancy. Some gentlemen came running up for our poker and tongs. One or two took station at the top of the stairs; while I fixed the bedstead in a way to let the door open no wider that to admit one man only at a time, and stood with a sword. I had pulled off my coat, and was prepared to give with a clear conscience as hearty a thrust as was ever given by man.

However, their cowardice soon put an end to the siege. They entered the passage, stabbed one man twice in his arm and did some other mischief: retreated hastily into the street. The thing went off without bodily hurt to any but our friends! And the natural consequence was, that the poor men who wished to vote for me dared no longer even talk of it! We got some firearms, and were quite secure in the house; but, as to the election, there remained nothing belonging to it worthy of the name. I stood at the bottom of the poll.

[*The Autobiography of William Cobbett*, 1947]

Cobbett's electoral disappointment did not diminish his output as a journalist or his activities as an agitator, but from 1821 onwards he began those rides through England which he reported in the Political Register *and which later formed the basis for his most famous book.*

I . . . put an end to my ride of August, September, and October, 1826, during which I . . . travelled five hundred and sixty-eight miles, and . . . slept in thirty different beds, having written three monthly pamphlets, called the *Poor Man's Friend*, and . . . also . . . eleven *Registers*. I was in three cities, in about twenty market towns, in perhaps five hundred villages; and I saw the people no-where so well off as in the neighbourhood of Weston Grove, and nowhere so badly off as . . . Uphusband. During the whole of this ride I was very rarely abed after daylight; I . . . drank neither wine nor spirits. I ate no vegetables, and only a very moderate quantity of meat; and it may be useful to my readers to know that the riding of twenty miles was not so fatiguing to me at the end of my tour as the riding of ten miles at the beginning of it. Some ill-natured fools will call this egotism. Why is it egotism? Getting upon a good strong horse, and riding about the country has no merit in it; there is no conjuration in it; it requires neither talents nor virtues of any sort; but health is a very valuable thing; and when a man has had the experience which I have had in this instance it is his duty to state to the world, and to his own countrymen and neighbours in particular, the happy effects of early rising, sobriety, abstinence, and a resolu-tion to be active. It is his duty to do this; and it becomes imperatively his duty when he has seen, in the course of his life, so many men, so many men of excellent hearts and of good talents, rendered prema-turely old, cut off ten or twenty years before their time, by a want of that early rising, sobriety, abstinence, and activity from which he himself has derived so much benefit and such inexpressible pleasure. During this ride I was several times wet to the skin. At some times of my life, after having indulged for a long while in coddling myself up in the house, these soakings would have frightened me half out of my senses; but I care very little about them; I avoid getting wet if I can; but it is very seldom that rain . . . has prevented me from performing the day's journey that I had laid out beforehand. And this is a very good rule: to stick to your intention whether it be attended with inconveniences or not; to look upon yourself as *bound* to do it. In the whole of this ride I . . . met with no one untoward circumstance, properly so called, except the wounding of the back of my horse, which grieved me much more on his account than on my own. I have a friend who, when he is disappointed in accomplish-ing anything that he has laid out, says he has been *beaten*, which is a very good expression for the thing. I was beaten in my intention to go through Sussex and Kent; but I will retrieve the affair in a very few months' time, or perhaps a few weeks . . . I shall take my horse and set off again to . . . the foot of Butser Hill . . . and, with a resolution not to be beaten next time, go along through the whole length of Sussex and sweep round through Kent and Surrey till I come to Reigate again, and then home to Kensington; for I do not like to be beaten by a horse's sore back or by anything else; and besides that there are several things in Sussex and Kent that I want to see and give an account of.

[*Rural Rides*, 1830]

During these years I made, at Kensington, a nursery ground, which had been, for the greater part, a rough and sour meadow in 1823. By 1827 on about four acres of land, disposed in about four hundred and fifty beds, there stood, more than a million of seedling forest trees and shrubs, and about three thousand young apple trees. Yet, as if this place were insufficient to provide occupation for my leisure hours, I had another nursery ground on the Surrey side of the Thames, which also was a walled-in-plot. There I made experiments. There, too, I was as safe from the world as a monk of Latrappe. I positively shut all out, except the gardeners and one gardener's wife, who kept the key of the door. I did this, not for the sake of secrecy; but because I would be certain of being uninterrupted when I was in that place. I got in time at Barn Elm, a farm of nearly a hundred acres, the richest land I believe in this whole world, except those marshes which bring diseases along with their riches. My farm was taken care of by my only surviving brother, who had been either gardener or farmer all his lifetime. He, from the fruit of his own labour, raised a family of ten able children, who brought him a score of grandchildren.

I never could go out 'to take a walk' in the whole course of my life; nor to take a ride: there had to be something to make me take one or the other, and though it would be pretty difficult to make me lie abed late in the morning, without actually tying me down with ropes, I might, I daresay, have degenerated in time into that disgraceful thing called a sluggard, if I had not had my work to call me out into the gardens or the fields.

I derived the greatest of pleasures from the reflection that I caused millions of trees and shrubs to be planted in England, that would never have been planted in England for ages yet to come had it not been for me . . . What a deal I did in my lifetime to produce real and solid good to my country! And how different was the tendency of my pursuits to that of the pursuits of the noisy, canting, jawing, popularity-hunting, newspaper-puffing fellows!

In June 1829 I began to publish my famous *Advice to Young Men*.

The work was intended to contain twelve Numbers, and the price of each Number was sixpence; so that, for six shillings, expended in one year of his life, any youth or young man might acquire that knowledge which would enable him to pass the rest of his life with as little as possible of those troubles and inconveniences which arise from want of being warned of danger in time. At any rate, I who had passed safely through as many dangers as any man that ever lived, gave my young countrymen the means of acquiring all the knowledge which my experience had given me.

[*The Autobiography of William Cobbett*, 1947]

By the year 1830 as the working people went on getting poorer and poorer they became more and more immoral, in innumerable instances men committed crimes for the purpose of getting into jail; because the felons in jail were better fed and better clad than the honest working people. As the working people became poor, the laws relating to them were made more and more severe; and the Poor Law, that famous law of Elizabeth, which was the greatest glory of England for ages, had by degrees been so much mutilated and nullified that, at last, it was so far from being a protection for the working people that it had, by its perversions, been made the means of reducing them to a state of wretchedness not to be described. The sole food of the greater part of them had been, for many years, bread, or potatoes, and not half enough of these. They had eaten sheep or cattle that had died from illness; children had been stealing food out of hog-troughs; men were found dead . . . lying under a hedge, and when opened by the surgeons nothing but sour sorrel was found in their stomachs. The spot on which these poor creatures expired was surrounded with villas of Jews, and fund-robbers, living in luxury, and in the midst of pleasure-gardens, all the means of which living they had derived from the burdens laid on the working people.

Besides suffering from want the working people were made to endure insults and indignities such as even Negroes were never exposed to. They were harnessed like horses or asses and made to draw carts and wagons; they were shut up in pounds made to hold stray cattle; they were made to work with bells round their necks; and they had drivers set over them, just as if they had been galley slaves; they were sold by auction for certain times, as the Negroes were sold in the West Indies; the married men were kept separated from their wives, by force, to prevent them from breeding; and, in short, no human beings were ever before treated so unjustly, with so much insolence, and with such damnable barbarity, as the working people of England had been. Such were the fruits of public debts and funds! Without them this industrious and moral and brave nation never could have been brought into this degraded state.

All across the South, from Kent to Cornwall, and from Sussex to Lincolnshire . . . commotion extended. It began by the labourers in Kent entering the buildings of the great farmers and breaking their thrashing machines; for, please to observe, one effect of heavy taxation was the invention of machinery. The farmer or manufacturer was so pressed for money by the government that he resorted to all possible means of saving the expense of labour; and as machines would work cheaper than men, the machines were preferred. The labourers saw . . . that the thrashing machines robbed them of the wages that they should have received. They therefore began by demolishing these machines. This was a crime; the magistrates and jailers were ready with punishments; soldiers, well-fed and well-clothed out of the taxes, were ready to shoot or cut down the offenders. Unable to resist these united forces the labourers resorted to the use of fire, secretly put to the barns and stacks of those who had the machines or whom they deemed the cause of their poverty and misery. The mischief and alarm that they caused by this means was beyond all calculation . . .

Such was the state of England. Here you saw a people, inhabiting the most productive land in the world, a people to whom God had given a large portion of all his choicest blessings, safety from foreign foes, climate, soil, mines, woods, downs, flocks and herds, and, above all, industry perfectly unparalleled; a people, too, whose forefathers gave them the best laws that ever existed in the world; here you saw this people, who were famed for their willing obedience to the laws, and whose forefathers had scorned the thought of maintaining even a single soldier except in case of war; here you saw this people, whose laws said that no man should be taxed without his own consent; first reduced to a state of half-starvation; next setting the laws at defiance; and then attacked by a standing army sent against them to capture them and put them in prison. Such were the effects of heavy taxes, and particularly when raised for the purpose of upholding a funding system, which was a system of usury and monopoly added to that of grinding taxation.

[*Political Register* LXX, 4 DECEMBER 1830]

I was accused by the Government of being engaged in inciting these labourers in their work of destruction, and I was indicted by the Whigs . . . When the news of this indictment was brought to my house in Bolt Court by a reporter of *The Star* newspaper, about eight o'clock in the evening, and when the servant came up and told me of it, after I was in bed, I prayed to God to protect me, turned myself round, and fell fast asleep.

On the day of my trial,* I, having had seven hours' sound, unbroken sleep, got up at four o'clock, went into the garden and gave instructions for the day, came off for Bolt Court at six, arrived there and found breakfast ready for me and a good many friends; and now . . . ate about half a pound of good fat leg of mutton, roasted the day before, ate no bread or anything else with it, and no salt, and never drank one drop of anything that whole day until after the conclusion of my speech, when I drank two stone bottles of milk, out of a horn, given me the summer before by a pretty little American lady, the wife of Mr Cooke, the portrait painter.

When I went into the Court, which was about ten minutes before the Judge entered it, I found the whole of the Court crowded in every part, so as to find great difficulty in getting in; and, indeed, a body of doorkeepers made a desperate effort to keep out my three sons and three other gentlemen who accompanied me. The moment I entered there was a great and general clapping and cheering for some time. When I got to my station I, in order to produce silence, turned round, and, addressing myself to the audience, said, 'Be patient, gentlemen, for, if truth prevail, we shall beat them.' Soon after this the Chief-Justice entered the court and took his seat. Soon after him came in the Attorney-General; and he, in opening his address to the Jury, told them that I had come into court with a great mob at my heels; and, that a shouting had taken place, which showed the spirit in which the defence was to be conducted. This was an abominable falsehood. I had come to Kensington in a close-carriage, hired at Kensington. At Bolt Court I had taken into the carriage Sir Thomas Beevor, Mr Palmer, Mr Blount, and my attorney, Mr Edward Faithful, of Staple's Inn, and one of my sons rode on the box with the coachman.

I had forced the Whig ministers to come by subpoena; and I intended to question them every one, if the Judge permitted me, with regard to the grounds on which they had advised his Majesty in dealing with the rural disorders. For this purpose I brought

* 7 July 1831. Cobbett was acquitted of the charges brought against him.

together, to sit upon the bench in front of me, Lords Grey, Brougham, Melbourne, Durham, Goderich, and Palmerston. There they sat, ranged in a row, to hear my defence; and there sat between two and three thousand intelligent men to witness the scene. From every county in England, I believe, some one man or more was present. Well might I say it was a day of joy to me! It was a reward going ten thousand times beyond all that I had ever merited.

[*Political Register* LXIII, 16 JULY 1831]

In 1832 I visited the North of England and Scotland: the most interesting spots of earth that I ever set foot upon in the course of my long and rambling life. It is hard to say which part of England is the most valuable gift of God; but everyone must see how perverse and injurious it is to endeavour to produce in the one that which nature has intended to confine to the other. In the north there were unnatural efforts made to ape the farming of Norfolk and Suffolk; it was only playing at farming, as stupid and loyal parents used to set their children to play at soldiers during the last war. It was a most lamentable thing that the paper-money price of corn tempted so many men to break up their fine pastures; the turf thus destroyed could not be restored, probably in a whole century; the land did not yield a clear profit, anything like what it would have yielded as pasture; and thus was destroyed the goose with the golden eggs . . .

In Scotland it was very fine: cornfields, woods, pastures, villages; a church every four miles, or thereabouts; cows and sheep beautiful; oak trees, though none very large; and, in short, a fertile and beautiful country, wanting only the gardens and vine-covered cottages that so beautify the South and West. All the buildings were of stone. Here were coal-works and railways every now and then. The farms were all large; and the people who worked on them either lived in the farm-house or in the buildings appertaining to the farm-house; and they were well fed, and had no temptation to acts like those which sprang out of the ill-treatment of the labourers in the South . . . I never liked to see machines, lest I should be tempted to endeavour to understand them. I constantly resisted all the natural desire which people had to explain them to me. As in the case of the sun and the moon and the stars I was quite satisfied with witnessing the effects. These things afforded nothing interesting to me, who thought a great deal more about the condition of the people, than I did about the cause of the movement or about the mechanical effects of the machines.

Being at New Lanark, however, I was rather curious to know whether there was any reality in what we had heard about the effects of the Owen 'feelosofy'. The building which Owen had erected was used as a schoolroom; and here I saw boys in one place and girls in another, carrying on what was called 'education'. There was one boy pointing with a stick to something stuck up upon the wall, and then all the rest of the boys bawling out what that was. In one large room they were all singing out something at the word of command. In another great apartment there were eighteen boys and eighteen girls, the boys dressed in Highland dresses, without shoes on, naked from three inches above the knee, down to the foot, a tartan plaid close round the body, in their shirt sleeves, each having a girl by the arm, duly proportioned in point of size, the girls without caps, and without shoes or stockings; and there were these eighteen couples marching, arm in arm, in regular files, slow march, to the sound of a fiddle, which a fellow big enough to carry a quarter of wheat was playing in a corner of the room. They seemed to perform with great regularity and elegance; and it was quite impossible to see the half-naked lads and girls, without clearly perceiving the manifest tendency of this mode of education to prevent 'premature marriage' and to 'check population'.

It was difficult to determine whether, when people were huddled together in this unnatural state, this sort of soldier-ship discipline might or might not be necessary to effect the purposes of schooling; but I thought it a very strange thing, if a man, calculated to produce effect from his learning, should ever come to perfection from a beginning like this. It was altogether a thing that I abhorred. I do not say that it might not be useful when people were thus unnaturally congregated; and above all things I was not disposed to bestow censure on the motives of the parties promoting this mode of education; for the sacrifices which they made, in order to give success to their schemes, clearly proved that their motives were benevolent; but I was not the less convinced that it was a melancholy thing to behold; that it was the reverse of domestic life, that it reversed the order of nature, that it made minds a fiction; and, which was among the greatest of its evils, it fashioned the rising generations to habits of implicit submission. However, the consolation was that it was impossible that it ever should become anything like general in any nation. The order of the world demands that nine-tenths of the people should be employed on, and in, the affairs of the land; being so employed they must be scattered about widely: and there must be homes and domestic life for the far greater part of the rising generation. When men contract a fondness for anything which has a great deal of novelty and of strangeness in it; when they brood over the contemplation of some wonderful discovery which they think they have made; when they suffer it long to absorb all the powers of their minds; they really become mad, as far as relates to the matter which has thus absorbed all their mental faculties; and they think themselves more wise than all the rest of mankind.

[Tour of Scotland, 1833]

On my own personal account I set not the value of a straw upon a seat in Parliament. I had, for a long while, wished to be in the Commons' House; but never for the sake of any advantage or personal pleasure of my own. From a very early age I had imbibed the opinion that it was every man's duty to do all that lay in his power to leave his country as good as he had found it. I knew that my country presented a scene of wretchedness and disgrace, compared with the scene it had presented at the time that I was born. I hated the life of the great cities; I hated their everlasting noise and bustle: my taste, all my own personal enjoyments, would have led me far away from them forever. I could, if I had been so minded, have secured out of my own earnings much greater possessions and in a state of tranquillity, much greater than I had the desire to be master of. But, feeling that I possessed the mind to enable me to assist in restoring my country to the state in which I found it, a sense of duty to that country restrained me from consulting my own ease and my own enjoyments . . .

The invitation to become a candidate for Parliament came first from Manchester. The people of Oldham, about eight miles distant from Manchester, knowing how difficult it would be to carry an election for Manchester by mere voluntary support, came to the resolution to secure my return for Oldham, which, though inferior to Manchester in point of population, was still a very large and opulent town. Had the invitation come first from Oldham I should certainly have declined that from Manchester because my object was not to disturb any place, but to take the seat with as much quietness as possible.*

* Under the traditional electoral laws it was permissible for a candidate to contest more than one constituency, since constituencies did not all poll at the same

I was at the opening of the elections at Manchester; where . . . having, upon these hustings, seen hooted off that very Mr Sharpe, who was the Borough-reeve that forbade me to enter Manchester on my return from America in 1819 . . . I went off to Oldham, there to remain until I should come back to Manchester a member of Parliament. The election at Manchester was, doubtless, greatly influenced by the election at Oldham, which was known at the former place by twelve o'clock of the first polling day. So that, after that it was naturally to be expected that the electors of Manchester who had intended to vote for me would either transfer their votes, or that they would not vote at all. Yet, in spite of this, the state of the poll, at its close, was as follows:

Phillips	2923
Thompson	2069
Loyd	1823
Hope	1560
Cobbett	1305

This result was sufficiently honourable to me. Not one single pint of beer, or glass of gin, had been given to any human being on my part; no attorney, and no attorney's clerk, had been employed, and not a single person hired, I believe, to do any one thing connected with my election. All, except the mere printing, and the hire of a few carriages, was the effect of voluntary exertion, chiefly by young men in the middle rank of life, whose zeal and activity I never can sufficiently applaud.

So much for the election at Manchester. At Oldham the polling was over on the 13th of December, when the numbers stood as follows:

Fielden	670
Cobbett	642
Bright	153
Burge	101
Stephen	3

At this election not one single farthing's worth of victuals or drink was given to anybody, for any services whatsoever. The committee,

---

time. But if elected for two constituencies a successful candidate could only sit for one. This was not the first time Cobbett had contested a seat: see 48, 61–4 above.

composed of sensible and sober manufacturers and tradesmen, paid
for the printing that they had done, and paid all the expenses of the
hustings, polling-places, clerks etc. They paid also for the entertain-
ment of the candidates at the hotel: and even the carriages to and
from Manchester that I went in I found paid for; and not a man nor
a woman in this excellent town attempted to obtain from me either
money, drink, or any promise to do anything for them in their private
concerns. This was purity of election indeed. It was an honour,
indeed, to represent a people like this. Neither Mr Fielden nor myself
ever canvassed in any shape or form, either individually or collec-
tively; neither of us ever asked the people to give us a vote; but we
contented ourselves with saying that, if they chose us to represent
them, we would be their true representatives to the best of our
power.

Of one thing we were both of us particularly proud; and that was
that the people had the good sense; that sense of their own worth and
our rights as to scorn to attempt to chair us or to drag us through the
streets. In my address to them, I besought them not to think of
imitating the slaves of the boroughmongers. 'Now,' said I, 'my
friends, I shall come down from the hustings, and the first handloom
weaver I meet with, I shall take by the arm and walk with him up to
the hotel from which I came.' I did this, and Mr Fielden did the same;
and thus, in this appropriate manner, we closed this election, which
should be an example to every borough and every county in the
kingdom. Not a disturbance of any sort; not a blow given in anger;
scarcely an abusive word from one person to another; not a single
drunken man seen about the streets; much singing, much playing
music, much joy, much triumph; but all was peace and decorum
from the beginning to the end. As a mark of victory over the combined malignity of factions I set a very high value upon this seat in
Parliament. But I set a higher value upon it as vindicating the
character of the Commons, or common people of England. I always
stood firmly up in defence, not only of the rights, but of the character
of the common people, who, of late years, were looked upon by both
the political factions, and by all the hordes that lived upon the taxes,
as not being of the same flesh and blood with themselves.

[*Political Register* LXXVIII, 22 DECEMBER 1832]

For many years there existed a fashion of looking upon the working
people, and particularly the labourers in husbandry, as an inferior

race of human beings, and of treating them as such. They are the contrary of this; they are the superior race, and they have always been so; they are content as to their station in life; they are un-presuming; they are honest; they are sincere; and he who says the contrary is a base and infamous slanderer. It has been amongst the greatest delights of my life to see them happy, and amongst my most ardent desires to contribute to that happiness. I have admired their character and their conduct ever since I was able to estimate them; and I would willingly strike dead at my feet the insolent brutes who speak contemptuously of them.

[*Political Register* LXX, 25 DECEMBER 1830]

I was born and bred a farmer, or a sort of labourer; and I have never desired to have any rank, station, or name, or calling, more and other than that of a farmer . . . I wanted nothing for myself, but . . . I wanted to take away the power of oppressing and pillaging the order to which I belonged; admire my industry, my perseverance, my won-derful exertions; but there was at the bottom, to balance against all these, my strong and implacable hatred of oppression of all sorts, and particularly the partiality of taxation; the stripping of the working people of their earnings, and the heaping of these earnings upon idlers. This has been the constant ground of hostility to me; and I must say, that I trust in God that I shall so conduct my-self as to cause the hostility to continue until the last hour of my life.

[*Political Register* LXXXV, 30 AUGUST 1834]

For . . . more than twenty-five long years I was the great and constant and only really sharp and efficient thorn in the side of that system which, at last, brought this great country to the edge of convul-sive ruin. I was the evening and the day star, the moon and the sun and the aurora of the press; all other parts of it have come twinkling behind me, shining now and then, indeed, but shining with borrowed light. I always led the way at a great distance forward; I foresaw, foretold every event, every effect; my predictions in due succession became history; I was the teacher of the nation; the great source of political knowledge, and of all those powerful arguments by which so many hundreds of thousands were able to combat the nefarious and desolating system of sway.

[*Political Register* LXIX, 10 APRIL 1830]

It was my intention to close the *Register*, and then I intended to publish, as the work of another year, *The History of My Life*; and then I intended to go into Hampshire, there to cultivate a garden and a few fields to the end of my life, the close of which I hoped to pass amongst that class of society that I have always most loved and cherished, the people employed in the cultivation of the land. I have it rooted in me that happiness and riches are seldom companions; I have seen too much of the misery and opprobrium attending the living upon the public money not to have long ago resolved never to pocket a single farthing of it; and as to what are called honours they have always been with me objects of contempt.

[*Political Register* LXXI, 8 JANUARY 1831]

Born amongst husbandmen, bred to husbandry, delighting in its pursuits even to the minutest details, never having, in all my range of life, lost sight of the English farm-house and of those scenes in which my mind took its first spring, it is natural that I should have a strong partiality for country life, and that I should enter more in detail into the feelings of labourers in husbandry than into those of other labourers.

[*Political Register* XXXIX, 5 MAY 1821]

If the cultivators of the land be not, generally speaking, the most virtuous and most happy of mankind, there must be something at work in the community to counteract the operations of nature. This way of life gives the best security for health and strength of body. It does not teach, it necessarily produces early rising; constant forethought; constant attention; and constant care of dumb animals. The nature and qualities of all living things are known to country boys better than to philosophers. The seasons, the weather, the causes and effects of propagation, in cultivation, in tillage, are all known from habit, from incessant repetition of observation. The nature, the properties, the various uses of different soils and woods are familiar to the mind of country boys. Riding, climbing, swimming, nothing comes amiss . . . Rural affairs leave not a day, not an hour, unoccupied and without its cares, its promises, and its fruitions. The seasons, which wait for no man; the weather, which is no respecter of persons, and which will be what it will be, produce an habitual looking forward, and make the farmer provident, whatever might have been his natural disposition. The farmer's cares are pleasing cares. His misfortunes can seldom be more than lessons. His produce consists of things wanted by all mankind. His market day is a ready money one. No day-books, bills, and ledgers haunt his mind. Envy can, in the natural state of things, find no place in his breast; for the seasons and the weather are the same to all; and the demand for his produce has no other measure than the extent of his crops.

[*Political Register* XXXVIII, 17 MARCH 1821]

But now I am once more in a farm. I might have been, I am aware of it, possessed of bags of public gold or of landed domains, purchased with that gold. I trudge through the dirt, and I might have ridden in the ring at Hyde Park, with four horses to draw me along in a gilded carriage, with a coachman before me and footmen behind me. What I might have been it is hard to say; what I have been and what I am the world knows; I was a plough-boy and a private soldier, and I am a Member of the House of Commons, sent thither by the free voice of a great community. I started at the same age, or thereabouts, with Canning, Liverpool, and Huskisson. I always told them that it was judgement as well as taste that led me into a path different from theirs. Time has shown that my judgement was as sound as my taste; for, if we are to estimate the future as well as the past, they are already rotten; and the kingdom hardly recollects that there were such men. Whereas, some generations, at least, will pass away before the name of William Cobbett will cease to be familiar in the mouths of the people of England; and for the rest of the world, I care not a straw.

If I have one wish more ardent than all other, it is this: that I, enjoying my garden and few fields, may see England as great in the world, and her industrious, laborious, kind and virtuous people as happy as they were when I was born; and that I may at last have a few years of calm at the close of a long life of storms and of tempests.

[*The Autobiography of William Cobbett*, 1947]

But Cobbett's last years were very active ones. Although not a great success in the House of Commons as M.P. for Oldham, he continued to play a vigorous part in agitation and controversy, especially over the Poor Law of 1834, which he resolutely opposed. But in 1835 his health began seriously to fail, as the account of his death, written by two of his sons, testifies.

The Last Illness and Death of William Cobbett

(Written by J. P. and J. M. Cobbett)

A great inclination to inflammation of the throat caused him annoyance from time to time, for several years, and, as he got older, it enfeebled him more. He was suffering from one of these attacks during the late spring, and it will be recollected that when the Marquis of Chandos brought on his motion for the repeal of the malt-tax, my father attempted to speak, but could not make his voice audible beyond the few members who sat around him. He remained to vote on that motion, and increased his ailment; but on the voting of supplies on the nights of Friday the 15th and Monday the 18th of May, he exerted himself so much and sat so late that he laid himself up. He determined, nevertheless, to attend the House again on the evening of the Marquis of Chandos's motion on agricultural distress on the 25th of May, and the exertion of speaking and remaining late to vote on that occasion were too much for one already severely unwell.

He went down to his farm early on the morning after this last debate, and had resolved to rest himself thoroughly and get rid of his hoarseness and inflammation. On Thursday night . . . he felt unusually well, and imprudently drank tea in the open air; but he went to bed apparently in better health. In the early part of the night he was taken violently ill, and on Friday and Saturday was considered in a dangerous state by the medical attendant. On Sunday he revived again, and on Monday gave us hope that he could yet be well. He talked feebly, but in the most collected and sprightly manner upon politics and farming; wished for four day's rain for the Cobbett corn and root crop; and on Wednesday he could no longer remain shut up from the fields, but desired to be carried round the farm; which being done, he criticized the work that had been going on in his absence, and detected some little deviation from his orders, with all the quickness that was so remarkable in him. As he was carried to see the fields a little boy in a blue smock-frock happened to come by us, to whom my father gave a laughing look, at which I thought I should have dropped, I knowing what was passing in his mind. He seemed refreshed at the sight of the little creature, which he had once precisely resembled, though now at such an immeasurable distance.

On Wednesday night he grew more and more feeble and was

evidently sinking; but he continued to answer with perfect clearness every question that was put to him. In the last half-hour, his eyes became dim; and at ten minutes after one p.m. he leaned back, closed them as if to sleep, and died without a gasp.

[*Autobiography of William Cobbett*, 1947]

COBBETT AND
HIS CONTEMPORARIES

Mr Addington and Mr Pitt

Cobbett had originally supported Pitt as the national leader in the war against France, but he became increasingly suspicious of Pitt's financial policies after the suspension of cash payments in 1797 and he criticized Pitt for not opposing Addington more energetically after Addington succeeded him as Prime Minister in 1801. Addington was, in Cobbett's eyes, the supine author of the Peace of Amiens.

From the result of the elections in general we are led to hope that the race of 'well-meaning men', of 'economists' and 'philanthropists' will have experienced a considerable diminution. The disorder of this nation is not a fever but a palsy. Anything that will enliven is good. An actual rebellion would not be half so dangerous as that torpor, that total indifference, which has lately prevailed; the former might be quelled, but the latter, if it continue for any length of time, must end in radical destruction. The decline of life and of genius has ever been marked by a return to childish fancies and amusements; and really the last House of Commons, with its Bills about 'bull-baiting' and 'rabbits' dung', exhibited a scene strongly resembling the last stages of mortality; a scene so disgusting, so humiliating to the nation, and so pleasing to its enemies, we hope never again to behold within the walls of St Stephen. With the new Parliament we hope to see also a new ministry; or at least an efficient and respon-sible ministry. We believe Mr Addington to be a very *honest* man, but what is that? Honesty alone is not a recommendation for a footman, and shall it be for a first minister? He is not altogether destitute of talents as an orator, and even, perhaps, as a financier. In truth, he is what may be called a clever man. But he wants those great and commanding qualities, which mark the statesman, and which are at this time, more than ever, necessary to the preservation of the country. There are several persons in the ministry possessed of very good talents, nor are they at all deficient in point of industry and zeal; but they want weight, they want consequence, they want birth. At no period of our history were the powers of Government ever shared by so few men of family. The ancient nobility and gentry of the kingdom have, with very few exceptions, been thrust out of all public employments: this part of the aristocracy has been, in some measure, banished from the councils of the State. A race of merchants, and manufacturers, and bankers, and loan-jobbers, and contractors, have usurped their place, and the Government is very fast becoming what it must be expected to become in such hands.

We think it probable that Mr Pitt may again be Minister, and if he should, we hope he will perceive and avoid the evil consequences of surrounding himself with *low* and *little men*. In a minister who is himself a little man it may be excused; but Mr Pitt must always be great, even among the greatest. If Mr Pitt should ever cast his eye upon this page, we are well persuaded he will not impute any selfish or malicious motive to the writer of it, and we therefore beg leave to tell him what many good men think, what is thought by many of his warmest admirers, but what he will never hear from any body but ourselves; and that is, that his preference of low churchmen has excited great jealousy and suspicion in those who are sincerely attached to the hierarchy, amongst whom are certainly to be reckoned a vast majority of the clergy; that the project imputed to him, for rendering the clergy pensioners of the State, has greatly strengthened this suspicion; that, in short, the clergy do not regard him as a friend of the church. While Jacobinism was at our doors, while all was in jeopardy, the clergy supported him, because the existence of the Church and State was, in some sort, identified with his adminis-tration; but, now that the danger of commotion and rebellion is past, the minds of men will return to consideration of a nature some-what more private, and, he may rest assured, that the attachment of this powerful body, powerful by their numbers, their talents, their characters, and their local situations, is to be preserved by nothing short of unequivocal testimony, that he harbours no intention of invading or undermining the Established Church; to effect which was, as many persons believe, the sole object of the establishment of the Board of Agriculture, a belief which has been but too strongly corroborated by the proceedings and publications of that Board. We also beg leave to tell him, that his partiality for young and new men, for persons of his own creation, to the almost total exclusion of the old nobility and gentry, is a subject of complaint with a great number of very good men. In the present state of this country a minister might set the nobility and gentry at defiance, if the ill-will excited amongst them could be confined to their own breasts; but it cannot; the people, we mean the better sort of the people, resent the neglect and ill-treatment of those whom they have been, from their infancy, in the habit of respecting, more especially when the honours and favours due to them are conferred on persons of mean birth. *Il vaut mieux qu'une cité périsse qu'un parvenu la gouverne*, is an old Norman proverb; and though the age of chivalry is certainly gone, men yet retain soul enough to dislike the power that places them beneath an upstart. This upstart system naturally grew out of the peculiar circumstances under which Mr Pitt came into power. It was adhered to, with some exceptions, from the first moment of his administration to the last: he appears never to have voluntarily and cordially given the hand to anything great, whether of birth, character, or talent. Let us hope that, if he should again come into power, he will discard a system so injurious to the harmony and welfare of the State. Another error, which it is to be hoped Mr Pitt will correct, is that superabundant caution which prevents him from clearly and unequivocally stating his object and resolution, which leaves the public mind for ever in a state of uncertainty, and which has, in so many instances, proved injurious to the country. To this very error, and to this error alone, the French Republic owes all its successes. The British Parliament never, at any one time, knew the real object of the late war; how then should Europe know it? From an over-anxiety not to fail in any enterprise, the British Prime Minister acted in a way in which he never could be said to undertake; and therefore he was never cordially joined, either at home or abroad. No man voluntarily embarks to be drifted to and fro by the tide, or to shift his course with every change of the wind; but, tell him his destination, and he cheerfully braves the toils and dangers of the sea.

Mr Pitt's forte lies in the domestic rather than the foreign department of politics. Having, from his very youth, had one eye constantly upon the Bank and the other upon the Parliament House, he has never been able to look abroad into the great world of politics. Without therefore at all detracting from the powers of his mind, we may venture to say, that he has discovered no great degree of penetration as to the conduct, the interests, and views of other nations. This is a science, however, which he must now apply himself to. The career on which he is now about to enter bears no resemblance to that which he has heretofore run. The present peace has laid the foundation for an entirely new distribution of power, the effects of which must be felt in a very few years. We must then have war; and it behoves him to consider how we shall be able to resist the confederacy which France can, and will, form against us. It behoves him to consider, *in time*, how the people of this country are going to be roused to arms. 'Husbanding our resources' will not save us. France has neither 'commerce, capital, nor credit', yet, at only six weeks' notice, she ships off an army of thirty thousand men across the Atlantic. She has, in the whole, sent 45,000 men, and more are preparing. This shows that 'commerce, credit, and capital' are not essentially necessary to the power of France; and we hope that Mr Pitt will not longer regard a contest with that power as 'a war of finance'. Men are very apt to attach the greatest degree of importance to that science which they best understand. 'You may,' said the currier, 'think what you please about stone and oak, but if you have a mind to have the town well fortified, take my word for it, there is nothing like leather.' We have opposed money to a military spirit, and we have failed. Let the eloquence of Mr Pitt be employed to create something more efficient than wealth; something that France cannot rob us of; then will he acquire a renown more lasting than brass and marble.

[JULY 1802, *Political Works* I 260–2]

Mr Robert Owen

Robert Owen was a successful factory-owner who also expounded unorthodox views on religion, education, marriage, capital and labour. Owen's schemes for industrialized villages made no appeal to Cobbett.

A Mr Owen, of Lanark, has, it seems, . . . his schemes, which are nothing short of a species of *Monkery*. This gentleman is for establishing innumerable 'communities' of paupers! Each is to be resident in an *inclosure*, somewhat resembling a barrack establishment, only more extensive. I do not clearly understand whether the sisterhoods and brotherhoods are to form distinct bodies, like the nuns and friars, or whether they are to mix together promiscuously; but, I perceive, that they are all to be under a very *regular discipline*; and that wonderful peace, happiness, and national benefit are to be the result! How the little matters of black eyes, bloody noses, and pulling of caps, are to be *settled*, I do not exactly see; nor is it explicitly stated whether the novices, when once they become confirmed, are to regard their character of pauper as indelible, though this is a point of great importance. Mr Owen's scheme has, at any rate, the recommendation of perfect novelty; for of such a thing as a *community of paupers*, I believe no human being ever before heard. Mr Owen has provided an hospital and a chapel for each of his communities; I wonder that he, who appears to have foreseen every other want, should have forgotten a *madhouse*. The formation of so many convents for paupers, with all their kitchens and 'dormitories', and other innumerable buildings, and with all the seeds, cattle, implements, household goods, &c. would require *a sum of money*, the amount of which would have staggered a man whose mind had been fashioned in any common mould. But this is nothing with Mr Owen, who says it may be *borrowed* of individuals, or of the *Sinking Fund*! Adieu, Mr Owen of Lanark.

[*The Last Hundred Days of English Freedom*, AUGUST 1817, *Political Works* V 230]

The Errors of Parson Malthus

The Reverend T. R. Malthus became famous as the author of an Essay on the Principle of Population *in 1798. He was pessimistic about notions of progress. Since population expanded in a geometrical ratio, while the means of subsistence expanded only in an arithmetic ratio, he urged the value of moral restraint in controlling the birth-rate. The alternative was economic disaster: hence Cobbett's wrath.*

PARSON:

I have during my life detested many men; but never any one so much as you. Your book on Population contains matter more offensive to my feelings even than that of the Dungeon Bill. It could have sprung from no mind not capable of dictating acts of greater cruelty than any recorded in the history of the massacre of St Bartholomew. Priests have, in all ages, been remarkable for cool and deliberate and un-relenting cruelty; but it seems to have been reserved for the Church of England to produce one who has a just claim to the atrocious pre-eminence. No assemblage of words can give an appropriate designa-tion of you; and, therefore, as being the single word which best suits the character of such a man, I call you *Parson*, which, amongst other meanings, includes that of Boroughmonger tool.

It must be very clear to every attentive reader of your book on *Population* that it was written for the sole purpose of preparing before-hand a justification for . . . deeds of injustice and cruelty . . . The project will fail: the tyrants will not have the *power* to commit the deeds which you recommend, and which they intend to commit. But that is no matter. It is right that the scheme should be exposed; in order that, as we ought to take the will for the deed, we may be prepared to do justice to the schemer and to the intended executors of the scheme.

In your book you show that, in certain cases, a *crowded* popula-tion has been attended with great evils, a great deal of unhappiness, misery and human degradation. You then, without any reason to bear you out, predict, or leave it to be clearly inferred, that the same is likely to take place in England. Your principles are almost all false; and your reason, in almost every instance, is the same. But it is not my intention to waste my time on your abstract matter. I shall come at once to your practical result; to your recommendation to the Borough-mongers to pass laws to *punish the poor for marrying* . . .

The bare idea of *a law* to punish a labourer and artisan for *marrying*; the bare idea is enough to fill one with indignation and horror. But when this is moulded into a distinct proposal and strong recommenda-tion we can hardly find patience sufficient to restrain us from breaking out into a volley of curses on the head of the proposer, be he who he may. What, then, can describe our feelings, when we find that this proposition does not come from an *eunuch*; no, nor from a *hermit*; no, nor from a man who has condemned *himself* to a life of *celibacy*; but from a *priest* of a church, the origin of which was the incontinence of its clergy, who represented views of chastity as amongst the damnable errors of the Church of Rome, and have, accordingly, fully indulged themselves in carnal enjoyments: what can describe our feelings, when we find that the proposition comes from a priest of this luxurious, this voluptuous, this sensual fraternity, who, with all their piety, were unable to devote their own vessels to the Lord!

But before I proceed further, let us have your proposition before us in your own insolent words; first observing that, at the time when you wrote your book, the Boroughmongers began to be alarmed at the increase of the *Poor Rates*. They boasted of wonderful *national prosperity*; wonderful ease and happiness; wonderful improvements in agriculture; but still the Poor Rates *wonderfully increased*. Indeed, they seemed to increase with the increase of the Boroughmongers' *national prosperity*; which might, I think, very fairly be called the eighth wonder of the world . . .

You talk of the '*punishment of nature*'; you talk of 'the *laws of nature* having doomed him and his family to starve'. Now, in the first place, the laws of nature; the most imperative of all her laws, bid him *love* and seek the gratification of that passion in a way that leads to the procreation of his species. The laws of nature bid man as well as woman desire to produce and preserve children. Your prohibition is in the face of these imperative laws; for you punish the illegitimate as well as the legitimate offspring. I shall not talk to you about *religion*, for I shall suppose you, being a parson, care little about that. I will not remind you, that the Articles of the Church, to which Articles you have *sworn*, reprobate the doctrine of celibacy, as being hostile to the World of God; that the same article declares that it is lawful for all Christian men to marry; that one of the Church prayers beseeches God that the married pair may be fruitful in children; that another prayer calls little children as arrows in the hand of the giant, and says that the man is happy who has his quiver full of them; that the Scriptures tell us that Lot's neighbours were consumed by fire and brimstone, and that Onan was stricken dead; that adultery and fornication are held, in the New Testament, to be deadly sins; I will not dwell upon anything in this way, because you, being a parson, would laugh in my face. I will take you on your own ground; the *laws of nature*.

The laws of nature, written in our passions, desires, and propensities; written even in the organization of our bodies; these laws compel the two sexes to hold that sort of intercourse which produces children. Yes, say you; but nature has *other laws*, and amongst those are, that man shall live by *food*, and that, if he cannot obtain food, he shall *starve*. Agreed, and if there be a man in England who cannot find, *in the whole country*, food enough to keep him alive, I allow that *nature has doomed him to starve*. If, in no shop, house, mill, barn, or other place, he can find food sufficient to keep him alive; *then*, I allow, that the laws of nature condemn him to die.

'Oh!' you will, with parson-like bawl, exclaim, 'but he must not commit *robbery* or *larceny*!' Robbery or larceny! what do you mean by that? Does the law of nature say anything about robbery or larceny? Does the law of nature know anything of these things? No: the law of nature bids man to take, whenever he can find it, whatever is necessary to his life, health, and ease. So, you will quit the law of nature *now*, will you? You will only take it as far as serves your purpose of cruelty. You will take it to sanction your barbarity; but will fling it away when it offers the man food.

Your muddled parson's head has led you into confusion here. The *law of nature* bids a man *not to starve* in a land of plenty, and forbids his being punished for taking food wherever he can find it. Your law of nature is sitting at Westminster, to make the labourer pay taxes, to make him fight for the safety of the land, to bind him in allegiance, and when he is poor and hungry, to cast him off to starve, or to hang him if he takes food to save his life! That is your law of nature; that is a parson's law of nature. I am glad, however, that you blundered upon the law of nature; because it is the very ground on which I mean to start in endeavouring clearly to establish the *rights of the poor*; on which subject I have, indeed, lately offered some observations to the public, but on which subject I have not dwelt so fully as its importance seemed to demand; especially at a time when the poor ought to understand clearly what their rights are.

When nature (for God and religion is out of the question with parsons): when nature causes a country to exist and people to exist in it, she leaves the people, as she does other animals, to live as they can; to follow their own inclinations and propensities; to exert their skill and strength for their own advantage, or, rather, at their pleasure. She imposes no shackles other than those which the heart and mind themselves suggest. She gives no man dominion over another man, except that dominion which grows out of superior cunning or bodily strength. She gives to no man any portion of the earth or of its fruits for his own exclusive enjoyment. And, if any man, in such a state of things, cannot get food sufficient to keep him alive, he must die; and it may truly enough, *then*, be said that 'the laws of nature have *doomed* him to be starved'.

But, when this state of things is wholly changed; when the people come to an agreement to desist, *for their mutual benefit*, from using their cunning and strength at their sole will and pleasure: when the strong man agrees to give up the advantage which nature has given him, in order that he may enjoy the greater advantage of those regulations which give *protection to all*, he surely must be understood to suppose, as a condition, that no state of things is ever to arise, in which he, without having broken the compact on his part, is to be refused, not only protection from harm, but even the bare means of existence.

The land, the trees, the fruits, the herbage, the roots, are, by the law of nature, the common possession of all the people. The social compact, entered into for their mutual *benefit* and *protection*; not Castlereagh's *'social system'*, which means the employment of spies and blood-money men and the existence of mutual suspicion and constant danger to life and limb. The social compact gives rise, at once, to the words *mine* and *thine*. Men exert their skill and strength upon particular spots of land. These become *their own*. And when laws come to be made, these spots are called the *property* of the owners. But still the property, in land especially, can never be so *complete* and *absolute* as to give to the proprietors the right of withholding the means of existence, or of animal enjoyment, from any portion of the people; seeing that the very foundation of the compact was, the *protection* and *benefit* of the whole. Men, in agreeing to give up their rights to a common enjoyment of the land and its fruits, never could mean to give up, in any contingency, their right to *live* and to *love* and to seek the gratification of desires necessary to the perpetuating of their species. And, if a contingency arise, in which men, without the commission of any crime on their part, are unable, by moderate labour that they do perform, or are willing to perform, or by contributions from those who have food, to obtain food sufficient for themselves and their women and children, there is no longer *benefit* and *protection* to the whole; the social compact is at an end; and men have a right, thenceforward, to act agreeably to the laws of nature. If, in process of time, the land get into the hands of a comparatively small part of the people, and if the proprietors were to prevent, by making parks, or in any other way, a great part of the land from being cultivated, would they have a right to say to the rest of the people, you shall *breed no more*, if you do, nature has doomed you to starvation? Would they have a right to say, 'We leave you to the *punishment of nature*'? If they were fools enough to do this, the rest of the people would, doubtless, snap them at their word, and say, 'Very well, then; nature bids us live and love and have children, and get food for them from the land: here is a pretty park; I'll have a bit here; you take a bit there, Jack'; and so on. 'What!' say the proprietors, 'would you take our *property*?' 'No: but if you will neither give us some of the fruits without our labour, nor give us some of them for our labour, we will use some of the land, for starved we will not be.' 'Why do you *love* and *have children* then?' 'Because nature impels us to it, and because our right to gratify the passion of love was never given up either expressly or tacitly.'

But there are the *helpless*; there are those who are *infirm*; there are babies and aged and insane persons. Are the proprietors to support them? To be sure they are; else what *benefit*, what *protection*, do these receive from the social compact? If these are to be refused protection, why is the feeble and infirm rich man to be protected in his property, or in any other way? Before the social compact existed, there were no sufferers from *helplessness*. The possession of everything being in common, every man was able, by extraordinary exertion, to provide for his helpless kindred and friends by the means of those exertions. He used more than ordinary industry; he dug and sowed more than ordinary; all the means which nature gave were at his command according to his skill and strength. And when he agreed to allow of proprietorship he understood, of course, that the helpless were, in case of need, to be protected and fed by the proprietors. Hence the *poor*, by which we ought always to mean the *helpless* only, have a right founded in the law of nature, and necessarily recognized by the compact of every society of men. Take away this right; deny its existence; and then see to what a state you reduce the feeble shadow of a man, who calls himself a landowner. The constables and all the whole *posse* of the county are to be called forth to protect *him*. The able and hearty labourer is to be *compelled* to fight for this frail creature; but if the father of this labourer becomes *helpless*, this father is to be handed over to the *punishment of nature*; though nature would enable the son to provide most amply for the father, if there were not laws to restrain the son from using for the supply of the father that same strength which he is compelled to use in the defence of the feeble proprietor! Oh, no! Mr Parson! If we are to be left to the *punishment of nature*, leave us also to be *rewarded* by nature. Leave us to the honest dame all through the piece; she is very impartial in rewards as well as in her punishments: let us have the latter and we will take the former with all our hearts. Their Boroughmongerships were extremely angry with the Spenceans for their talking about a common partnership in the land; but the Spenceans have as much right as you to propose to recur to the state of nature; yet *you* have not yet been *dungeoned* . . .

To suppose such a thing possible in a society, in which men, who are able and willing to work, cannot support their families, and ought, with a great part of the women, to be *compelled* to lead a life of celibacy, for fear of having children to be starved; to suppose such a thing possible is monstrous. But if there should be such a society, every one will say, that it ought instantly to be dissolved; because a state of nature would be far preferable to it. However, the *laws of England* say that no person shall be without a sufficiency of food and raiment; and, as we shall see, this part of our laws is no more than a recognition of those principles of the social compact of which I have just been speaking.

The lands of England, like those of any other country, were, at one time, and before society was formed, the common property of all the people in England. *Proprietorship* in individuals arose as I have above stated; till, at last, all the land was appropriated. But, so far (when society came to be formed completely) was the proprietorship of individuals regarded as *absolute* that it was made a thing wholly dependent on the sovereign power of the nation. The sovereign power (which with us, is in a king as chief of the nation) was regarded as *the proprietor of all the land*: as the *lord* of it all. And, at this very hour, there is not an inch of land in the kingdom, to which any man has any *title*, which title does not acknowledge that the land is *held under the king*. There are lands held under Lords of Manors; but then these Lords of Manors hold their manors *under the king*. So that, as the king has no Divine Right to rule, but rules and holds his office for the good of the people, and as he may, in the case of violation of the laws, be set aside and see another put in his place, he, as Lord Paramount of the land, is only the chief of the nation; and, of course, all the lands are *held under the nation*.

Agreeably to this notion we daily see the lands of men taken away for public uses sorely against their will. We know that armies may be encamped on them without liability to actions of trespass. We know that men are *paid*, indeed, for their lands taken away; but they are *compelled* to give up lands. Nay, their lands may be ceded to foreign nations. All which, and many other things that might be mentioned, prove that the nation never gives up its paramount right to the lands.

Now, Parson Malthus, were there not some *conditions*, on which the lands of England were granted to, or made the property of, individual persons or families? Every one, who knows anything at all of the laws of England, knows that to every grant of land was attached the performance of some *service* or *duty* towards the *sovereign*, or chief of the nation. Sometimes the service was of a military nature;

sometimes of an agricultural nature; sometimes of a pecuniary nature. Nay, the hold which the sovereign still kept of the lands was so strong, that he was regarded, and he acted too, as guardian of all heirs and heiresses; and, in default of regular heirs, took back the lands, no one being able to give his lands by *will*.

Thus, the king or sovereign held an estate in the lands. From this estate the sovereign drew his means of carrying on the government, of making war, alliances, and so forth. These services have, for the greater part, been abolished by Acts of Parliament; and taxes have been raised to supply their place.

As to the *poor*, when the lands were at first granted to individuals, those individuals were the heads of *bands* or little *knots* of men. The leader, in time, called himself the *Lord*, and those under him his *vassals* or *villeins* or under-tenants, and almost slaves. The lords had the services of the vassals and villeins, and the vassals and villeins were protected and taken care of by the lords. So that, in this, the worst state of things (always excepting the *present*) the *poor* must, of course, have had provision, they being in some sort the property of the lords.

When Christianity came to make considerable progress in England, and the lords of the lands became Christians, they caused churches and parsonage-houses to be erected; they were allowed to give lands to, and to settle tithes on, the priest. And now mark me, Parson, for we are now coming to the point at which you will be pinched. These priests, you will observe, were to have *no wives*, and of course, *no children*, to keep. Therefore, it would have been preposterous to give them the tenth part of the produce of the lands, seeing that, besides, they disclaimed all worldly possessions. *What should they do* with this tenth part of the fruits of the earth? The fact is that the endowment was made upon the condition that the priest should expend a fourth in his own way; a fourth was to go to the bishop of the diocese; a fourth was to maintain the edifice of the church; and a fourth was to *maintain the poor*. For a long while there was no *general law* for the yielding of tithes; but when that charge was legally imposed on all the lands, the poor were, of course, everywhere entitled to this fourth part. *Villeinage* being at this time greatly diminished, it was proper to provide a resource for helplessness other than that of the tables of the lords, and, therefore, this species of hospitality was transferred to the Church, from which the poor had a *right* to demand maintenance, and from which they received it, too, until the *robbery of the poor* (which has been called a *robbery of the church*) took place in the reign of King Henry the Eighth.

Before that time, the poor were, according to the *common law*, that is, the settled law of the whole kingdom, to be *sustained by those who received the tithes*, in the several parishes or districts, which, indeed, all became parishes, except some particular spots, now called extra-parochial. That this was the *law of the land*, at and before the grand robbery of the poor in the time of Henry the wife-killer, and defender of the faith, is certain, not only from the *law-books*, but from the *statute-book*.

This is so important a matter that, though I have . . . gone pretty fully into it, I will not be deterred, by the fear of a charge of repetition, from doing the same again.

When the regular clergy, or monks, or, more properly speaking, the persons of whatever order, who lived in religious houses, or monasteries, came to be in high repute for their piety and for the efficacy of their prayers in behalf of the souls of rich persons, they very soon persuaded those persons to give them a part, at least, of their property; and some of these rich persons gave *advowsons* to the monasteries.

When churches were founded and endowed, the founder and endower became the *patron* or *protector* of it; and he had the right to *present* to the bishop the *priest* who was to officiate in the church and receive its revenues. This right of presenting is called an *advowson*, and we know that *advowsons* are now become objects of *traffic*, and have been frequently *gambled* for.

Rich persons frequently gave to the monasteries advowsons as well as other things; and then the monasteries sent a priest of their own to act as parish-priest, who was allowed a small part for himself; but who was obliged to send away the far greater part of his revenues to the monastery. So that, out of this arose great distress to the poor, who thus lost *their share* of the tithes. This gave rise to two Acts of Parliament, one passed in the fifteenth year of the reign of Richard the Second, and one in the fourth year of Henry the Fourth, ordering that, in all such cases, a sufficiency of the revenues of the church should be retained in the parish for the sustenance of the poor.

Thus, then, clear as daylight stood the *legal* rights of the poor, previous to the grand robbery of them, in the reign of Henry the Eighth, when, and in a few years afterwards, they were despoiled of the whole of their reserved resources. The tithes were either *given to courtiers*, or to *priests with wives*, and thus they have continued to this day.

But still, there would be poor and helpless persons; and as there was no such man as you at hand to recommend the 'punishment of nature', provision was made for the poor in the way of *rate* or *tax*. Hence arose the present system of Poor Laws, which, for those unable to work, provide food and raiment; and, for those able to work, employment, whereby they may obtain food and raiment. And Blackstone, in his enumeration of the *Rights of Persons*, has this right to be sustained in case of need. 'The law,' he says, 'not only regards *life* and *member* and protects every man in the *enjoyment* of them, but also furnishes him with every thing *necessary for their support*. For there is no man so indigent, or wretched, but he may demand a supply sufficient for all the necessities of life from the more opulent part of the community, by means of the several statutes enacted for the relief of the poor; a humane provision, and *dictated by the principles of society.*'

Surely it was dictated by those principles; but the necessity of making it arose out of the *robbery of the poor* by Henry the Eighth's courtiers, and by priests of the succeeding reigns, which priests have, from that day to this, chosen to have wives and families. According to the law of the land, it is not *larceny* or *robbery* where a person (not owing to his own fault) is *reduced to extreme necessity, and steals victuals merely to satisfy present hunger, and to prevent starvation*; and I have no hesitation in saying that a jury, who convicts a person, under such circumstances, are guilty of *perjury*. The law is just here; for, if there be a state of society, which exposes persons to starvation, without any fault on their own part, such society is a monster in legislation; it is worse than a state of nature, and ought to be dissolved. What! a social compact, formed for the purpose of punishing persons (who have been guilty of no fault) for using the only means left within their power to preserve their lives! A social compact, which does not recognize the right to live! Oh, no! you do not deny anybody the right to *live*: you only wish for a law to make them *live on grass* or *dirt*, if they marry after a certain day, or are the fruit of any marriage, or of any cohabiting or carnal communication after that certain day! That is *all* you want. *Only* that! Those who are live now, whether married or single, may have a right to live; but all that marry, or that shall proceed from any marriage or any unlawful commerce, *after this time*, are to feed with the crows or the rabbits!

So that, at the end of about forty or fifty or, at most, eighty years, there shall be no person entitled to *relief*; and that, in a few years, the number of persons so entitled shall be very small.

Callous parson, hardened parson, I have proved that the relief now given, and that ought to be more largely given, by the statute law, to the poor, is their *right*; that it came to supply the place of that relief which the law of the land gave them before the thing called the Reformation; and that the law of the land only supplied, in this respect, the place of the law of nature. I have traced the rights of the poor; meaning the *helpless*, either from inability to labour or from inability to find labour; I have traced their rights down from the origin of the social compact to the present day, and have shown that men, when they originally gave up their right of possessing the land in common, never gave up, either for themselves or for future generations, the right of living, loving, and perpetuating themselves . . .

[LONG ISLAND, 6 FEBRUARY 1819, *Political Works* V 395–406]

An Open Challenge to William Wilberforce

William Wilberforce, the great Evangelical, was hated by Cobbett as a Tory M.P., a friend of Pitt, and the most famous opponent of slavery. His campaign on behalf of the negro slaves in West Indies was beyond Cobbett's comprehension.

WILBERFORCE,

I have you before me in a canting pamphlet; and, upon your conduct and character, as developed in that pamphlet, it is my intention to remark fully, at some future time. At present I shall use it only thus: to ask you what need there was, or what propriety there was, in spending your time in writing and publishing, 'An Appeal to the religion, justice, and humanity, of the Inhabitants of the British Empire, in behalf of the Negro Slaves in the West Indies'; to ask you what propriety, what sense, what sincerity, there could be in your putting forth this thing in the present state of this country? It is to the inhabitants of the 'British *Empire*' that you appeal, in this heap of shameless cant. '*Empire*' in your teeth, you retailer of bombast! The French do not call their country an *Empire*. They, possessing real wealth and strength, are content to call their country what it was always called; that is to say, a Kingdom. Take, therefore, this bombast and make what you can of it. But your appeal is to the inhabitants of this Kingdom: that is to say, to the People of England, Scotland, and Ireland.

Now Wilberforce, what do you want these people to do; you appeal to them for *something*. It is hardly to be believed that you do not want them to do something in consequence of your appeal. You call upon them in behalf of the slaves in the West Indies. In short, this is what you appeal to them for, to cause the 'transmuting the wretched Africans into the condition of *free British labourers*'. There is a great deal of canting trash; a great deal of lying; a great deal of that cool impudent falsehood for which the Quakers are famed; a monstrous quantity of hypocrisy is there evident in these seventy-seven pages of yours; but this would appear to be the substance; this would appear to be what you want; namely to make the West Indian Negro slaves *as well off as the labourers in this kingdom*. As to 'transmuting the wretched Africans into the condition' and so forth, that is nonsense too beastly to be used by anyone but a son of cant. To put your meaning into plain English, it comes to this, that you want the inhabitants of this country and of Scotland and Ireland, to do something that shall make the West Indian Blacks *as well off* as the working part of the Whites in these countries.

Now, this being your meaning, there is no man who knows anything at all of the real situation of the Blacks, who will not declare you to be totally ignorant of the subject on which you are writing; or to be a most consummate hypocrite. Why do you not give us something of a description of the labours, the lodging, the food, the drink, the state of health, and particularly, of the nature and quantity of the food, and the nature and quantity of the labour, in the West Indies. You do not give us any account of these. You pretend to want the Blacks to be *as free* as British labourers; but you do not tell us what you mean by the word *freedom*. The devil a bit do you make any *comparison* between the lives which the Blacks lead and the lives which the White labourers lead. When there were a parcel of bothering petitions before the House of Commons last winter, relative to the Black slavery, Mr James, Member for Carlisle, observed that he was sorry to perceive that, while the Black slaves had so many friends, the poor White slaves in this kingdom appeared to have no friends at all in the House . . . You talk a great deal about the partiality of the laws in the West Indies. What you say about the inhumanity of these laws is right enough; but have you, Wilberforce, have you ever done anything to mitigate the laws which exist in this country with

regard to those free British labourers of which you so cantingly talk?
Never have you done one single act, in favour of the labourers of this
country; but many and many an act have you done against them. In
this canting and rubbishy pamphlet, you bring forward in the way of
charge against the West Indian planters and Assemblies, the following: that 'the killing of a slave was not to be punished, according to
their laws, unless the killing were committed wantonly, or from
bloody-mindedness or *cruel intention*. And,' say you, 'lest there should
be any disposition to visit the crime too severely, it was specially
enacted that, if any negro or other slave, while under punishment by
his master, or master's order, for running away, or any other crimes
or misdemeanours towards his said master, unfortunately *shall suffer
in life or member*, which seldom happens, *no person whatever shall be
liable to any fine therefore*.' This is perfectly damnable, to be sure;
this is tyranny: here is horrible slavery: the tyrants ought to be
stricken down by thunderbolts, or to be otherwise destroyed. But,
Wilberforce, listen to me a bit; did you ever hear of a parcel of
people, who were assembled at Manchester on the 16th August 1819?
These were persons whom you call *free British labourers*. Well, then,
these labourers had not run away from any masters. They had committed no crimes or misdemeanours towards any masters. About five
hundred were, nevertheless, killed or wounded: they suffered *in life
or member*. And, pray, Wilberforce, was anybody punished for killing
and wounding them? Did anybody pay any fines for killing and
wounding these free British labourers? Were not those who committed the killing and wounding *thanked* for their good conduct on that
occasion? Did you ever object to those thanks? Did you not object
to any Parliamentary inquiry into the conduct of those who caused
that killing and wounding? Well, then, this was all right, was it? The
killing and wounding at Manchester was right: the thanking of the
killers and wounders was right: it was right to applaud the conduct
of the Ministers, and to object to inquiry. I find no fault of anybody
about this, mind. I am not discussing this matter now, though this
matter will have to be discussed one of these days. But if these things
were all right, it being right that all these things should take place
with regard to 'free British labourers', pray tell us, Wilberforce, why
a person should suffer any fine for accidentally killing, for over-
punishing unto death, a runaway negro.

You cannot be ignorant that a coroner's inquest declared that an
English soldier died in Yorkshire, last year, in *consequence of having*

been over-flogged. This was not a free British labourer, to be sure; but it was a British soldier. Did you ever hear, Wilberforce, of anybody having been *fined*, or having suffered in any way, for causing death to come to that man by over-flogging? This was a parallel case to the one selected by you. The soldier had committed a crime. He was flogged, and died in consequence of the flogging. Nobody was fined for it, nor called to account for it. Well, then, why did you not, in fairness to the West Indian planters, quote this case? Why did you not show that British soldiers might suffer in life or member while under punishment, and that no persons were liable to fine for it? Why did you not make an appeal to the 'religion, justice, and humanity' of the nation, in behalf of British soldiers and of your famously free British labourers at Manchester? You have selected certainly the most odious, the most tyrannical, the most terrible part of the Colonial Code; and yet you see that a pitiful figure you make with it. Before you set about appealing again in behalf of the black slaves, pray say a little something about the two cases that I have just mentioned; and endeavour to recollect the state of the people of Ireland, living, or rather existing, under that renowned law, the Insurrection Act . . .

Your appeal is to the inhabitants of this country. You make your appeal in Piccadilly, London, amongst those who are wallowing in luxuries, proceeding from the labour of the people. You should have gone to the gravel-pits and made your appeal to the wretched creatures with bits of sacks round their shoulders, and with haybands round their legs: you should have gone to the roadside, and made your appeal to the emaciated, half-dead things who are there cracking stones to make roads as level as a die for the tax-eaters to ride on. What an insult it is, and what an unfeeling, what a cold-blooded hypocrite must be he that can send it forth; what an insult to call upon people under the name of free British labourers; to appeal to them in behalf of Black slaves, when these free British labourers, these poor, mocked, degraded wretches would be happy to lick the dishes and bowls out of which the Black slaves have breakfasted, dined or supped. What! while it is notorious that millions of human beings in these wretched countries never taste of food other than that which is not sufficient to nourish even a poor pig; when it is in evidence before the House of Commons itself, that English labourers, once so well fed, carry even to the field with them cold potatoes instead of meat and bread! Talk, indeed, of 'transmuting the wretched Africans into this condition'. If the West Indian planters were to attempt such transmutation, they would speedily have to repent of it. If they were to attempt to give their Black slaves potatoes instead of the Indian meal and pork and rice, which they do give them; if they were to attempt such transmutation, they would soon find that, to submit quietly to the eating of cold potatoes, men must be under that THING which is called the '*envy of surrounding nations and the admiration of the world*'! But, and this brings you to the test, can you produce us any instances of negro slaves *starved to death*? Away with all your trash about '*free* British labourers' and about 'moral sentiment'. You seem to question in one place whether the Blacks be 'as yet *fit for the enjoyment of British freedom*' . . . Fit for the enjoyment of *what*, Wilberforce? You seem to doubt whether they be as yet fit for the enjoyment of this blessed thing. But, surely, they may be fit to be shut up in their huts from sunset to sunrise. A part of these free British labourers are so shut up; and if they transgress they are, without trial by jury, liable to be transported for seven years. That is pretty well for a British labourer; but let me bring you back to the point. You never attempt to tell us; you never so much as insinuate, that the Blacks perish or even suffer for want of food. But it is notorious that great numbers of your '*free* British labourers' have actually *died from starvation*; and that, too, at a time when the Minister declared from his seat in Parliament that there was in the country an over-production of food. This is notorious. This can be denied by no one. The devil himself, if he were to come to the assistance of the hypocrites, could not embolden them to deny this fact. This being the case, then; and it being equally notorious that no black slave ever suffered for want of food, will not the care, will not the anxiety of a really humane Englishman be directed towards the Whites, instead of towards the Blacks; until, at any rate, the situation of the former be made as *good* as that of the latter. A very large portion of the agricultural labourers of England; a very large portion of those who raise all the food, who make all the buildings, who prepare all the fuel, who, in short, by their labour sustain the community; a very large part of these exist in a state of almost incessant hunger. The *size* of the people is diminishing from this cause. They are becoming a feeble race, they suffer from numerous ailments engendered by the poverty of their food. Their dress is fast becoming nothing but rags; and, in short, every hardship and every suffering that labour and poverty and starvation can inflict, are becoming their lot. You know this as well as I do; but instead of being, as I am, engaged in constant endeavours to put an end to this degradation and suffering, you are constantly endeavouring to perpetuate them. Never do you utter a syllable against any of the measures by which the suffering of the labouring classes has been produced: never do you propose, second, approve of, or in any way give countenance to, anything tending to turn the villainous cold potatoes into bread; and you do all the mischief which it is in your power to do, by endeavouring to draw public attention away from the real sufferings of the people at home to the imaginary sufferings of the Blacks. In many respects your charges against the West Indian planters and Assemblies are false; and the whole of what you say about them is a tissue of disfigurings and misrepresentings. But suppose the *whole to be true*. Still it is manifest from your own showing, or, at least, upon the supposition that you have shown all; it is manifest that your '*free* British labourers' are worse off than your Black slaves. This fact alone is sufficient to characterize you and your endeavours. But my charge against you is this: that you do the labourers of England great harm, or, at least, all the harm in your power; that you not only do them no good; that you, the great canter and noise-maker about humanity, never seem to admit that they have anything to complain of; but, on the contrary, that you describe their situation as desirable, by putting it in contrast with that of the Blacks, by the use of the words *free* and *freedom*, as applicable to their situation; and in short by every trick that the invention of a crafty political hypocrite can furnish . . .

The Combination Law was passed in the year 1799; that is to say, in the thirty-ninth year of the reign of the 'good old King'. Before he had blessed us with another year's reign, that Act was repealed and another passed in its stead. This last Act, which is now in force, was passed on the 29th of July 1800. The first Act sets out with saying, 'That great numbers of journeymen, manufacturers, and workmen have, by unlawful meetings and combinations, *endeavoured to obtain advance of their wages*'. The Act keeps on talking of unlawful combinations, and illegal purposes; but then it takes care, in the very first clause, to declare such meetings and combinations *to be illegal.* After this it goes on jovially; and enacts the punishments which are to attend the commission of such illegal doings. In other words, it first makes the thing criminal, and then allots the punishment. That punishment is imprisonment, in the common gaol, or in the House of Correction; and that too *without any trial by jury* . . .

Well, Wilberforce; the combiners are to go to gaol or to the House of Correction, to the former for not more than three months, and to the latter for not more than two months, for the first going off. *Two justices of the peace*, who are appointed and displaced at the pleasure of the Ministers; two of these men are to hear, determine, and sentence, without any *trial by the peers of the party*. It being very difficult to get proof of this combining for the raising of wages, there is a clause in the Act compelling the persons accused to give evidence against themselves or against their associates. If they refuse, these two justices have the power to commit them to prison, there to remain, without bail or mainprize, until they submit to be examined and give evidence before such justices.

Now you will observe, Wilberforce, that this punishment is inflicted in order to prevent the workmen from uniting together, and by such union, to obtain an addition to their wages, or . . . to prevent their wages from being reduced. Every man's labour is his *property*. It is something which he has to sell or otherwise dispose of. The cotton spinners had their labour to sell; or at least they thought so. They were pretty free to sell it, before this Combination Law of 1800. They had their labour to sell. The purchasers were powerful and rich, and wanted them to sell it at what the spinners deemed too low a price. In order to be a match for the rich purchasers, the sellers of the labour agree to assist one another, and thus to live as well as they can; till they can obtain what they deem a proper price. Now, what was there wrong in this? What was there either unjust or illegal? If men be attacked, either in the market or in their shops; if butchers, bakers, farmers, millers be attacked, with a view of forcing them to sell their commodities at a price lower than that they demand, the assailants are deemed rioters and are hanged! In 1812 a poor woman who seized, or rather assisted to seize, a man's potatoes in the market at Manchester, and, in compelling him to sell them at a lower price than that which he asked for them: this poor woman, who had, very likely, a starving family at home, *was hanged by the neck till she was dead*! Now, then, if it were a crime worthy of death to attempt to force potatoes from a *farmer*, is it a crime in a cotton-spinner to attempt to prevent others from getting his labour from him at a price lower than he asks for it? It is impossible; statutes upon statutes may be passed, but it is impossible to make a man believe that he has fair play, if a farmer's property is to be protected in this manner, and if it be a crime to be punished by imprisonment, without trial by jury, to endeavour to protect the labourer's property.

This Combination Act does, however, say that the 'masters shall not combine against the workmen'. Oh! well then, how fair this Act is! . . . Does not this law say that all contracts between masters and other persons for reducing the wages of men; does it not say, in short, that all such combinations of masters against workmen, 'shall be, and the same are hereby declared to be, *illegal*, null and void, to all intents and purposes whatsoever'? Does not the law say this; and does not it empower the two justices to *send the masters to the common gaol and the House of Correction*? No, the devil a bit does it do such a thing! No such a thing does it do. However flagrant the combination; however oppressive; however cruel; though it may bring starvation upon thousands of persons; though it may tend (as in numerous cases it has tended) to produce breaches of the peace, insurrections and all their consequences; though such may be the nature and tendency of these combinations of masters, the utmost punishment that the two justices can inflict is a *fine of twenty pounds*! But, and now mark the difference. Mark it, Wilberforce; note it down as a proof of the happiness of your '*free* British labourers': mark that the masters cannot be called upon by the justices to GIVE EVIDENCE AGAINST THEMSELVES AND THEIR ASSOCIATES. Mark this, you who have so much compassion for the Blacks. This is the happy state to enjoy which you seem to be almost afraid that the Blacks are, as yet, not quite fit! The 'transmuting of the wretched Africans into the condition' of these cotton spinners; these *free* British cotton spinners, the elevating of them, as you call it, might, indeed, be apt to turn their poor shallow brains. You are for giving them '*free scope* for their industry and for their *rising* in life'. You are for giving them an interest in defending the community. To be sure these cotton spinners have, living under this Combination Law, a very free scope for their industry; a great deal of chance of rising in life; and a monstrous deal of interest in defending the community! The cotton spinners are not, however, so beastly; such complete brutes as not to be able to discover something of the nature of their real situation.

I shall not stop, upon this occasion, to ask whether you, Wilberforce, know anything about the passing of this Combination Law. I shall not ask how such a law came to be passed; for there is no man in his senses that does not clearly see the reason for passing it . . . There has been, for many years past, an almost continual struggle between the cotton labourers and their employers. Recently there has been, if there be not at present, a struggle of this sort going on at

Bolton in Lancashire. The workmen . . . have published a statement . . . of their case . . . Read it, Wilberforce, and then go back
to the West Indies, collect a parcel of Black people together, and
offer them a comfortable situation amongst these '*free* British
labourers'. The things related are so monstrous, so horribly degrading; so beyond all measure cruel and insulting to the poor people,
that I could fain believe them not to be true . . .

Look at the fines! See the crafty invention for mulcting the poor
creatures of their earnings. Think of the horrid state of things when
a fine for . . . *two men being together*, can be thought of as a thing
necessary to be imposed! Think of a fine, amounting to a large part
of a week's wages, for a man's opening a window to get a breath of
cool air, after having been shut up for many hours in a heat of from
eighty to eighty-four degrees! Look at the regulation to prevent the
thirsting creatures from drinking even the rain-water! Look at the
SHOP: in short, look at all the artifices, all this ingenious mixture of
force, menace, and fraud: look at the wretched creatures: look at
their miseries: look at their perishing and emaciated frames: then
look at your fat and laughing and singing and dancing negroes and
negresses; and then believe, if you can; flatter yourself, if you are
able, that we shall think you a man of humanity, making, as you do,
such a bawling about the imaginary sufferings of the latter, and
saying not a word about the sufferings of the former, who are your
own country-people, who are living under your very nose, and with
those miseries and degradation you must be acquainted . . .

When the Parliament shall meet again, there will, I trust, be
Petitions for the repeal of this Combination Law. Any of us can
petition. The '*admiration*' has not yet been made that criminal, and
while you, Wilberforce, are petitioning for the Blacks, I am resolved
to see if I cannot find somebody to join with me in a petition for the
Whites. You seem to have a great affection for the fat and lazy and
laughing and singing and dancing negroes; they it is for whom
you feel compassion: I feel for the care-worn, the ragged, the
hard-pinched, the ill-treated, and beaten down and trampled upon
labouring classes of England, Scotland, and Ireland, to whom, as
I said before, you do all the mischief that it is in your power to do;
because you describe their situation as being good, and because you
do, in some degree, at any rate, draw the public attention from their
sufferings.

It is not my intention to enter into a full examination of your hypocritical pamphlet; but I cannot conclude this letter without observing on the malignity which you discover towards the West Indian planters. You talk of the good example '*afforded in many of the United States of America*'. You must know that this conveys a falsehood as gross as ever was put on paper. It is more than thirty years since the negro slavery was mitigated in the middle and northern States of America; but you must know that in more than *three-fourths* of the territory of the United States negro slavery exists without limit. You must know that the number of negro slaves in the United States has increased with the number of the inhabitants of that country; you must know that not a single pound of tobacco, rice or cotton, the three great exportable articles of the country, proceeds from any but the sweat of slaves. You must know that even the free negroes are taken in the Northern States, and carried and sold in the Southern States; you must know that the seat of the Congress itself is a grand mart of negro slavery; you must know that, in spite of the laws to the contrary, ships in great numbers are fitted out from the United States to fetch negroes from the coast of Africa. Knowing all these things, how very sincere a man you must be to represent the United States as holding forth a laudable example . . .

Away with your cant about the happiness and the morality of the Blacks. You will next take us to the baboons and the monkeys; and, indeed, anywhere to make us lose sight of those who are suffering under our eyes, and screaming aloud to us for help. You can see the miserable Irish stretched out by thousands, expiring from hunger; and you can coolly invite us, in the name of humanity and of Christian charity, to come forward and bestir ourselves in 'transmuting the wretched Africans into the condition' of those *free* and stretched and starving creatures! . . .

Indefatigable as you are, your cant shall make no progress while I hold a pen to expose it. *Answer* me, with regard to the overflogged soldier: answer me with regard to the people killed and wounded at Manchester. To make comparisons of this sort you have the cool impudence to call sophistry. Those who have long been your dupes may be incorrigible; but your power to cajole is departed. Your craft has worn itself out: your name now excites, at the best, a smile or a shake of the head. Seldom has there been a man, who, with the advantages which you once possessed; with all that wonderful combination of cant-cherishing circumstances that once enveloped you; seldom has there been a man to spin himself out so completely as you have

done. I think it very probable that you will live to see the repeal of every Act in the passing of which you have ever been instrumental . . .
[KENSINGTON, 27 AUGUST 1823, *Political Works* VI 351–67]

On Dissenters, Methodists and Catholics

That men, that *all* men, should be allowed to worship their Maker in their *own way*, is, I think, not to be doubted; but if the government once begins to meddle it must establish somewhat of a *uniform creed*, and that this creed will not suit all men is very certain. Whether the government *ought ever to meddle* with religion is a question that I will not now attempt to discuss; but this I am not at all afraid to assert: that without *a state religion*, a kingly government and an aristocracy will never long exist, in any country upon earth; therefore, when the Dissenters . . . come forward and volunteer their praises of kingly government, and boast so loudly and so perfectly gratuitously of their '*ardent loyalty* to their venerable Sovereign' whose goodness to them 'has made an indelible impression upon their hearts'; when they do this they do, in effect, acknowledge the utility and the excellence of a state religion; because, as I said before, and as all history will clearly prove, *without a state religion a kingly government cannot exist*.

If this be the case, it must be allowed that the government is bound to protect its own religion, which is to be done only by *keeping down others* as much as is necessary to secure a predominance to that of the state. And then we come to the question: whether it ought not, for this purpose, now to do something to lessen the number of Dissenting Ministers, who are daily increasing, and whose influence increases in proportion beyond that of their number. Indeed, *if we allow that a state religion is necessary*, this is no question at all; for, in proportion as these Dissenting Ministers increase, the Church of England must lose its power.

But, in another view of the matter, in a *moral* view, I mean, it may still be a question with some persons, whether the increase of these Ministers be a good or an evil. I say in a *moral* view; for, as to *religion* without morality, none but fools or knaves do, or ever did, profess it.

Now, as to the moral benefit arising from the teaching of Dissenting Ministers, it is sometimes very great, and I believe it is sometimes very small indeed, and, in many cases, I believe, their teaching tends to immorality and to misery.

Amongst the Ministers of some of the sects there are many truly learned and most excellent men; and even amongst the sects called Methodists there have been, and doubtless are, many men of the same description. But, on the other hand, it must be allowed that there are many of the Methodist Preachers who are fit for anything rather than *teaching* the people *morality*. I am willing to give most of them full credit for sincerity of motive, but to believe that the Creator of the Universe can be gratified with the ranting and raving and howling that are heard in some of the Meeting-Houses, is really as preposterous as any part of the Mahommedan Creed; and if possible it is still more absurd to suppose that such incoherent sounds should have a tendency to mend the *morals* of the people, to make them more honest, industrious, and public-spirited, for this last is a sort of morality by no means to be left out of the account.

I have heard it observed by very sensible and acute persons that even these ranters *do more good than harm*; but if they do any harm at all the question is, I think, at once decided against them; for that they can do any *good* appears to me utterly impossible.

I am clearly of the opinion that, to lessen the number of this description of Ministers (for so they are called) would be a benefit to the country, provided it could be done without creating a *new source of political influence*. And, as to the politics of the whole sect of the Methodists, they are very bad. Never has anything been done by them, which bespoke an attachment to *public liberty*. 'Their kingdom', they tell us, is 'not of this world'; but they do, nevertheless, *not neglect the good things of it*; and some of them are to be found amongst the rankest jobbers in the country. Indeed, it is well known, that that set of politicians, ironically called THE SAINTS, who have been the main prop of the PITT system; it is well known, that under the garb of sanctity they have been aiding and abetting in all the worst things that have been done during the last twenty years. These are very different people from the *Old Dissenters*, who have generally been a public-spirited race of men. The *political* history of THE SAINTS, as they are called, would exhibit a series of the most infamous intrigues and most rapacious plunder, that, perhaps, ever was heard of in the world. They have *never* been found wanting at any dirty job; and have invariably lent their aid in those acts which have been the most inimical to the liberty of England . . .

I must say that when I hear the Dissenters complaining of persecution, I cannot help reflecting on the behaviour of some of them towards the *Catholics*, with respect to whom common decency ought to teach them better behaviour. But, whether I hear in a Churchman or a Dissenter abuse of the Catholics, I am equally indignant; when I hear men, no two of whom can agree in any one point of religion, and who are continually dooming each other to perdition; when I hear them join in endeavouring to shut the Catholic out from political liberty on account of his religious tenets, which they call idolatrous and damnable, I really cannot feel any compassion for either of them, let what will befall them. There is, too, something so impudent; such cool impudence in their affected contempt of the understanding of the Catholics, that one cannot endure it with any degree of patience. You hear them all boasting of their *ancestors*; you hear them talking of the English Constitution as the pride of the world; you hear them bragging of the deeds of the Edwards and the Henrys; and of their wise and virtuous and brave forefathers; and, in the next breath, perhaps, you will hear them speak of the Catholics as the vilest and most stupid of creatures, and as wretches doomed to perdition; when they ought to reflect that all these wise and virtuous and brave forefathers of theirs were *Catholics*; that they lived and died in the Catholic faith; and that notwithstanding their Catholic faith they did not neglect whatever was necessary to the freedom and greatness of England.

It is really very stupid as well as very insolent to talk in this way of the Catholics; to represent them as doomed to perdition, who compose five-sixths of the population of Europe; to represent as beastly ignorant those amongst whom the brightest geniuses and the most learned men in the world have been and are to be found; but still the most shocking part of our conduct is to affect to consider as a sort of out-casts of God as well as man those who have, through all sorts of persecution, adhered to the religion of *their* and *our* forefathers. There is something so unnatural, so monstrous, in a line of conduct in which we say *that our forefathers are all in Hell*, that no one but a brutish bigot can hear of it with patience.

Why, if we pretend to talk of toleration, should not the exemptions from *military discipline**∗** extend to *Catholic* Christians as well as *Protestant* Christians? What good reason can be found for the distinction? None; and, while this distinction exists, and while I hear not the Protestant Dissenters complain of it, I shall feel much less

∗ It was possible for men, other than Catholics, Jews, or Infidels, to buy exemption from service in the militia.

interest in any thing that concerns *them* . . . They were quiet enough while none but the Catholics were the object of attack . . . they have not even glanced at the hardships on the Catholic, who was expressly shut out from the benefit of the Toleration Act. They could, and still can, see him treated in that way, without uttering a word in his behalf. He is in the very state they were petitioning not to be placed in; and yet they say not one word in his behalf.

Lord Holland is reported to have said, that 'every man had a right to preach if he pleased to anybody that would hear him'. Agreed, my lord, but surely every man ought not to have the right to *exempt himself from the militia service*? Yet this right he has unless he be a *Catholic*, a *Jew*, a *Turk*, or an *Infidel* of some sort or other . . . Is every broad-shouldered, brawny-backed young fellow that chooses to perform what he calls preaching to be excused from service in the Militia? Who is there that would not much rather sit and hear a score or two of young women sing at a meeting-house two or three times a week than be liable to be a hearer, much less a *performer*, at a military circle, though it were but once a year? It is easy enough to TALK about *carrying the Cross* and *mortifying the flesh*; but when it comes to the pinch, when the hour of *performance* comes, we find men disposed to act by a figure of rhetoric, rather than to do the thing in their real, proper, natural person . . .

The great increase of the congregations of the Methodists in particular, and the consequent diminution in the congregations of the Church of England . . . has long been a subject of alarm to the Clergy of the Church, who imagine that, in time, people, from so seldom seeing the inside of a church, will begin to wonder why the *tithes* should be given to the clergy of that Church; and, we may be very sure, that the *Dissenting teacher* will put himself to no very great pains to prove to his flock that the tithes are *due* to the Clergy. This defection from the Established Church bears a strong resemblance to the defection from the parochial Clergy in the second and third century of the Catholic Church of England, when the laziness and neglects of those Clergy and their endless pluralities had thrown the people into the hands of the *itinerant* monks and friars, who appear to have been a most active and vigilant description of men, and, indeed, to have borne a strong resemblance in most respects to the itinerant Methodist preachers of the present day. Such a hold did they get by means of their exertions that, as the benefices fell in, the patrons bestowed many of them in fee upon the Abbeys and Priories, who thus became the patrons, and who, of course, supplied the churches from their own houses, and took the greater part of the tithes to their own use, but who, having become rich in their turn, became also in their turn lazy and neglectful as the parochial clergy had been; and hence came that change which we call the REFORMA-TION, which *originated* not in any dislike on the part of the people to the tenets or ceremonies of the Catholic Church, but in the laziness, the neglects, and, in some cases, oppressions of the Clergy, aided by a quarrel between the King and the Pope.

Men looked back into the cause of the existence of the *tithes* and *benefices*. They inquired into the *grounds* upon which they stood. They asked *why* they were granted. They came to a clear understanding as to what was expected and what was due *from the Clergy* in return for them. And, at every step, they found that *endowment* and *residence* went together. They found, in short, that the parish churches, the parsonage-houses, the glebes, and the tithes, had been originally granted for the purpose of insuring the *constant residence* of a Priest in each parish, there to teach the people, to give them religious instruction, to feed the poor, and to keep hospitality. These were the express conditions, upon which the grants were made; and when, instead of fulfilling these purposes, the livings were given away to Abbeys and Priories and religious communities of various descriptions, who merely kept a sort of journeyman in the parishes, called Vicars, to whom they gave the nails and the hair, while they took the carcase home to be spent at the Convent; when this was the case, and when, in another way, the Popes were bestowing living after living upon one and the same person; when, in short, a very considerable part of all the parishes in the kingdom were thus deprived of nearly all that they had a right to expect in return for their tithes; when this was the case it was no wonder that the people were ready to listen to reformers. And I beg the reader to bear in mind that these were the real efficient causes of what we call the *Reformation*, and not any fault that the people discovered in the *doctrines* or *ceremonies* of the Catholic Church; for after all we believe in the Creed of St Athanasius, and what can any Catholic or Pope want us to believe more? We hold that a man *cannot be saved* unless he believes the whole of this Creed; and will any man believe, then, that the Reformation had a quarrel about doctrine for its cause.

Such being the short but true history of the causes of the *Reformation*, that is to say, *the taking of the tithes from Catholic Priests and giving them to Protestant Priests, keeping back a part to be given to favourite Lords and Ladies,* and which are now called lay impropriations; such being the history of this grand event, which, after all, was merely a shifting of the *Church Property* from one set of hands to another, is it not worth while for the present Clergy, that is to say, the present possessors of that property, to consider a little of the state in which they are with regard to their parishioners? They evidently have considered this, or somebody else has for them. The complaint, on the part of the Church, of the increase of the Methodists, has been made for some years. The evil increases; and dangers, greater than those of former times, menace; because, if once the church property be touched now, it *never returns* . . .

It is notorious that to the neglect of the Clergy the rise of the Methodists is owing. And how neglectful, how lazy, must they be to suffer any sect to raise its head only an inch high! When one looks over the country and sees how thickly the churches are scattered; when one considers how complete is the possession of the country by the Clergy; when the force of habit is taken into view; when we consider that they are the keepers of the records of births and of the bones of ninety-nine hundredths of the dead; when we behold them and their office having all the large estates, all the family consequence and pride on their side; when one considers all this, one cannot help being astonished that there should be any such thing as a Meeting-House; but, when we reflect, that the Clergy have the *power of speaking, as long as they please, to the people, in every parish in the kingdom, once-a-week at least,* and in a place where no one *dares to contradict them,* or would ever think of such a thing; when we reflect upon this, and calculate the number of hours that the Pitt system would exist, if we Jacobins had the use of the pulpits for one fortnight, when we consider this, we cannot find words to express our idea of the *laziness,* the incomprehensible laziness, that must prevail amongst the Clergy of the Established Church.

There are, however, some worthy and diligent men amongst them; and at any rate I do by no means believe that public liberty would gain anything by exchanging the Clergy for THE SAINTS, who have been the most steady abettors of the PITT system, and who have been full as eager as any of the Clergy in the cry of 'No Popery'.

In short, they are *Dissenters* merely because they have *no tithes,* and in that name only do they resemble the Dissenters of the times before the Revolution: they are as much like the Dissenters of old times as *horse-dung* is like an *apple*. Those were fanatics but they were honest and just men, full of courage and full of talent; they understood well the rights and liberties of Englishmen, and upon the maintenance of them they staked their lives. The mongrel SAINTS of our days are as keen for places, pensions, contracts and jobs as the inhabitants of any perjured borough in the kingdom; and indeed if I were to be put to it to find out the most consummate knaves in all England, I should most assuredly set to work amongst those who are ironically denominated SAINTS. They were the great corps of scouts in the famous times of *No Popery*, and did more with that base and hypocritical cry than all others put together. One of the bawling brutes in my neighbourhood told the people that 'the King, Lord bless him! had saved them all from being burnt by the *papishes*'. Was it for a service like this that he was to be exempted from Lord Castlereagh's Local Militia? A congregation of these SAINTS in a neighbouring county, *cashiered their Minister* because he spoke at a town meeting against the clamorous outcry of 'No Popery'; and in consequence thereof a gentleman gave him a living in the Church.

Many, very many, instances of their base time-serving in politics might here be mentioned; but enough has, I think, been said to show that the increase of their Members cannot be expected to be attended with any good effect. I would let them alone; but I would give them no *encouragement*. There are persons who like them, because they look upon them as hostile to *the Church*. Their hostility is for the *tithes*, which they would exact with as much rigour as the present Clergy, and would, if possible, deserve them less. But *my* great dislike to them is grounded on their politics, which are the very worst in the country; and though I am aware that there are many very honourable exceptions amongst them I must speak of them as *a body*; and as a body I know of none so decidedly hostile to public liberty. This is an age of *cant*. The country has been ruined by cant; and they have been the principal instruments in the work, and have had their full share of the profit.

[*The Dissenters*, MAY 1811, *Political Works* IV 52–60]

The Quakers

In one article the wishes of our wise government appear to have been gratified to the utmost; and that too without the aid of any express form of prayer. I allude to the hops, of which, it is said, that there will be, according to all appearance, none at all! Bravo! Courage, my Lord Liverpool! This article, at any rate, will not choke us, will not distress us, will not make us miserable by 'over-production'! . . . The hop affair is a pretty good illustration of the doctrine of 'relief' from 'diminished production'. Mr Ricardo* may now call upon any of the hop-planters for proof of the correctness of his notions. They are ruined, for the greater part, if their all be embarked in hops. How are they to pay rent? I saw a planter, the other day, who sold his hops . . . last fall for sixty shillings a hundred. The same hops will now fetch the owner of them eight pounds, or a hundred and sixty shillings.

Thus the *Quaker* gets rich, and the poor devil of a farmer is squeezed into a goal. The *Quakers* carry on the far greater part of this work. They are, as to the products of the earth, what the *Jews* are as to gold and silver. How they profit, or, rather, the degree in which they profit, at the expense of those who own and those who till the land, may be guessed at if we look at their immense worth, and if we, at the same time, reflect that they never work. Here is a sect of non-labourers. One would think that their religion bound them under a curse not to work. Some part of the people of all other sects work; sweat at work; do something that is useful to other people; but here is a sect of buyers and sellers. They make nothing; they cause nothing to come; they breed as well as other sects; but they make none of the raiment or houses, and cause none of the food to come. In order to justify some measure for paring the nails of this grasping sect, it is enough to say of them, which we may with perfect truth, that if all the other sects were to act like them, *the community must perish*. This is quite enough to say of this sect, of the monstrous privileges of of whom we shall, I hope, one of these days, see an end, If I had the dealing with them I would soon teach them to use the *spade* and the *plough*, and the *musket* too when necessary.

[REIGATE, 26 JULY 1823, *Rural Rides* I 163–4]

---

* David Ricardo was famous as an advocate of economic expansion, which could be brought about only by increased investment. He criticized the financial policies of successive governments as inflationary, but his belief in the iron law of wages made him an opponent of government intervention in the economic life of the nation.

COBBETT THE
PARLIAMENTARY REFORMER

Parliamentary Reform

Of what has been denominated *Parliamentary Reform* I have always disapproved; because I never could perceive, in any one of the projects that were broached, the least prospect of producing a *real reform*. Of universal suffrage I have witnessed the effects too attentively and with too much disgust ever to think of it with approbation. That the people of property; I mean *all* persons having real property, should have some weight in the election of members of Parliament I allow; but, even if this were provided for by law, the funding and taxing and paper system still continuing in existence to its present extent, I should be glad to hear the reasons, whence anyone is sanguine enough to conclude, that the evil complained of by Mr Tierney, the evil of leaving the making of laws in the hands of men of mere money, who have little or no connection with or feeling for the people; I should be glad to hear the reasons whence, the present money system continuing in full force, any man can conclude that this evil, as to the magnitude of which I agree in opinion with Mr Tierney, is to be gotten rid of. To me it appears that, while the present means of acquiring such immense fortunes, at the expense of the people, remain, there can be found out no effectual cure for this evil; and this is, I think fully proved by the uniformity in the Parliamentary irresistance from the time the funding system began to the present hour. Without laying too much weight upon the theories of Montesquieu, De Lolme, Paley and others, who have written in praise of the English constitution, we must allow that the real protecting power of the House of

Commons lies entirely in their being able to *refuse money*. There was a pensioned Parliament in the reign of Charles II. But in that reign the most excellent of our modern statutes were passed; and, let it be remembered, they were wrung from the throne solely by the power, the real and active and frequently exercised power, of refusing money; not little paltry sums for this public purpose or for that private job; but of refusing *supplies*, and thereby checking the will of the king and his ministers, and effectually controlling their measures, with regard to foreign as well as to domestic affairs. Since the establishment of the funding system we have seen many just and virtuous measures originating in the House of Commons; we have seen kings thwarted, and ministers turned out by that House: whether the main object of these struggles has generally been for public good or party triumph; whether they have generally tended to the happiness and honour of the country, or merely to the emolument of the victors, are points that may admit of dispute; but that no House of Commons, since the establishment of the funding system, has ever refused to grant supplies, however large and burdensome, and for whatever purpose wanted, is a fact which admits of no dispute; and, as to the present, we all know that when the minister now comes for money the question for the consideration of the House of Commons is not, in fact, whether it shall, or shall not, be raised upon the people, but simply in *what manner* it shall be raised. Viewing the House of Commons, therefore, as 'the guardians of the property of the people', as Mr Pitt in his better days described them; and not as assembled merely to discuss, or rather to sanction, executive measures, I cannot, with the above facts before my eyes, perceive any ground for hoping that any practical good would, while the funding system exists in its present extent, result from the adoption of any of those projects, which have professed to have in view what is called *Parliamentary Reform*; to which I must add that, in my opinion, every such project would be found utterly impracticable; that it would, at once, drop lifeless from the hands of the projector, or, which is infinitely worse, would disseminate the seeds of a convulsion, to be freed from the numerous torments and horrors of which, the people would gladly resort to the at once protecting and deadly shield of a military despot. When the funding system, from whatever cause, shall cease to operate upon civil and political liberty, there will be no need of projects for Parliamentary reform. The Parliament will, as far as shall be necessary, then reform itself; and until then no attempt at alteration in this

respect should, in my opinion, and for the reasons I have above-stated, be made, either in or out of the House of Parliament . . .
[*Parliamentary Reform*, *Political Register*, MARCH 1806, *Political Works* II, 51–2]

To the Electors of the City of Westminster

It being now become almost certain that a dissolution of the present Parliament will speedily take place I propose to address to you about four or five letters thereupon, and upon your duties which will there-from arise; which letters, that they may not be confounded with any others, I shall number from one to as many as they shall amount to.

Before I proceed to submit to you the observations and sugges-tions, which, upon the above-mentioned subject, present themselves to my mind as being likely to be useful at the present moment, give me leave to express a hope that you are duly impressed with the importance of the subject itself; for, if you regard, or if you act as if you regard, the days of an election as a time merely for keeping holiday and making a noise; as a time for assembling in a tumultuous manner, without running the risk of smarting under the lash of the law; if, like the slaves of Rome, whose tyrannical and cunning rulers let them loose, once in a while, to commit all manner of foolish and beastly acts, in order thereby to terrify their own children from the commission of such acts; if, like these degraded creatures, you suffer yourselves to be made the sport of those who solicit your votes, then, indeed, will you . . . deserve to be slaves all the rest of your lives. But my hope is, and indeed my expectation is, that your conduct will be exactly the reverse, that 1st you will look back to the days of your forefathers, and revive in your minds the arduous and successful efforts, which, at various times, they made for the preservation of the privilege which you will soon have an opportunity of exercising, and that you will duly reflect upon the nature of that privilege; that, 2ndly, you will view, in its true light, the present situation of your country, and that you will diligently and impartially inquire whether all the evils we endure, and all the dangers that threaten us, are not to be ascribed to the folly and baseness of those who have possessed, and who have so shamefully abused, their privilege of choosing members of Parliament; that, 3rdly, you will inquire, whether at any time heretofore, the members whom you have chosen, have held to their professed principles or their promises, and that you will endeavour to ascertain the cause of their desertion of their principles and of you; that, 4thly, you will, beforehand, while you have time well to weigh and to consider, inquire and resolve upon what sort of men those ought to be whom you shall elect, and what sort of security you ought to demand for their holding to the principles which they profess; and that, 5thly, you will, as soon as may be, determine upon the very men for whom you will vote, and in support of whom, as your representatives in the Parliament, as the makers of the laws to which you are to submit, as the guardians of your property and your personal freedom, you will use all the lawful means in your power. To assist you in these considerations and inquiries is the object of the letters that I am now beginning to address to you; and though I am well aware that the far greater part of you stand in need of no such assistance, yet I am persuaded, that want of the habit of reflecting in some, and want of leisure in others; have heretofore prevented them from forming right opinions upon the subject, and, under that persuasion I cannot refrain from endeavouring to do some little in the way of guiding those opinions upon the present important occasion, begging you to bear in mind, however, that it is not my intention to offer *myself* to you as a candidate unless it shall be found that no other man in the kingdom has the public spirit to stand forward upon that ground, whereon alone I think any man ought to be chosen as a member of the House of Commons, and particularly as a member to represent the City of Westminster.

1. In looking back to the days of our forefathers we find them, in ancient times, fallen into a state of personal bondage to the few great possessors of the soil, who were the only part of the subjects of the king enjoying anything worthy of the name of freedom; we find that, from this degraded state, they began to rise under those kings of England who carried the English banners in triumph over the fields of France, who won and left, as an everlasting memorial of the valour of Englishmen, those Lilies which, only six years ago, were effaced from their arms; we find that the right or the duty of voting for members of the House of Commons, which right had, by those gallant kings, been conferred upon every man not a mere bondsman, was, by a foolish and cowardly successor, restricted, in many cases, to persons having a certain portion of property of a particular kind; we find, that, in more recent times, the advisers of the kings, the creatures who swarm about a court, and who rob the people of their substance

as the drone robs the industrious bee, contrived various means of rendering the representatives of the people the mere tools of the court, and that, when unable to succeed in corrupting them to their purposes, they caused the Parliament to be dissolved; we find, that, when this scheme had been tried to its utmost without success, a weak and bigot king endeavoured to govern without a Parliament, and soon after we find him driven from his throne, the crown being settled in succession upon another family, and provision being made, a solemn compact being entered into that, forever afterwards, the people should have an opportunity of choosing a new House of Commons once in *three* years; we find, however, that a House of Commons, so elected, became parties to a law for depriving the people of this right, and for making the term *seven* years instead of three, from the passing of which law we may date the rapid decline of public liberty, and the no less rapid increase of public burdens. Until that fatal day great and almost constant were the exertions of the people to maintain their due weight in the Government; since that day they have made but few and those very contemptible exertions; but, now, when they see that there is no hope left of safety from any other source, ought they not to rouse themselves? Ought they not to exert their power as often as it comes into their hands? The object of our ancestors in contending, with their lives, for their rights as relating to the choice of members of Parliament, was, to keep a check upon the power of the crown; to prevent the king, or his favourites, from taking from them any more of their property than what should be found necessary for the support of the government and for the carrying into effect such measures as should be found requisite for the good of the nation in general; to prevent their substance from being drawn from them to fatten idlers and profligates; to prevent any part of their fellow subjects from becoming oppressors of the rest; to prevent, in short, the loss of their freedom and of the enjoyments therefrom arising. The *means* was the power, given to representatives of the people, of *refusing to grant money to the king*. And, when I say the power, I mean the *real* power of refusing, and not the mere *nominal* power of refusing; for, if the power be merely nominal, it is no power at all; and, if it be *never exercised*, it is merely nominal.

'To what,' some one may say, 'does all this tend, but to convince me that all exertions on the part of the electors would be useless?' Yet this is not so. The fault has been with the *independent* electors; for, owing to several causes, there always will be, until a material

change in the representation takes place, a great majority in favour of
whomsoever is minister; though the representation arising from the
decayed boroughs will always produce, in point of mere numbers, the
means of overbalancing anything that can be done by the independent
electors, still, these latter are able, if they were willing, to make such
a choice as would be a sufficient means of protection against all the
schemes of oppression that ambition or rapacity could devise. The
electors of boroughs, where their numbers are small, or where they
are, in some way or other, dependent upon one or two rich men; the
electors of such places, whether they actually take bribes or not, have
some excuse for becoming the miserable and degraded tools of a
corruptor. Their crime is, indeed, detestable; they deserve to be held
in execration; their names ought to be inscribed upon the gallows-
tree, after their carcasses have therefrom been carried piece-meal by
the fowls of the air; 'BE SUCH THE FATE OF THE VENDORS OF
THEIR CHILDREN'S LIBERTIES AND HAPPINESS' ought to be
uttered from the lips of every honest man; but still *they* have some
excuse; they have the excuse of the hungry robber and assassin
whose crimes they equal and whose fate they deserve. But for you,
electors of Westminster, what excuse shall be made for *you*, if you
fail in the performance of your duty; if you violate so sacred a trust?
If you, who have all the political advantages that time and place can
give; who well understand what is right, and who have no temptation
to do what is wrong; who can plead neither ignorance nor want; who
are, in short, as free as you could possibly be made by any scheme of
liberty that human art is capable of devising; what shall be said for
you, if, setting at nought all considerations of country and of individual honour, you become the passive instruments, the trodden-down
things, of some half-dozen of opulent men, whose only merit, in the
eyes of the world, would be that they would hold you in a degree of
contempt, surpassing that which they entertain for the beasts that
perish?

To hear some persons talk of an election for Westminster, a
stranger to the state of things would believe, that the electors were
the bondsmen, or at best the mere menial servants of a few great
families. The question, upon hearing such persons talk, seems to be,
not what man the electors may wish to choose, but what man is
preferred by a few of the noblemen, though, by-the-by, it is well
known that the law positively forbids such noblemen to interfere in
elections. Notwithstanding this law we hear the boroughs called after

the names of the peers who are the *owners* of them; we hear that such
a peer has so many members in the House of Commons, and such
a peer so many more; and this we, at last, have come to hear and to
talk about with perfect unconcern; but this is no excuse for *you*.
Neither peers nor any body else can render you dependent if you are
disposed to be free. You are nearly *twenty thousand* in number. Your
trades and occupations are, generally speaking, full as necessary to
your employers as their employment is necessary to you. If you are
turned out of one house there is always another ready to receive you;
if you lose one customer you gain another; you need court the smiles,
you need fear the frowns of no man, and no set of men, living. Some
few unfortunate dependants there may be amongst you; but the
number is so small as to be unworthy of notice, when compared to
the whole . . . To make use of any interested motive for the purpose
of inducing an elector to give, or to withhold, his vote, is a crime in
the eye of the law, which has provided injunctions and oaths, which
has prepared shame and punishment for every such crime; but to
attempt to induce an elector to vote contrary to his conscience is also
a personal offence, that every honest man will resent with as much
indignation as he would an accusation of perjury. How scandalous,
then, is it that tradesmen should patiently listen to the commands of
their customers, nay, that they should obey those commands, in
direct opposition to the dictates of their own minds, from the paltry
consideration of gain, which, when compared to the weight of taxes,
brought upon them from the want of real representatives, is as a
farthing to a pound!

Men who have been *born* slaves, who, and whose fathers before
them, have never had an idea of freedom, may be pitied, but they
cannot reasonably be blamed, any more than the Pagans of Peru
could be blamed for their want of Christian faith. Yet it is not rare to
hear Englishmen speaking contemptuously of those r tions who
quietly submit to the absolute will, and who lick the foot of a ruler;
but if such nations be objects of just contempt, what shall be said of
us, if, with all the noble examples of our ancestors before us, with all
the laws which their valour obtained and their wisdom has secured,
we give up, and that, too, from the basest of motives, all the *real*
freedom, which we enjoy, or which we might enjoy? In the exercise
of perfect freedom at elections, we are not only secured by the law;
not only does the law say, that we shall be permitted freely to make
our choice of persons to represent us; but, it commands us not to be

biassed, and it provides heavy penalties for all those who attempt to bias us. In short, men must arrive at a state of sheer baseness of mind, before they can suffer themselves to be induced to vote for persons, of whom, in their consciences, they do not approve; and this must be more especially the case in a city like Westminster, where it is morally impossible that any motive of real *interest* should exist sufficiently powerful to bias a rational man.

The possessor of the elective franchise is the holder of a trust; he acts not only for himself, but for his country, and more especially for his family and his children. To violate his trust, or to neglect the performance of what it imposes upon him, is, therefore, not merely an act of baseness, not merely a degradation of himself, but a crime against others; and a man so acting, ought to be regarded by his neighbours as a public offender: as an injurer of every other man; as a person to be shunned and abhorred; as a person very little, if at all less detestable than one who betrays his country into the hands of an enemy. It is no justification of such a man to say that those who bias him are his superiors or that his temptation is great. In the case of Westminster there is no temptation at all; and besides what crime is there which might not, upon such a principle, be justified? And, as to the 'superiors' who bias, they may be superior in riches; but in every other respect are they not the basest of mankind, except only those who are biassed by them? Are they not violators of the law? Are they not hypocrites of the most odious description? Are they not, with the sound of loyalty and patriotism on their lips, the worst of enemies to their King and their country? I shall be told that, in some instances, even the Clergy have used the means of corruption at elections. I hope such instances are rare; and it cannot but shock any one to know that they at all exist; but, if they existed in ever so great a number, no countenance would thereby be afforded to the corrupted; for, of all detestable characters, the most detestable assuredly is what is called 'an *electioneering parson*'. From the chalice of such a priest one would flee as from a goblet of poison; and if ten such instances could exist, without producing an ecclesiastical censure and punishment, the Church ought to be destroyed, root and branch, for ever.

[*First Letter to the Electors of Westminster*, AUGUST 1806, *Political Works* 11, 85–90]

Our country is not yet subjugated; let us hope that it never will; but it is, by every one, confessed to be in a perilous situation; it is, by every one, confessed to be in a situation in which it cannot possibly for many years maintain its independence; and if you see it in that light, does it not behove you, at this moment in particular, 'diligently and impartially to inquire whether all the evils we endure, and all the dangers that threaten us, are not to be ascribed to the folly and baseness of those, who have . . . so shamefully abused their privilege of choosing members of Parliament'?

These evils are, FIRST, a system of taxation so extensive as to leave to no man scarcely any thing, scarcely any species or article of property, in which the tax-gatherer does not, in one way or another, come to claim a share on the part of the government; SECOND, an universal prevalence of disguise, insincerity, suspicion, fraud, and ill-will between man and man, engendered by the system of taxation; and THIRD, the existence of nearly a million and a half of paupers, in England and Wales only, upon a population of less than nine millions of souls. The dangers that threaten us are an increase of taxes, an increase of immorality thereby engendered, an increase of paupers, and, as the natural consequence of all these, a further decrease of public spirit, and in short, such a state of things as may finally render England what Holland now is.*

The greater part, the far greater part of the evils which we now endure have been brought upon us by the councils and measures of PITT . . . but it was, at all times, in the power of *the House of Commons* to have prevented the minister from adopting the measures by which that necessity was created, it being the chief use of that House to watch over the expenditure of the public money, and to withhold it, unless in cases where the granting of it is evidently necessary for the public good. Yet during the twenty years squandering of Pitt; during the whole of the time that he was more than doubling the national debt, never did the House of Commons, in any one instance, refuse him the money he asked for, however enormous the sum, and however foolish or profligate the purpose . . .

The fault, then, lay in the House of Commons. That House we have to look to for all the evils we feel, and all those we apprehend. But the House of Commons is called the *representative of the people*, and in many cases it is so; and, if that House do wrong, it is because the people themselves have made a bad choice. I shall, perhaps, be

* Cobbett was afraid that the ascendancy of the financial interest would make England as powerless as Holland, which had been unable to resist the aggressions of the French Republic.

reminded, that Mr GREY, now Lord Howick, asserted in Parliament, that there were 300 of the members, whose seats were the private property of noblemen and others, and who came into the House without having had any connection or acquaintance with those who were called their constituents. But, though we cannot deny this, the people have still power enough, if they had the virtue, to elect such a House of Commons as should protect them against the effects of every weak or wicked measure, on the part of a minister. There are upwards of 70 *county* members; there are 50 more sent by cities or boroughs, over the electors of which no man can have any other control than that which is given him by the folly or the baseness of the electors; and, though 120 members are but few in comparison with the whole number of which the House now consists, every one must perceive that, against the decided will of 120 such members as might be selected, no minister would be able to carry any measure whatever; because in the mind of the nation those members would be estimated according to their real worth, and not merely according to their numbers. Nay it is my opinion that if there had been, for the last twenty years, but twenty members, chosen upon principles such as ought to prevail, we should have avoided great part, if not the whole, of our present calamities and dangers. We have, upon particular occasions, seen what only one or two members are capable of effecting; what, then, might not be effected by 20 members, entering the House with a fair resolution to do their duty, and particularly with a resolution *never to touch the public money, either by their own hands, or by those of their relatives?* This is the great *test*. All professions, short of this, I account as nothing; for experience has proved to us that the moment the patriot begins to pocket the profits of a place or a pension he changes his tone, or he becomes a mute, and seems to forget every thing that has theretofore passed in his lifetime.

These are the truths which hardly any man will attempt to deny; but the worst of it is, that the electors are, but in too many instances, participators in all the worst feelings of the elected. They can complain, most bitterly complain, of oppression; but, comparatively speaking, there are very few of them who will scruple to avail themselves, as often as they can, of the advantages, or imaginary advantages, to be derived from assisting those who are the cause of such oppression; and, perhaps, in their complaints against the government none are more clamorous than those who find themselves compelled to refund in a tax the price of their vote at an election. Such men may complain; but who will be weak enough to pity them? A nation of such men may be subjugated, and crawl along the remainder of their days under the lash of a conqueror; but is there any man that will not say that those who have sold their liberty ought not to be slaves? . . .

Let no man deceive himself by the subterfuge, that it is not *money* for which he gives his vote. To give money to all, or to half the electors of Westminster, would strain the purse even of a Nabob or a contractor; but, to bribe with the hopes of gain, with the hopes of increased trade, or with the more seducing hope of causing the elector or his relations to be maintained at the expense of the government: or, in other words, of enabling them to cheat the public; to bribe in this way is easy enough; and in this way has bribery been most successfully practised. Weak, however, must that elector be who hopes, by pitiful evasion, to escape from the punishment which awaits such conduct; who hopes to escape from the contempt of mankind and from those stripes of oppression which, by his own baseness, he has enabled others to inflict upon him. To hear such a man complaining of the weight of taxes, and to see him, with that complaint upon his lips, go to the hustings and give his vote for a man, from whom he has no reason to expect anything but a tame acquiescence in every measure proposed by any and by every man who happens to be minister, is something too disgusting to admit of an adequate description.

[*Second Letter to the Electors of Westminster*, SEPTEMBER 1806, *Political Works* ii, 90–2]

That the king has a right to dissolve the Parliament whenever he pleases has never been denied by any man, who did not feel an interest in a Parliament's continuing undissolved. It is, in fact, the only *constitutional* means which the king has of protecting himself and his authority, of preserving his due weight in the scale, or of preserving to the Lords their due weight, against the encroachments of the House of Commons; for that assemblies of men are as apt to encroach as individuals history affords us many and striking proofs. This prerogative is also necessary to the protection of the people, seeing that it is possible for a House of Commons to betray its trust, and, by the means of the power of granting or withholding supplies, to tyrannize over both king and people. It is now, however, contended that the Parliament itself has the right of inquiring whether this prerogative be justly exercised. We are told . . . that it was 'given to the king not to enable him to get rid of honest and virtuous counsellors, but to protect him against the exuberance of independence'. . . . Than this principle nothing can be more false, nothing more contrary to the constitution of our government, nothing more degrading to both king and Parliament and nothing better calculated to keep alive a constant jealousy and hatred of the former. The true doctrine is, that the Parliament has nothing at all to do with the choosing, or the dismissing, of the king's ministers, who are called and who ought to be regarded as *his servants*. The true office of the Parliament is, to propound, to discuss, to pass laws, and to present them to the king for approbation or rejection; and it is the peculiar office of the House of Commons to grant, or refuse, money to the king for any and for every purpose whatever. In this and this alone consists its power as a check upon the other branches; and in the just and wise exercise of this power consists the only constitutional security that the people have, either for property, liberty, or life. Take away this power, or render it of no use, *no matter by what means*, and all we have, life included, is placed at mere hazard. Such a well-poised government, supported by laws so just and of so long standing, does not, all at once, sink down into an open and merciless tyranny, crushing every man without exception: but, by degrees, and with a motion continually accelerating, down it must come, if this power be once destroyed, or, by whatever means, rendered of no effect. If this doctrine be sound, and I think that no reasonable and disinterested man will deny that it is, what despicable nonsense is this that we hear about the *confidence of Parliament* in the king's ministers? A man cannot serve two masters. It is certain that the Parliament, viewed in the constitutional light as a *check* upon the king, are the very last of his subjects who ought to be able to interfere in the choice of his servants. If there be a limit upon the prerogative; if the exercise of it be subjected to any considerations of expediency, in any body besides the king himself, it is evident that the Parliament must be the judge; and if the Parliament are of opinion that it is inexpedient to dissolve them of course they will not be dissolved. What then becomes of the prerogative? But, gentlemen, the fact is that the people who preach such doctrine as this wish to make a mere tool of Parliament; a mere mouthpiece wherewith to remonstrate against every measure of the king that may militate against their interests, whether in the way of power or of profit. They never tell us that the House of Commons, upon seeing the affairs of the nation committed to dishonest or childish men, ought to *refuse money*, till they see those affairs in honester or abler hands; these writers never call upon the House to exercise this, its constitutional and efficient power. That would not suit their purpose. It is always some dispute about *who shall have power and profit*, in which such men wish to engage the Parliament; and it is, to be sure, ridiculous enough to see the whole nation engaged in the same disputes, taking the side of one place-hunting faction or another, and seeming to think it of no consequence at all who compose the House of Commons, that House, which . . . forms the only constitutional check upon the exercise of the royal authority! . . .

[*Twelfth Letter to the Electors of Westminster*, APRIL 1807, *Political Works* 11, 149–50]

On Placemen in the House of Commons

I confess that my wish would be that men who are chosen members of Parliament should *never* become servants of the king. A man cannot serve two masters; and it matters very little whether he be nominally the servant of both at one and the same time; or whether he be the nominal servant of one of them, while he is paving his way for being taken into the service of the other . . .

But the debates (it is said) would become frivolous and unimportant if the king's counsellors and servants were not in the House. The *debates*! All is debate. Why, there is a standing order of the House against publishing any debate; and moreover any member may, when he pleases, cause the galleries to be cleared, and the doors to be locked against all spectators and hearers. It is, to be sure, a very valuable thing that we possess; a mighty thing for our liberties, that any one member, either of those for Old Sarum, without even a seconder, may, at any time, totally deprive us of.

But . . . why should the debates become of no importance? Of no interest at all to us, if the ministers and other placemen were kept out of the House? They might indeed be of little interest to those who are now seeking for place through the means of debates; but to the people: it is possible, that you can think that the discussions of men who were the real representatives of the people; who could scarcely have any views towards gain of any sort; who would be under no temptation to vote this way or that way to serve themselves, or to serve a party: is it possible that you can think that the discussions of such men would be less interesting to the people than the wranglings of two parties, *always* opposed to each other, taking opposite positions in the House as naturally as two hostile armies, and well known to be contending for the places and emoluments which the Crown has to bestow? No, it is not possible; I assert that it is not possible for you to believe that the discussions of an assembly where, upon all great occasions, it is known beforehand on which side each member will speak and vote; where it is known beforehand what the result will be; I assert it to be impossible for you to believe that the debates of such an assembly can be so interesting as the debates of an assembly where there is no such foreknowledge, and where there is known to exist, generally speaking, nothing to bias the judgement of the members. . . .

As to the advantage of 'questioning the ministers face to face', they were so questioned when they were excluded from Parliament. They were sent to the House by the king to bear his messages; to ask for money in his name; and to give such explanations as the representatives of the people required at their hands. There is, surely, nothing difficult in this. It is the regular and natural course of proceeding; but can any one pretend that it is natural; can any one pretend that it is not a monstrous absurdity that ministers, that the servants of the king . . . should be *called to account by themselves*; that they should sit in judgement, and vote, and assist in the deciding, upon the merits or demerits, of their own conduct; and especially when it is known beforehand, when it is acknowledged to be essential to the very system, that they have, and must have, a majority in their favour, it being, according to that system, impossible for them to hold their places any longer than they have that majority?

. . . What have they, as long as they can preserve their majority, to tremble at? When did you see a ministry tremble, except for the loss of their places? And why should they? But if there were a House of Commons without placemen or pensioners, consisting of men not capable of being placed or pensioned; if the race could not be for power and emolument; if the members could not, in the future, discover any motive for indulgence, and lenity with respect to the past; then, indeed, wicked and foolish counsellors would have good cause to tremble at the moment of meeting, not an *able* minority, but an *honest* majority in Parliament, who would not waste their time in making long lawyer-like speeches, in order to show their fitness for conducting wars and negotiations; but who, having only their own good, as connected with that of the public, in view, would busy themselves in doing that which belonged to their office, as guardians of the public treasure and the public liberty.

If the House of Commons contained no placemen; if it were unmixed with the servants of the king; if it were composed of men who never could touch the public money, can it be believed that the public money would not be better taken care of? Besides the incompatibility of the two situations, in this respect, is it not evident that a man who has, for one half of the year, to fight daily battles in the House of Commons for the preservation of his place must neglect the duties of that place? Is it not evident that, if a man be compelled to give his mind up to debate and the preparation for debate, the duties of his office must be left to underlings or be wholly neglected? Nay, is it not evident that, if the possession of the place is to depend upon debates in the House of Commons, he will fashion his measures and especially his appointments and other favours to that mould which is likely to ensure him the greatest number of friends in that House; which fashioning would be useless for his purpose were the members and the relations of the members incapable of receiving emoluments from the public purse?

The king, too, would, if this were the case, be left free in his choice of servants. He would not be compelled to take into his council a whole pack together. He would not be compelled to consider who could make the best, or rather the longest, speeches, and who would carry with them the greatest number of votes. He would be free to select whomsoever he thought most able and most trustworthy; while the Commons, on their side, could have no reason for undue bias or partiality in this respect, at the same time that, if the king had counsellors whom they disapproved of, they would, at all times, have the power of censuring them, of impeaching them, or of causing their removal by following the old constitutional course of *refusing money*; which is now, all the world knows, a power that is never exercised, nor is it ever thought of being exercised.

Is there an evil we complain of, or feel, which cannot be traced to this source? . . .

[*Members of Parliament*, JANUARY 1809, *Political Works* III, 2–5]

Parliamentary Reform the Cure for Excessive Taxation

It is now become pretty evident to every body that if the people had been fully represented in Parliament this enormous load of taxes would never have existed; and it is not less evident that the load will continue, as far as the taxes can be collected, as long as we are in want of a reform. It is clear enough, indeed, that the taxes to their present nominal amount cannot be collected; but still the weight will be felt as severely, and still more severely, because the burden will be as great as can possibly be borne, and will continue to spread ruin around us. There is nothing, therefore, short of a reform of the Parliament that can be of any real service; and it is of the greatest importance that the people should be cautioned against being amused with any petty schemes and devices. If the enemies of reform choose to assail church property; if they choose to begin any revolution of this sort, in the name of all that is ridiculous let them do it. But I hope that the work will be theirs; that it will be their own undertaking, and that the reformers will not be thereby amused, and withdrawn from their own proper object.

All sorts of schemes are afloat. Never was a nation so stocked with *schemers*. There is nothing too high or too low for them. They soar at one moment, and dive the next. Expedients which could put pickpockets and shoplifters to shame are brought forward with serious faces and pompous accents. There must be a reform in Parliament, or a Bethlem* big enough to hold half the nation.

[*Letter to Sir Francis Burdett*, SEPTEMBER 1816, *Political Works*
IV, 482]

What would a Reform of Parliament achieve?

It would be impossible for a Reformed Parliament to restore to affluence or competence the hundreds of thousands of persons who have lately become insolvent. It would be impossible for a Reformed Parliament to find the means of paying away 60 or 70 millions a year. It would be impossible for a Reformed Parliament to prevent mortality from taking place in cases where the mortal stab has been given. It is impossible for the present Parliament to pay much longer

* Cobbett is here referring to the Hospital of St Mary of Bethlehem, which had been used as a lunatic asylum since 1547, and which was familiarly known as Bethlem or Bedlam.

the interest of the debt in full; and a Reformed Parliament certainly would not attempt it. But a Reformed Parliament would do a great many good things *at once*; and in the space of *a very few years* it would restore the country to ease and happiness.

I. It would do away with the profligacy, bribery, and perjury of elections, and it would, thereby, in one single act, do more for the morals of the people than has, since the system has existed, been done by all the Bible Societies and all the schools that have ever been set on foot, and all the sermons that have ever been preached.

II. A Reformed Parliament would instantly put an end to that accursed thing called *Parliamentary interest*. Promotion and rewards and honours in the army, navy, the church, the law, and in all other departments would follow *merit*, and not be bestowed and measured out according to the number of votes that the party or his friends were able to bring to the poll in support of this or that set of people in power. Thus would the nation be sure to have the full benefit of all that it needed of the best talents and the greatest virtues that it possessed. It was from this cause . . . that America shone so bright in the late contest. The world was *surprised* to see naval and military commanders spring up as it were spontaneously out of lakes and woods; and the people of England were utterly astonished to see their ships and armies either captured by, or fleeing in disgrace from men who had never before been heard of. But, if we had considered, that the President of the United States had, in the choice of his commanders, the whole of the nation lying open before him, and that he had no particular interests to consult in the determination, we should have been less surprised. If he had had boroughmongers or members of corporations to consult in his appointments; if the lady of this man, or the sister of that man, or the father of another, and so on, had had the dictation of his appointments, the Porters and Decaturs and Chaunceys and M'Donnoughs and Jacksons and Browns, might have remained to till the land, while the protegés of corruption were letting in the legions of the enemy to devour its produce and enslave its inhabitants. This . . . is the people to whose conduct and institutions we are to look. They are a people like ourselves in all things, except where our institutions have an effect different from theirs. What should make crimes so rare amongst them, and great public virtues and talents so abundant? Why should that soil more than this be fertile in great military and naval skill and courage, caught up, all at once, out of common life? Nothing but this; that there the executive is unbiassed in its choice, and has the whole of society to choose from; while here there is a borough faction, whose pretensions and power supersede the legitimate power of the executive, a power which would instantly be restored to it by a Reformed Parliament. It is well known what heart-burnings there are in the army and navy on this score. *Parliamentary interest* is well understood amongst the gentlemen of those professions. *Merit* is a thing, therefore, little sought after, because worth very little when acquired. Of all the professions and ranks of society none ought more anxiously to wish for a Reformed Parliament than the officers in general, and even the privates, of the army and navy; and yet there are men so stupid as to suppose that these bodies would present a great obstacle in the way of reform. As ambassadors, consuls etc., the Americans send their *most able* citizens, while ours consist of persons chosen from the motives before mentioned. The superior talent of the American diplomatists is universally acknowledged. Indeed, what Englishman can refrain from blushing at the endless proofs, which the last twenty years have given to the world of this superiority, which is made the more conspicuous by the language of both countries being the same? Yet there is no scarcity of talent of this sort in England. But the talent, to be available by our executive, must have the borough interest at its back; and as that is seldom the case we are exposed to all the shame which bungling agents never fail to bring upon a nation; and, notwithstanding that a tribe of underlings of greater talents than the chief are generally selected to accompany him, we have seen many of their public papers so obscure and ungrammatical as hardly to have a meaning; to say nothing of the want of knowledge, of argument, and of force which they almost invariably exhibit. All this a Reformed Parliament would put to rights. The best talents would, in this department also, be called forth into the country's service. There could exist no motive for sending an unfit person on any foreign mission. Every person so sent would know that reward and honour would follow his merits, and that disgrace and punishment would follow misbehaviour. In the Church too, the Crown, the Bishops, and even private patronage would be freed from this source of undue bias. Borough interest would no longer open the path to rich livings, while it closed them against learning and piety and true charity unsupported by that interest. And thus it would be in every department. And . . . would this not be *a good*? This good would operate *instantly*. It would be completely in the power of a Reformed Parliament to effect it; and it is hardly to be believed that it would be possible to find a king, who would not be glad to be thus restored to the free use of his lawful authority.

III. A Reformed Parliament would, in the space of one single week, carefully examine the long list of Sinecures, Pensions, Grants, and other emoluments, of individuals, derived from the public purse. They would critically distinguish between those which had been granted for public services, known and acknowledged, or capable of being proved, and those for the granting of which no good reason could be assigned. They would inquire also into the *duration* of these several grants, would ascertain the aggregate sums which the parties had received in this way, would ascertain the means of the present possessors, would trace the public money back to its source, and would then adopt such measures thereon as justice might point out. And would this be doing *nothing*? Would this be *no good*? Would it be no good to curtail this enormous head of expenditure? Would it be no good to leave a large part of this money in the hands of the farmers and tradesmen, in order to assist them in paying the poor-rates and other necessary taxes? . . .

IV. A Reformed Parliament would, without a day's delay, set a Committee to work to inquire into the amount of the salaries of all persons in public employ. They would ascertain whether the said salaries of such persons had been raised in consequence of the rise in the prices of provisions and labour which took place some years ago. It would soon be discovered that the salaries of the Judges, for instance, have been doubled within the last twenty years, and that the ground, upon which the augmentation took place, was the rise in the prices of provisions and labour. This being the undeniable fact, and it also being undeniable, that the prices of provisions and labour have come down to their former amount, a Reformed Parliament, *freely chosen by all the tax-payers*, would say, that the Judges' Salaries ought to be reduced to *their former amount*; and if any one grumbled at this reduction a Reformed Parliament would call him a most unreasonable and unjust man. The same would be done with regard to the *Police Justices* and other persons appointed by the Government. Great crowds of people in office would be *dismissed* wholly and their salaries saved; but a Reformed Parliament would not be under the necessity of turning *clerks* out to starve. The fault has not been theirs if they have been unprofitably employed. The expense of affording them a decent maintenance, in proportion to their talents and length of service, would be trifling, and they would receive it, except in cases where their introduction or promotion had sprung notoriously from the *Borough interest*; for between men thus fostered, and other men, a distinction would necessarily be made. More than a million a year of expense would thus be lopped off in a week, without any one act of cruelty or injustice. Let the spawn of the Borough-corruption return back to feed on the flesh that its parent has collected; but let the hard-working clerk and his family find food at the hands of national generosity.

V. Precisely the same principle would guide a Reformed Parliament in its reduction of the army and its siftings of the navy. In all cases where promotion or rewards could be traced back to the borough interest the hand of a Reformed Parliament would be unsparing; but to all meritous men, of all ranks, it would show how liberal a people fairly represented can be. Be the cause, in which sailors and soldiers have fought, what it may they have incurred no blame. Their wounds ought to be regarded, and so does the length of their service, as proofs only of their valour; and it would be one of the first principles of a Reformed Parliament to reward and hold in honour valiant men. A Reformed Parliament would suffer no man to be in a sailor's or soldier's coat. If an imposter they would whip him; if a real soldier or sailor they would give him ample means to have house and home and to be well fed and clothed. But a Reformed Parliament would see no necessity, I imagine, of a Commander-in-Chief's office, with an enormously expensive Staff. They would see as little necessity for supporting, at an enormous expense, academies where the sons of borough-voters and other protegés are educated (in some cases under foreign masters) *in the art of war*, and who are thus, from their earliest youth, separated and kept as a *distinct caste* from the rest of the nation. A Reformed Parliament, adopting the maxim of BLACKSTONE that all such establishments are abhorrent to the principles of the English Constitution, would support no such thing; but would look upon the nation as most secure when under the protection of the arms of freedmen; commanded by their natural leaders, the gentlemen of England, selected for their skill and courage by a king uncontrolled and unencumbered by borough interest and family intrigue. If possible still less necessity would a Reformed Parliament see for Barracks, Fortresses, and Depots in the heart of England. Such a Parliament would devote these places to demolition and sale for useful purposes. Rows of officers joined together by the arm, like chain-shot, lounging up and down the streets of towns, and thrusting the tradesman and farmer from the pavement, would be an object of which a Reformed Parliament would soon rid the country. Long swords dragging the ground; lofty caps and brass helmets, tied under the chin; whiskers, muffs, tippets, jackets, bark-boots, false-calves, false-shoulders, and the whole list of *German* badges and frippery, would fly away before the acts of a Reformed Parliament as the dust and dead leaves and rotten limbs of trees fly through the air before a thunder-storm in Carolina; and we should once more behold the plain and warm English coat envelope the bodies that contain the brave and honest hearts of our countrymen. In examining the *half-pay list* a Reformed Parliament would proceed, not so much with an eye to *economy*, as with an eye to *impartiality*; for, as to compassion, no man who has served as a soldier or a sailor ought to be exposed to the pain of exciting such feeling . . . Whatever else a Reformed Parliament might do in this respect, certain I am that they would never suffer hundreds of midshipmen, who have faced death in a thousand shapes, to starve in our streets, or become paupers. As to this matter, a Reformed Parliament would first take care that an *impartial distribution* was made; and having seen that they would rely upon the justice of the people to afford the means of any necessary augmentation.

VI. A Reformed Parliament, elected by the people themselves, and having no reason to suspect that any *secret* enemies of the Government could have any power to do mischief, would have no occasion to expend money in 'secret services'. Here would be a saving at once equal to the comfortable support of all the discharged midshipmen. A Reformed Parliament, chosen by the people and re-chosen *yearly*, would have no idea of expending money for any *secret* purpose. It would openly avow all its objects, and would scorn to owe its safety to the aid of spies and informers. It would need no eaves-droppers and pot-house topers to give it information of the people's feelings and complaints. The poll yearly taken would fully instruct it upon these heads . . . A Reformed Parliament would, therefore, want no 'secret-service money'; it would need no hired scoundrels to inform against this man or that man; to mark out this man as a friend, and that man as an enemy of the Government; this man as loyal and that man as disloyal; there would be none of this disgraceful spy-work; none of these devices by which neighbours, friends, families are set together by the ears; none of those infamous proceedings which tyrants adopt upon their favourite maxim of '*divide and destroy*' . . .

VII. Nothing would be improved by a Reformed Parliament more than the reputation of the Bar. The Government under the influence of, and controlled by, a Reformed Parliament, would stand in need of no acute men, bred to the law, to lay traps for, and catch, the people. It would have no desire to find out the means of prying into every man's mind and purse. The taxes would be such as were necessary; they would be simple in their nature, obvious in their source, impartial in their distribution amongst the payers, and easy in their assessment and collection. It would require no law-lords at the Boards; it would not require the keen education and inexorable habits of a lawyer to be a collector or supervisor. Acts of Parliament on fiscal affairs would not swell into volumes any more. The people would understand the duties they had to perform towards their government; and the gentlemen of the Long Robe, rescued from the disgrace of being tax-gatherers and surchargers would, as they formerly did, raise their heads boldly in the Courts of Law and Justice, having their eyes fixed upon fair fame, won in their profession, which, in itself, has always been considered as learned and honourable . . . We should again see the Bar possessed by men who would scorn to truckle to the underlings of ministers and, for the sake of mere bread, become the third or sixth clerks in the offices of Government.

VIII. The *Press* would be what it ought to be. Perfectly free to utter the words of any man who confined himself within the bounds of *truth*, as to public men or public matters. A Reformed Parliament would want nobody to assist it in blinding the people. It would stand in need of no deception, no fraud, no falsehood. The hireling crew of editors and authors would, indeed, severely suffer. They would be reduced to beggary or exalted to the gallows for robbery or theft; but what do the people owe them, except it be ill-will and curses? They have been amongst the most efficient instruments in producing our ruin; and they, at this moment, are labouring with a degree of malignity, which, while it demonstrates their sense of the desperateness of their cause must go to the account of their demerits, whenever that account shall be settled. A Reformed Parliament need care nothing about the press, in any way, but for the protection of the freedom of that guardian of public morals. The Parliament would have to meet their constituents *annually*. Their conduct could never be misrepresented with any degree of effect. There could, therefore, be no motive for hiring the press, which would become what the press ought always to be. A Reformed Parliament would naturally be anxious for the instruction of the people in political matters, but it would effect this desirable object by the frequent discussions which annual elections would give rise to, and by the promulgation of its acts amongst all classes of the people, the acts being written in plain and intelligible language, and stripped of all that uncouth jargon and that cumbrous tautology, by which craft obstructs the pursuit of common sense. All the filthy and base intercourse between the underlings of office and the hirelings of the press would cease . . .

IX. A Reformed Parliament would not leave the Civil List and the 'Crown Lands' as they are called in their present state. In this time of public distress a Reformed Parliament would think it reasonable, and, indeed, necessary, that the Civil List should be greatly reduced. The enormous sums now swallowed up under that name almost surpass belief. We see that the President of the United States of America, who is the Chief Magistrate of a people equal in number to the people of England and Wales, including Scotland, perhaps; whose country has a quantity of trade and commerce not much less than this country has; and who was able single-handed to carry on a successful war against the undivided power of England; that Chief Magistrate, a man chosen for his wisdom, experience, and great talents, has no more allowed him than *six thousand pounds a year*! Yet America is well governed, and so well governed and so happy are the people that there is no misery in the land, and there are not as many crimes committed there in a year as are committed in England and Wales in one week, or perhaps one day! To what . . . are we to ascribe a difference so disgraceful to us? Shall we hear it asserted that we are *naturally a murdering and a robbing race*? If our Government were to do this, it would not answer its purpose, for the Americans are of the same race. But we reject with indignation the unjust idea. We are naturally as honest and as kind as the Americans are. It is our *misery*, and that alone, which produces such a mass of crimes in England, compared to what is committed in America. And this misery arises, as every one now sees, from that pressure of taxation, which forces men into the lists of paupers and beggars. When a man becomes a pauper or a beggar; when want is continually staring him in the face; when hunger gnaws his stomach and cold pinches his limbs; when his present sufferings are merely a foretaste of that which awaits him later in life; when hope has ceased to linger in his bosom, then comes despair, and with the remaining energies of his mind and body *he seizes by force or by fraud on that which he cannot obtain by labour*. This is the beginning of crime; and here we have the true and only cause of the difference between us and the Americans in this respect. The President's six thousand pounds a year is an example worthy of imitation in England, especially in this season of horrible distress. The hirelings of the press tell us that we have *secured our Constitution* by the *sacrifices* that we have made. You know, and the people now see, what they have secured; but, be this as it may, if it be acknowledged that we have made sacrifices, let us ask what sacrifices the Royal Family, the Judges, the Placemen, the Sinecure-men, the Pensioned Ladies, the Police Justices, and others, have made. Their incomes have been augmenting during the whole of this long season of sacrifices! . . . It is now acknowledged, even by the very hirelings themselves, even by that most corrupt of prints, the *Times* newspaper, which was conceived in sin and brought forth in iniquity, and which has never belied its origin; even by this vile hireling it is now acknowledged *that great and general distress prevails*. Well, then, will none of those who wallow in luxury, out of means derived from the public purse, do anything in the way of making sacrifices? . . . Surely the Civil List, which has had so many hundreds of thousands added to it during the season of the people's sacrifices, ought now to be greatly reduced. If each of the junior branches of the Royal Family were allowed as much as the President of the United States is allowed, and if the king were allowed ten times as much; this surely would be enough. It will be time early enough to talk of splendour when the nation shall again be relieved from its distresses, and when the number of paupers shall have diminished. It will be time enough to have grand dinners and sumptuous fêtes. Besides the President governs America very well without any splen-dour at all. No country upon earth is so well governed; in no country are there so few breaches of the peace; in no country is the law so implicitly and cheerfully obeyed. Why, then, need our Royal Family be so anxious to secure the means of living in splendour? Splendour may serve to dazzle slaves, but it never can be an object of respect with free men. If a reduction such as I have here spoken of were made, a million pounds a year would thereby be left in the pockets of the people, instead of that sum being annually taken from them by the tax-gatherers. This would be the true way of enabling the farmers and the tradesmen to pay wages sufficient to keep labourers out of the poor house . . . A Reformed Parliament would therefore infallibly reduce the charges of the Civil List in somewhat nearly the amount that I have mentioned, and in doing this they would really render a great service to the Royal Family as well as to the people . . .

Now . . . though a Reformed Parliament could not, all at once, relieve *all* the existing distress, I think it is evident that a Reformed Parliament would be able to do a great many good things, and to afford the nation a great deal of relief. The question of our enemies is, therefore, already more than answered. They now see 'what good' a Reform of Parliament would do; and if they can turn round upon us and say that all these things can be done without a Reform of Parliament, we deny the fact upon the best possible ground, namely that nothing is to be done till Borough-elections are put an end to . . . There has been wanting either the *will* or the *power*, and it is to us no matter which, since the effect has been the same . . .

[*Letter to Sir Francis Burdett*, 7 OCTOBER 1816, *Political Works*
IV, 500–9]

In What manner Can a Reform of Parliament Take Place without Confusion?

Having . . . shown that a Reform of Parliament would do a great deal of good, it shall now be my business to answer the second of the questions which fear, at the suggestion of craft, is continually putting to us. Before, however, I proceed to show that a timely reform might be, and would be, effected without the smallest chance of creating confusion, a preliminary remark or two are called for on the conduct of those crafty and corrupt men who suggest this question to the ignorant and the timid.

Why should any body suppose that confusion would be created by restoring the people at large to the enjoyment of the most important of their undoubted rights? We know well enough what infamous confusion now reigns at every general election. Why, then, is confusion so much dreaded? It will be shown, by and by, that a Reformed Parliament would be chosen by means the most simple, the most quiet in their operation, the most fair, and the best calculated to prevent those scenes of tumult and violence and beastly conduct which now disgrace elections; but, before proceeding to the detail of these means, let us again ask these pretended lovers of peace and harmony, *why* they suppose that a Reform of Parliament, above all things in the world, would be likely to create confusion?

The Habeas Corpus Act could be suspended for seven years at one time; new treasons could be invented; addition upon addition to the severity of the penal code; punishment heaped on punishment for the sake of collecting revenue; a fiscal system diving into every man's most private concerns; persons empowered to enter our houses, take account of our windows, horses, dogs, carriages, and servants; numerous Acts of Parliament, each exceeding the New Testament in bulk, to impose taxes and penalties upon the people; a system of watching us so close that no man can be said to have anything private; balloting for a militia, for a supplementary militia; a volunteer system; a yeomanry cavalry system; an army of reserve system; a levy-en-masse system; a local militia system. All these, and a hundred other schemes and measures, adopted, undone, readopted, abandoned, exchanged, modified; and at every step *penalties* and *forfeitures*. All these have taken place, and no confusion seems ever to have been apprehended, though complexity and vexation, and pains and penalties, made the most conspicuous figure throughout the whole series. But, now alas! when a *reform* is talked of, though nothing be in contemplation but a mere restoration of the undeniable rights of the people, and the putting an end to corruption, profligacy, and waste, *confusion* is affected to be apprehended!

Confusion in what? In the mode of election? There is now a greater bulk of laws and cases and decisions and expositions and reports relative to elections; these now amount in bulk to more than any man could read through in seven years, allowing himself time barely sufficient for eating and sleeping! . . . And yet the harpies . . . affect to be alarmed at the confusion that putting an end to this shocking system will create! The confusion which exists at elections, as they are now carried on, is notorious. A considerable part of the people come out of the scandalous strife with black eyes, bloody noses, broken limbs, or disordered minds; and yet the peace-loving harpies fear confusion from the opposite of this system! No . . . what they really apprehend is that confusion amongst the people would cease and that confusion to themselves would begin. This is what they apprehend; and without saying another word, *they* are answered.

But for the satisfaction of persons who mean well, and who have been alarmed by the horrors hatched by these base and crafty deceivers, I will show *in what manner* a Parliamentary Reform would take place, without the smallest chance of creating any confusion other than confusion to the harpies who now prey on the nation's vitals. If a set of magpies, or carrion crows, were engaged in tearing out the eyes, and pecking away the flesh of a poor unfortunate flock of sheep, to fire amongst them with a good charge of shot would certainly *create confusion*; but not confusion to the sheep, who, on the contrary, would . . . find themselves relieved from confusion. In sultry summers the maggots, which are engendered in the fleeces of our flocks, proceed by degrees till they eat into the flesh of the animals, who discover their pain by stopping suddenly, then starting, then running their noses against the ground, then looking round at the part affected, then lying down, then jumping up and running away: they sweat all over; the tears run down their faces; fever leads to madness, and madness to death. But the faithful shepherd comes in time, and by the application of his shears and his wash creates confusion amongst the filthy devourers and restores the flock to ease and to happiness. No question . . . that the magpies and the carrion crows, and that the maggots too, if they could squall, would cry aloud against the reforming shepherds; but the flock, I take it, would be very grateful to them for their exertions, and would entertain no fear of experiencing *confusion* from the change.

When I say that a reform of Parliament might be, and would be, effected without the smallest danger of producing confusion, I must, of course, be understood to make the assertion with this condition, namely, *that the present Parliament would agree to the measure in the form that it shall be proposed*; for if they will not, if they be resolved to persevere in rejecting the prayers of the people for reform, then, of course, a reform cannot possibly be effected *without* confusion. If this be what the sons and daughters of corruption mean as the source of confusion, they are right enough as to the *effect*, but it will then remain for them to find out a *justification* for the *cause*. But I must presuppose the consent of the present Parliament to the prayers of the people: and, in that case, I am able to prove that the reform would take place without any chance of creating confusion amongst the people; and without putting at hazard the lives and properties of any portion of the rightful owners of the country.

Another objection of the harpies is that the Reformers are divided in opinion amongst themselves as to the precise details of the reform which they pray for. What petty and what case cavilling is this! Do we not know that no bill of any great importance was ever passed without such a division in the opinions of its advocates? Do we not always see that the principle of a bill is first made a matter of discussion, that blanks are left in it to be filled up in a Committee; that in this Committee alterations and additions are made; that after all this, the bill is frequently amended by the Lords? Nay, does not the bill, when it becomes law, frequently contain a provision for its being further altered during the same session of Parliament? Indeed, what proposition, what measure, ever was, amongst any body of men, introduced in any other way? And what impudence, then, is it in the advocates of bribery and corruption to tell us that, though these are as notorious as the sun at noon-day, they ought to continue to exist, because those who wish to put an end to them have not, every man of them, signed beforehand an instrument binding himself to the precise regulation to be adopted to prevent their return? At this rate, too, how could any law ever be passed? It is the *majority* who decide; but the Reformers are required to be *unanimous*. They are so as to the *principle* of the measure; and they will, as in all other cases, insist that the detail must and shall be left to a decision by a majority.

However, it is necessary to state somewhat of the outline of the Reform that we seek; because, as is the case in most other good causes, there are sham reformers, who mean anything but that which the people wish for and want. What the people seek is a real reform; a restoration of the whole of their own rights, without violating the rights of others. The rights of the people, according to Magna Carta, according to the constitution and the ancient laws of the kingdom are, *That they are to be taxed only by their own consent*; and that they *shall YEARLY choose their representatives*. That every man who pays a tax of any sort into the hands of the tax-gatherer shall, by his representative, *give his consent to such a tax*, which he cannot do, unless he vote at elections for members of Parliament, who impose the taxes. It is also an essential, that the election should be *annual*; because the ancient law says so; and because we know from fatal experience, that a three years' Parliament voted themselves into a seven years' Parliament; and that the seven years' Parliament have loaded us with a debt, the interest of which is pressing us to the earth, and the principal of which has been employed in supporting French emigrants, in subsidizing Germans, in restoring the Bourbons, the Pope, and the Inquisition, and in other ways equally beneficial to the country.

It is quite necessary that the people should be put on their guard against the *triennial trick*. It has already been begun to be played off by the hirelings of one of the factions. The object of it is to divide the friends of Reform. Mr Fox played it off thirty years ago; and he at last played a good pension into the hands of Mrs Fox and her daughters, though he never, after he was in place, once *talked* even, of a Parliamentary Reform. It is, therefore, quite necessary that the people should be cautioned against the tricks of these sham Reformers, who were only so many enemies' spies in the camp of Reform.

This is an old and has often been a very successful trick of a crafty enemy. 'Divide and destroy' is the maxim of tyrants. First they openly oppose; but, when that is like to fail, they seek to undermine by dividing. They, better than anybody, know the history of the bundle of sticks; and they seek to separate the bundle, that they may snap them one at a time. As to the detail of Reform it is of little consequence; but the main principles must be adhered to inflexibly; these are, that *every man who pays a tax of any sort into the hands of a tax-gatherer should vote for members of the Commons' House; and that Parliament should be chosen annually*. To make the right of voting consist in possession of this or that species of property; to make freehold or copyhold or leasehold or lifehold a title of voting would be to rob the people of their right; and to allow a man to be a representative for more than one year without being rechosen has in it neither justice nor common sense, to say nothing about its being contrary to the spirit of the Constitution, and to the very letter of the ancient laws of England . . .

Having thus shown what the principle of the Reform ought to be, and having supposed that the present Parliament will agree to and pass a Bill, brought in for carrying a reform into execution, I shall now proceed, not to state all the details of such a Bill, but to show how easily a new and Reformed Parliament might be chosen and returned.

As every male tax-payer would have a vote, and the number of members for every county in the three kingdoms would, of course, be proportioned to the number of inhabitants within each county, there would be very little difficulty in apportioning what number of members each county should send. We have the population-book, recently enough compiled. Suppose, therefore, the whole of the population to amount to 15,000,000, the whole number of members to 658, as it is now, and Hampshire to contain 300,000 inhabitants; the question with regard to Hampshire would be, if 15,000,000 return 658, how many ought 300,000 to return, and the answer would be 13 members. Thus would the proportion be determined with the utmost facility; or, to prevent fractional parts, it might be settled that every 20 or 30 thousand inhabitants should be a title to a member. These would be matters of minor consequence, however, and would admit of a very easy arrangement.

It may be thought by some persons that the number of members sent by each county ought to be proportioned to the numbers of taxpayers in each county, and not in proportion to the number of inhabitants. I am of a different opinion, because, after all, those who pay no direct taxes ought to have some weight; and they ought, at any rate, to be as nearly represented as possible. But if it were resolved on to take the numbers of tax-payers as the criterion, nothing would be more easy than to obtain an account of those numbers. It would be collected in less than a month. And I would engage to make out the scale of proportion, and to settle the whole matter with the greatest accuracy in the space of one week from the time of receiving such account. Where, then, is the difficulty so far? And where is the fear of confusion?

The number of members for each county in England, Ireland and Scotland being fixed on, and it being settled that every payer of a direct tax should have a vote, the next thing to be considered would be, *in what manner the election should take place*, 'Aye', say the harpies, 'now let us see what a pretty bustle you will kick up!' No . . . we would have no bustle at all. We shall have no canvassing attorneys and agents galloping throughout the country; no lying, fawning members, giving false shakes of the hand to a poor fellow, whom they pass by the next month as if he were a dog; no filthy knaves kissing men's wives and daughters, and spewing gold into their mouths, as my father told me he once saw at Haslemere, and as I myself very nearly saw in the borough of Honiton, where the people openly avowed that the sale of their votes was their 'blessing'. We shall have no ribbons and flags; no drums and trumpets; no election-balls, at which the higher and lower orders of the sons and daughters of corruption mix in base and filthy familiarity. No rattling of post-chaises to the county towns; no hogsheads of muddy beer served out in the streets to a deluded and debased populace; no drunkenness, no riots, no bruises, no murders. But, in lieu of all these, we should have

one day in each year spent by sober and thoughtful citizens, in deliberately exercising the important right, and performing the great duty, of
choosing proper persons to speak their wishes in the making of laws,
and in guarding the rights, the honour, and the freedom of their
country.

You have often said that you want NOTHING NEW; and so we say
all. Even in the regulations for the taking of the voice of the people,
I, for my part, see no necessity for any one new establishment, or for
any one new office, or new officer. Our excellent form of government;
our excellent ancient laws; our excellent modes of carrying on the
business of a nation, leave us nothing new to wish for. The Election
would take place on one and the same day throughout the whole of
the United Kingdom; and, as I shall proceed to show, might all be
completed, the returns made, and the new Parliament assembled in
the space of one month.

On the day fixed on by the law, of which due notice would be
given in every parish by posting at the church-doors, and also from
the pulpit, if that was thought necessary, the Churchwardens and
Overseers would meet at the Church, where there would be a box,
into which the Voters would put each his ballot, on which he would
have previously written, or caused to be written, the names of those
men whom he wished to be chosen for his county. Let us suppose,
then, the parish of Botley to be the particular scene before us. The
county is to give thirteen Members, and every voter is, if he chooses,
to vote for thirteen men. Nicholas Freemantle, for instance, having
heard all that has been said for this man and against that man (for
he would hear a great deal) writes down thirteen names upon a bit
of paper, takes it in his hand, and away he goes to the Church. The
Churchwardens, who have the charge of the ballot-box, ask his name;
the Overseers look into their rate-book to see whether he be a tax-
payer; finding his name there, they bid him put in his ballot; which
done, home he goes to his business. If the Overseers do not find him
to be a tax-payer, he, of course, does not vote.

Between nine in the morning, and five in the afternoon, should be
the hours of polling. In large cities there might be numerous ballot-
boxes, with additional copies of the rate-book, and deputies to the
Churchwardens and Overseers. At Botley, and in almost every parish,
there would need but one ballot-box, and the Election would be over
and completed without even a bustle by twelve o'clock in the day.

On the next day, the Churchwardens and Overseers would, being all assembled together, open the ballot-box, and make out their return. They would take out the several ballots, write the names of all the persons voted for upon a piece of paper, and ascertain from the ballots how many votes each had got. They would then, on the same day, transmit by the hands of the senior Churchwarden, not only the result of their investigation, but also the whole of the ballots, to the High Sheriff of the County, who should be ordered to be present, and in constant attendance at the County Town, for the purpose of receiving the parochial returns . . .

Now, I will venture to pledge my life that an election like this would take place, not only without confusion, but without the loss of one single day's work in the Parish, except with the Parish-officers themselves, which could not possibly be a matter of great moment, especially if they were allowed to charge for their time in their usual annual accounts and which no human being would grudge.

With what facility, with what celerity, would these returns all find their way to the High Sheriff, a copy of each being recorded in the Parish-book, to provide against accidents! Then would come the duty to be performed by the High Sheriff. He, with his Deputy, and with a sufficient number of Clerks (four would be amply sufficient), would first compare each parochial return with the ballots; when all the parochial returns were verified, or corrected, in the presence of the Chairman of the Quarter Sessions and the Clerk of the Peace, the High Sheriff would make out a County Return . . . This return might be sent to the Crown Office, and there kept till the Parliament should meet. The Sheriff, on the very day of closing his return, should make a proclamation in his county, and which proclamation should contain a copy of the return; so that the people would, at once, be informed on whom the election of their county had fallen.

Now . . . can you conceive it possible for any confusion to arise out of a series of proceedings like these? We should have no rioting, because there would be nothing to irritate; no drunkenness or bribery, because no fortune could drench, and much less bribe, forty or eighty thousand voters; no false-swearing, because we would have no swearing at all, from the first to the last; no ill blood and spite amongst neighbours, because no man (unless he chose it) would let any other man know whom he voted for . . .

All would, therefore, be regularity, celerity, truth, fairness, instead of the disorder, tardiness, the falsehood, the foul-play that now prevail . . .

The voting by *ballot* is, in my opinion, best; but the other mode would create no difficulty in the execution. *Viva Voce*, if that be thought best; and then the voter has only to read his names, sign his card, and put it in the box. There would arise from this no other difficulty than that which would arise from the possible ill-will, which, in some cases, a man's voting on one side, or the other, might excite against him from his friends and employers. I am for the ballot; but it is not a matter of very great consequence; because such ill-will would, if expressed, or acted upon, become extremely odious; and because there would be very little motive for its being entertained . . .

The exclusions from the right of voting should, it seems to me, be confined to foreigners and to persons convicted (by a common jury of course) of infamous crimes, and especially of crimes against the rights of election, which should be deemed infamous in the highest degree.

As to the qualifications of members, they should consist, not of a pocket full of money, nor of a sham estate, nor of a good thumping notoriously false oath; but of such qualities and endowments as the voters might take a fancy to. Who ought to judge of the qualifications of the persons employed besides the person who has to employ him? An estate, whether in money or in land, does not confer wisdom or integrity. The people would be the best judge of whom it was their *interest* to choose. If a whole people were left to choose measures for themselves, is it to be believed that they would choose measures injurious to their interest, expecially if free and ample discussion were on foot? Is it to be believed that the people would choose men whom any one could prove to have been guilty of what was injurious to them; or whom any one could prove to be likely to wish to do them harm? Is it to believed that we in the country should vote for gipsies or trampers? Or that the people in cities would vote for swindlers and pickpockets? 'Demagogues', of whom the sons and daughters of corruption are for ever telling the people to *beware*, would find few to vote for them. To hear demagogues harangue may possibly amuse a small part of the people; but it is one thing to be amused by a mountebank, and another to entrust him with the making of laws affecting our property and lives. But the fact is that the real 'demagogues' are all on the other side; for demagogues are *deceivers*, and not those who utter *truth*, in language however violent. Upon this head, therefore, there would need no one measure of precaution. The people would, for the far greater part, choose men of good character and of some ability; and if any county found itself deceived, the deception would not be very detrimental, seeing that, at the end of the year, they would take special care to choose other persons.

To those who have the insolence to affect to apprehend that the taxpayers, if left to their own free choice, would choose foolish and wicked men to represent them, and to impose taxes upon them, the *answer* is in America, where the people not only freely choose *one house*, but the *other house too*, and the *Chief Magistrate into the bargain*. And do they choose penniless Demagogues? Do they choose fools and robbers? It is notorious that they choose for the far greater part not only men of distinguished talent, but men of wealth and estate, whose means have enabled them to study, and whose fortune has kept them out of the reach of temptation to do wrong. Why, then, should we suppose that the people of England or Ireland would fix their liking upon fools or knaves? . . .

There need be none of those odious exclusions of Members of Parliament from being Ministers or Pensioners or anything else. These are only so many miserable palliations for a deep-rooted and wide-spreading disease. If a person was so remarkable for his talent or his wisdom as to be an object of choice both with the king and the people, why should not his talent and his wisdom be used by both? These pitiful exclusions are odious because they are grounded upon the presumption of *corruption* existing, and, indeed, upon the still more odious presumption that the king is the enemy of the people. Besides, we know how *nicely* they are got over now; and that they are, in fact, no exclusions at all. The whole of these miserable precautions would be rendered unnecessary by the annual occurrence of an election. If the king chose a Member of Parliament to be one of his Ministers, and the Constituents disapproved of their Member being a Minister, why they *would not rechoose him*; that would be all. He would soon be before them again. There would be no time for heart-burnings upon the subject. The evil, if it were thought one, would be speedily redressed, and that too without any clamour or any up-braidings . . .

Would a Reform, then, produce confusion? No: but it would, because it must, produce order, peace and harmony. This the harpies know as well as we do; but it is not order, peace and harmony they want. They want confusion amongst every body but themselves. They love to see one part of the people armed against the other part.

They want the country to be miserable, that they may wallow in ease and luxury.

But . . . it is time to *talk no longer*. The time of *acting* is come, and of this I am extremely happy to hear that you are fully sensible. There is *no violence* wanted. The country now understands the cause of its ruin; it knows that the remaining mode of seeking redress is, by *petition and remonstrance*; it is ready to perform its duty, and there only wants an *uniformity of movement* to send you to the House loaded with the people's prayers. The application for a Reform in the shape of a Bill, ready prepared, is all that will then be wanted, and for the making of this application the nation with confidence looks up to you . . .

One would imagine . . . that it was impossible for any body to be so blinded by their wishes as to expect that things can go on as they are. There is, indeed, nobody except downright fools that do expect it. Every one believes that some great change must take place. That it cannot, without reform, be a change for the better, I am quite sure; and I have heard of no man who pretends to point out any means of producing good without a reform. I have shown, I think, that a Reform may now take place without any chance of creating confusion; but I will by no means take it upon me to say, that at a future period even Reform will prevent confusion. The confusion and bloodshed, which took place in France, were laid to the charge of the Revolutionists; but those who merited the charge were the Government and its adherents. Mr Arthur Young, who was travelling through France during the first of the violences in that country, observes, in his Travels, written upon the spot, that all the outcry directed (in England and elsewhere) against those who were burning country-seats and ill-treating the noblesse and their families should have been directed against those, who by their loads of vexatious taxes and impositions and other acts of tyranny, and by the refusal of all redress, drove the people to madness and despair. It is in vain to tell men that they are in danger from violating the law, when they feel that it is impossible for them to be worse off than they are.

I have thus . . . I think, given the harpies an answer to their two questions, and proved that a Reformed Parliament would do a great deal of good even now, and, if speedily adopted, would take place without producing confusion.

[*Letter to Sir Francis Burdett*, 18 OCTOBER 1816, *Political Works* IV, 514–27]

The Only Choice is between Parliamentary Reform and Total Ruin

Innumerable are the instances in private life where men blindly and pertinaciously listen to those who are their worst enemies, who are undermining their characters and their fortunes, and who are fattening at their expense, while, towards those who are naturally, as well as by inclination, their friends, they wear an eye of constant suspicion, and entertain a feeling nearly approaching to that of enmity. That this failing, which is so common amongst individuals, is not without its influence on whole bodies of men, the conduct of the Country Gentlemen of these Islands, for many years past, most abundantly proves. And, as such conduct in private life seldom fails to produce ruin to the party or his family; so, in your case, total ruin to yourselves, or at least to your descendants, appears to be a consequence altogether inevitable, unless you immediately rouse yourselves, shake off the infatuation, and act as becomes men who have children whom they do not wish to become beggarly dependents.

Amongst the other marks of this fatal infatuation is an obstinate refusal, not only to follow the advice of those who propose a Reform of the Parliament, or who disapprove of the measures of the Gcvernment; but a refusal equally obstinate to *hear* what they have to say. A stubborn, a stupid, a contemptible obstinacy, to give way to which is justly punishable with ruin and disgrace. And, indeed, instead of patiently hearing what we have to say, no small part of you have repaid our endeavours with every species of persecution within your power. You have shown no sense of justice in these matters. You have not heard *both sides*, as common fairness pointed out; but you have suffered yourselves to be led along by Corruption's sons, as an ass is led by a gipsy; you have spitefully kicked at every man who has endeavoured to set you free; and even now, when your backs are breaking under your burdens, and your bones are sticking through your skins, you appear to feel a new *fit of alarm* at the proposition of that measure which alone can, by any possibility, afford you relief and security.

Under such circumstances, it is almost impossible for us so far to master our resentment as to entertain a desire that you should now act the part that becomes you; but, to harbour such resentment would be to injure the great cause of the country, and it is, therefore, our duty to bury it, if possible, in everlasting oblivion. For my own part, bred up in the country, and taught in early life to look towards your order with great respect; remembering the times when your hospitality and benevolence had not been swept away by the tax-gatherer; having still in my recollection so many excellent men, to whose grandfathers, upon the same spots, my grandfathers had yielded cheerful obedience and reverence, it is not without sincere sorrow that I have beheld many of the sons of these men driven from their fathers' mansions, or holding them as little better than tenants or stewards, while the swarms of Placemen, Pensioners, Contractors, and Nabobs, with all the keen habits of their former lives, have usurped a large part of the soil, and wholly changed the manners, and even the morals, of the country. Upon this occasion I wish to address you in the temper inspired by the recollection of early impressions, rather than in that which recent facts would naturally dictate. For more than ten years I have been endeavouring to convince you that that which has now taken place would take place. I have, hitherto, with regard to you, laboured in vain; and one more effort, though it should prove equally useless, will form but a trifling addition to the disappointments already experienced.

My opinion is, that you have now no choice remaining, except that which lies between *a Reform of Parliament* and the *loss of your estates*, through the means of taxation; and the soundness of this opinion I will, if you will give me a patient hearing, endeavour to prove in the clearest manner.

Let me first ask you a question or two applicable to this matter. Look, each of you, just around your neighbourhoods. Take a circumference of thirty or forty miles. Put all the Gentlemen's mansions within that compass down upon paper. Write against each who was the owner thirty years ago, and who is the owner now. And then tell me, what reason *you* have to hope that *your* sons will possess your estates? If you have any love for your children, can you take this survey without experiencing the most poignant anguish? Then, look at the numerous little farm-houses tumbling down, or suffered to dwindle into wretched sheds for labourers. Look at the out-stretchings of the Metropolis, and see the increase of glittering chariots that rattle through its streets and squares; then turn to the places where numerous hamlets once stood, inhabited by happy people; and then tell me whether the accumulation of property into great masses, by means of taxes and loans, has been for the glory or disgrace of the country? Search the poor-books of fifty years back, and when you find but one pauper for every hundred paupers that now are upon those books tell me whether you can behold the horrid sight without shame for the present and apprehension for the future? The sons of Corruption would fain induce you to believe that this dreadful change has been produced by a change in the morals and manners of the labouring people. This is not a very decent charge to make against them at the close of a war, during which those classes have shown so much valour, and have endured with patience so many and so great hardships. But the fact is, that there is less drunkenness than formerly; the labourers work harder than their forefathers worked; and it surely will not be denied that they are better educated, if by education we mean reading and writing . . . What then can have been the cause of this increase of human degradation? It is useless, besides being unjust, to rail against the poor. It is clear that they *ought* to be fed, that they have both a *legal* and *equitable* right to be fed out of the produce of the soil; but it is also clear that they *must* be so fed. They never *can* be made to die by thousands quietly under the hedges; and if they *could* the evil would be still greater; for then there would be nobody to labour and the country would become again a wilderness.

It is impossible for you to dwell upon reflections of this kind for ten minutes without being convinced that there is some great radical cause of all these evils. And does it not become you, then, patiently to investigate that cause? . . . But, at the present day, there is another and most important reason for your lending a patient ear; for your examining and well weighing what is tendered to you, which reason is this: that your farmers, your trades people, your workmen of all sorts are very attentively reading upon these subjects. It is quite useless for you to endeavour to discourage and check the progress of political knowledge. That knowledge has gone forth like the rays of the sun bursting a black cloud asunder; and it is as impossible to destroy the effect of that knowledge as it would be to smother the rays of the sun. Even error, when strongly imprinted on the mind, has always been found extremely difficult to efface. What, then, is to efface truth, when imprinted on the mind in fair and distinct characters? . . .

Now the Reformers say, and I for one, that a Reform would cause the peace of the country never to be broken, or attempted to be broken, except in such a trifling degree as to be easily restored by peace-officers. We say that, as to sinecures, pensions, etc., a Reformed Parliament would reduce them to the standard of strict public services. We say that, as to salaries and pay, they should be reduced in the proportion in which the wages of labourers and mechanics and manufacturers have been reduced. We say that if we were to stop here the drain upon your estates would become much less than it is. But I am not for stopping here. I am for making that reduction of the interest of the debt, which has been stigmatized as a breach of national faith, and, by others, as a robbery; and I will endeavour to prove that it is neither one nor the other.

At several of the public meetings it has been resolved that the debt is not national; that those only owe the money who have *voted* for those *who borrowed* the money; and that those who have filled the seats owe the debt. Without attempting to enter into this question at present, I shall proceed to say that those who have lent their money to the Government were the best judges of the security they received for repayment. They very well knew that they had no other security than that which the power of collecting a sufficiency of taxes gave them; and the simple question is, whether, in order to collect a suffi-ciency of taxes, the nation is bound to hazard the very lives of a great part of the people. I say that it is not; I say that the safety and hap-piness of millions is to be preferred to the safety and happiness of thousands; and I say that this is a principle that is consonant with every notion of justice and humanity . . .

It is impossible to take this view of the matter and not be con-vinced that things cannot go on in their present train for any length of time. The question, therefore, is not whether all shall remain as it is, or a change take place; for a change of some sort must take place; and the only question is, of what sort that change shall be . . .
[*An Address to the Country Gentlemen*, 20 DECEMBER 1816, *Political Works* v, 46–58]

Cobbett Reminds the King of the Wisdom of Parliamentary Reform

Amongst all your Majesty's subjects there is not one who has, in this season of advice-giving, fairer pretensions to offer you advice than I have. No one has addressed himself to you so many times, and no one has ever been proved, by time, to have been so correct and so sound in the advice which he has offered you. If your Majesty could now read the volume (and a large one it would be) of that advice, you could not but exclaim: 'If I had listened to *this*, my people could not now have exhibited to the world that mass of ruin and of wretchedness which they now exhibit' . . .

After all . . . there is no ground to hope for a just and peaceable result, except your Majesty be the chief mover; and I will now, in very plain language, tell your Majesty how I would act, the advice which I would give, if I were in your Ministry, and being resolved to give that advice, really giving it and standing by it, I should not be afraid of all the boroughmongers, both the factions, everything that could be mustered up against me, I would answer for success with my life, and I should have the inexpressible pleasure of seeing your Majesty the most justly popular sovereign that ever reigned upon the face of the earth. My first step would be, humbly but most urgently, to press upon your Majesty the necessity of issuing your Royal Proclamation, fully and frankly stating to your subjects the situation of the nation's affairs; describing the several evils that oppress them, and tracing those evils to their immediate causes; then tracing them to their more distant causes and stating the great cause of all to be a want of sufficient sympathy and community of feeling between those who make the laws and those who pay the taxes; calling upon them for mutual forbearance towards each other in their pecuniary affairs; calling upon the rich to be kind and benevolent towards the poor; enjoining most strictly on magistrates to see the laws well and duly enforced, for preserving the lives and health of the people of the poorer sort; promising to all everything in your power for their relief and for their speedy restoration to happiness, concluding with telling them that you would immediately suggest to your Parliament to make such a change in the representation as would be likely to repair the injuries inflicted upon the country.

The next step would be to advise your Majesty to send a message to both Houses of Parliament, recommending them to pass laws for making a constitutional reform of the Commons House; observing to them that you had examined into the source of the evils that now afflict your people; telling them that history informed you that, of all the people in the world, the English people had been, for numerous ages, the happiest, the best fed, the best clad, the freest, the most virtuous; that a long list of melancholy but undeniable facts now convinces you that they are, with the sole exception of your still more miserable subjects in Ireland, the most unhappy, the worst fed and worst clad people upon the face of the earth. Telling them that you had diligently inquired into the several causes which had produced this disgraceful, this deplorable change; that when you looked round the kingdom and saw everywhere new gaols, new modes of punishing criminals; that when you saw that a greater quantity of food was allowed to the convicted felon than to the honest labouring man, you could not but inquire into the causes of all this misery and degradation; that, after long and diligent inquiry, you had traced this mass of evil, this fearful change, this change which seemed to have destroyed everything of England but its bare name; that, in every instance, you had traced back the original cause to *some act or other of the Parliament*. That, to confine yourself to recent instances, the miseries of the year 1822, the agricultural distress of that year; the panic of 1825; that these you found came immediately as the effects of two Acts of Parliament; that, therefore, it could not be doubted that there must be something wrong in the manner of electing those who imposed the taxes; that this had been told you by your people a thousand times over; that Earl Grey, then Mr Grey, presented a petition to the House of Commons in 1793, in which the petitioners declared that they were ready to prove at the bar of the House that a decided *majority of the House were returned by only one hundred and fifty-four persons*; that you find, upon inquiry, that the petition was received, that it now lies upon the table of the House, and that it has never, from that day to this, been taken into consideration; and that, therefore, you recommended to the House of Commons to take that petition into their consideration without loss of time.

There is no man in his senses who must not be well assured that, if your Majesty were to take these steps, an effectual reform of the House of Commons would be the certain and speedy consequence. With such a House of Commons, and with the concurrence of your Majesty, everything would be speedily done which your dignity and our happiness demanded. This load would be taken from our shoulders, the uncertainty as to the value of property would cease; your corn, like that of your ancestors, would be the only money known to your people; wealth, wherever it existed, would be solid; men would seek to live by industry and not by trick; no fortunes of half a million would be made by watching the turn of the market; the cursed Jews must flee the land, or . . . be flung into the sea, and England would be once more a really Christian, a free and happy country . . .
[*To the King . . . on the Measures Necessary to Restore the Nation to Happiness*, 25 APRIL 1827, *Political Works* VI, 525-36]

COBBETT
THE TRADITIONALIST

Advice to a Youth

You are now arrived at that age which the law thinks sufficient to make an oath, taken by you, valid in a court of law. Let us suppose from fourteen to nearly twenty; and . . . let me here offer you my advice as to the means likely to contribute largely towards making you a happy man, useful to all about you, and an honour to those from whom you sprang.

Start, I beseech you, with a conviction firmly fixed on your mind, that you have no right to live in this world; that, being of hale body and sound mind, you have *no right* to any earthly existence, without doing work of some sort or other, unless you have ample fortune whereon to live clear of debt; and, that even in that case, you have no right to breed children to be kept by others, or to be exposed to the chance of being so kept. Start with this conviction thoroughly implanted on your mind. To wish to live on the labour of others is, besides the folly of it, to contemplate a *fraud* at the least, and, under certain circumstances, to meditate oppression and robbery.

I suppose you in the middle rank of life. Happiness ought to be your great object, and it is to be found only in *independence*. Turn your back on Whitehall and on Somerset House; leave the Customs and Excise to the feeble and low-minded; look not for success to favour, to partiality, to friendship, or to what is called *interest*: write it on your heart that you will depend solely on your own merit and your own exertions. Think not, neither, of any of those situations where gaudy habiliments and sounding titles poorly disguise from the eyes of good sense the mortifications and the heart-ache of slaves . . .

Indeed, reason tells us that it must be thus: for that which a man owes to favour or to partiality, that same favour or partiality is constantly liable to take from him. He who lives upon anything except his own labour, is incessantly surrounded by rivals: his grand resource is that servility in which he is always liable to be surpassed. He is in daily danger of being out-bidden; his very bread depends upon caprice; and he lives in a state of uncertainty and never-ceasing fear. His is not, indeed, the dog's life, '*hunger* and idleness'; but it is worse; for it is 'idleness with *slavery*', the latter being the just price of the former. Slaves frequently are well *fed* and well *clad*; but slaves dare not speak; they dare not be suspected to *think* differently from their masters; hate his acts as much as they may; be he tyrant, be he drunkard, be he fool, or be he all three at once, they must be silent, or, nine times out of ten, affect approbation: though possessing a thousand times his knowledge, they must feign a conviction of his superior understanding; though knowing that it is they who, in fact, do all that he is paid for doing, it is destruction to them to *seem as if they thought* any portion of the service belonged to them! . . .

And how comes it, then, that we see hale and even clever youths voluntarily bending their necks to this slavery; nay, pressing forward in eager rivalship to assume the yoke that ought to be insupportable? The cause, and the only cause, is that the deleterious fashion of the day has created so many artificial wants, and has raised the minds of young men so much above their real rank and state of life, that they look scornfully on the employment, and fare, and the dress, that would become them; and in order to avoid that state in which they might live *free* and *happy*, they become *showy* slaves . . .

Endless are the instances of men of bright parts and high spirit having been, by degrees, rendered powerless and despicable, by their imaginary wants, Seldom has there been a man with a fairer prospect of accomplishing great things and of acquiring lasting renown, than Charles Fox; he had great talents of the most popular sort; the times were singularly favourable to an exertion of them with success; a large part of the nation admired him and were his partisans; he had, as to the great question between him and his rival (Pitt) reason and justice clearly on his side: but he had against him his squandering and luxurious habits: these made him dependent on the rich part of his partisans; made his wisdom subservient to opulent folly or selfishness; deprived his country of all the benefit that it might have derived from his talents; and, finally, sent him to the grave without a single sigh from a people, a great part of whom would, in his earlier years, have wept at his death as at a national calamity.

Extravagance in *dress*, in the haunting of *playhouses*, in *horses*, in everything else, is to be avoided, and, in youths and young men, extravagance in dress particularly. This sort of extravagance, this waste of money on the decoration of the body, arises solely from vanity, and from vanity of the most contemptible sort. It arises from the notion that all the people in the street, for instance, will be *looking at you* as soon as you walk out; and that they will, in a greater or less degree, think the better of you on account of your fine dress. Never was notion more false. All the sensible people that happen to see you, will think nothing at all about you: those who are filled with the same vain notion as you are, will perceive your attempt to impose on them, and will despise you accordingly: rich people will wholly disregard you, and you will be envied and hated by those who have the same vanity that you have without the means of gratifying it. Dress should be suited to your rank and station; a surgeon or physician should not dress like a carpenter! But there is no reason why a tradesman, a merchant's clerk, or clerk of any kind, or why a shop-keeper or manufacturer, or even a merchant; no reason at all why any of these should dress in an *expensive* manner. It is a great mistake to suppose that they derive any advantage from exterior decoration. Men are estimated by other *men* according to their capacity and willingness to be in some way or other *useful*; and though, with the foolish and vain part of *women*, fine clothes frequently do something, yet the greater part of the sex are much too penetrating to draw their conclusions solely from the outside show of a man: they look deeper, and find other criterions whereby to judge. And, after all, if the fine clothes obtain you a wife, will they bring you, in that wife, *frugality*, *good sense*, and that sort of attachment that is likely to be lasting? Natural beauty of person is quite another thing: this always has, it always will and must have, some weight even with men, and great weight with women. But this does not want to be set off by expensive clothes. Female eyes are, in such cases, very sharp: they can discover beauty though half hidden by beard and even by dirt and surrounded by rags: and, take this as a secret worth half a fortune to you, that women, however personally vain they may be themselves, *despise personal vanity in men*.

Let your dress be as cheap as may be without *shabbiness*; think more about the colour of your shirt than about the gloss or texture of your coat; be always as *clean* as your occupation will, without inconvenience, permit; but never, no, not for one moment, believe that any human being, with sense in his skull, will love or respect you on account of your fine or costly clothes. A great misfortune of the present day is that every one is, in his own estimate, *raised above his real state of life*: every one seems to think himself entitled, if not to title and great estate, at least *to live without work* . . .

As to Drunkenness and Gluttony, generally so called, these are vices so nasty and beastly that I deem any one capable of indulging in them to be wholly unworthy of my advice; and, if any youth unhappily intitiated in these odious and debasing vices should happen to read what I am now writing, I refer him to the command of God, conveyed to the Israelites by Moses, in Deuteronomy, chap. xxi. The father and mother are to take the bad son 'and bring him to the elders of the city; and they shall say to the elders, This our son will not obey our voice: he is a *glutton* and a *drunkard*. And all the men of the city shall stone him with stones, that he die.' I refer downright beastly gluttons and drunkards to this; but indulgence short, *far short*, of this gross and really nasty drunkenness and gluttony is to be deprecated, and that, too, with the more earnestness because it is too often looked upon as being no crime at all, and as having nothing blameable in it; nay, there are persons who *pride* themselves on their refined taste in matters connected with eating and drinking: so far from being ashamed of employing their thoughts on the subject, it is their boast that they do it . . .

This *love* of what are called 'good eating and drinking', if very unamiable in grown-up persons, is perfectly hateful in *a youth*; and, if he indulge in the propensity, he is already half ruined. To warn you against acts of fraud, robbery and violence, is not my province; that is the business of those who make and administer *the law*. I am not talking to you against acts which the jailor and the hangman punish; nor against those moral offences which all men condemn; but against indulgences which, by men in general, are deemed not only harmless, but meritorious; but which the observation of my whole life has taught me to regard as destructive to human happiness, and against which all ought to be cautioned even in their boyish days . . .

Such indulgences are, in the first place, very *expensive*. The materials are costly, and the preparations still more so. What a monstrous thing, that, in order to satisfy the appetite of a man, there must be a person or two *at work every day*! . . . And then the *loss of time*: the time spent in pleasing the palate: it is truly horrible to behold people who ought to be at work, sitting, at the three meals, not less than three of the about fourteen hours that they are out of their beds! A youth, habituated to this sort of indulgence, cannot be valuable to any employer . . . I am certain that, upon an average, I have not, during my life, spent more than *thirty-five minutes a day at table*, including all the meals of the day. I like, and I take care to have, good and clean victuals; but, if wholesome and clean, that is enough. If I find it, by chance, *too coarse* for my appetite, I put the food aside, or let somebody do it, and leave the appetite to gather keenness. But the great security of all is, to eat *little*, and to drink nothing that *intoxicates*. He that eats till he is *full* is little better than a beast; and he that drinks till he is *drunk* is quite a beast.

Before I dismiss this affair of eating and drinking, let me beseech you to resolve to free yourselves from the slavery of the *tea* and *coffee* and other *slop-kettle*, if unhappily you have been bred up in such slavery. Experience has taught me, that those slops are *injurious to health*: until I left them off (having taken to them at the age of 26), even my habits of sobriety, moderate eating, early rising; even these were not, until I left off the slops, sufficient to give me that complete health which I have since had. I pretend not to be a 'doctor'; but I assert that to pour regularly, ever day, a pint or two of *warm liquid matter* down the throat, whether under the name of tea, coffee, soup, grog, or whatever else, is greatly injurious to health. However, at present, what I have to represent to *you is the great deduction, which the use of these slops makes, from your power of being useful*, and also from your *power to husband your income*, whatever it may be, and from whatever source arising . . .

So much for indulgences in eating, drinking, and dress. Next as to *amusements* . . . It is certain that there ought to be hours of recreation . . . but . . . those hours ought to be *well-chosen*, and the *sort* of recreation ought to be attended to. It ought to be such as is at once innocent in itself and in its tendency, and not injurious to health. The sports of the field are the best of all, because they are conducive to health, because they are enjoyed by *day-light*, and because they demand early rising. The nearer that other amusements approach to these, the better they are. A town-life, which many persons are compelled, by the nature of their calling, to lead, precludes the possibility of pursuing amusements of this description to any very considerable extent; and young men in towns are, generally speaking, compelled to choose between *books* on the one hand, or *gaming* and the *play-house* on the other. *Dancing* is at once rational and healthful: it gives animal spirits: it is the natural amusement of young people, and such it has been from the days of Moses: it is enjoyed in numerous companies: it makes the parties to be pleased with themselves and with all about them; it has no tendency to excite base and malignant feelings; and none but the most grovelling and hateful tyranny, or the most stupid and despicable fanaticism, ever raised its voice against it. The bad modern habits of England have created one inconvenience attending the enjoyment of this healthy and innocent pastime, namely, *late hours*, which are at once injurious to health and destructive of order and of industry. In other countries people dance by *day-light*. Here they do not; and, therefore, you must, in this respect, submit to the custom, though not without robbing the dancing night of as many hours as you can.

As to Gaming, it is always criminal, either in itself, or in its tendency. The basis of it is covetousness; a desire to take from others something, for which you have given, and intend to give, no equivalent. No gambler was ever yet a happy man, and very few gamblers have escaped being miserable; and, observe, to *game for nothing* is still gaming, and naturally tends to lead to gaming for something. It is sacrificing time, and that, too, for the worst of purposes. I have kept house for nearly forty years; I have reared a family; I have entertained as many friends as most people; and I have never had cards, dice, a chess-board, nor any implement of gaming, under my roof. The hours that young men spend in this way are hours *murdered*; precious hours, that ought to be spent either in reading or in writing, or in rest, preparatory to the duties of the dawn . . .

The *Theatre may be* a source not only of amusement but also of instruction; but, as things now are in this country, what, that is not bad, is to be learned in this school? In the first place not a word is allowed to be uttered on the stage, which has not been previously approved by the Lord Chamberlain; that is to say, by a person appointed by the Ministry, who, at his pleasure, allows, or disallows, of any piece, or any words in a piece, submitted to his inspection. In short, those who go to playhouses *pay their money to hear uttered such words as the government approve of, and no others*. It is now just twenty-six years since I first well understood how this matter was managed; and, from that moment to this, I have never been in an

English play-house. Besides this, the meanness, the abject servility of the players, and the slavish conduct of the audience, are sufficient to corrupt and debase the heart of any young man who is a frequent beholder of them. Homage is here paid to every one clothed with power, be he who or what he may; real virtue and public-spirit are subjects of ridicule; and mock-sentiment and mock-liberality are applauded to the skies.

'Show me a man's *companions*', says the proverb, 'and I will tell you *what the man* is'; and this is, and must be true; because all men seek the society of those who think and act somewhat like themselves; sober men will not associate with drunkards, frugal men will not like spendthrifts, and the orderly and decent shun the noisy, the disorderly, and the debauched. It is for the very vulgar to herd together as singers, ringers, and smokers; but there is a class rather higher still more blamable; I mean the tavern-haunters, the gay companions, who herd together to do little but *talk*, and who are so fond of talk that they go from home to get at it. The conversation amongst such persons has nothing of instruction in it, and is generally of a vicious tendency. Young people naturally and commendably seek the society of those of their own age; but, be careful in choosing your companions; and lay this down as a rule never to be departed from, that no youth, nor man, ought to be called your *friend*, who is addicted to *indecent talk*, or who is fond of the *society of prostitutes*. Either of these argues a depraved taste, and even a depraved heart; and absence of all principle and of all trust-worthiness; and I have remarked it all my life long, that young men, addicted to these vices, never succeed in the end, whatever advantages they may have, whether in fortune or in talent. Fond mothers and fathers are but too apt to be over-lenient to such offenders; and, as long as youth lasts and fortune smiles, the punishment is deferred; but it comes at last; it is sure to come; and the gay and dissolute youth is a dejected and miserable man. After the early part of a life spent in illicit indulgences, a man *is unworthy* of being the husband of a virtuous woman; and, if he have anything like justice in him, how is he to reprove, in his children, vices in which he himself so long indulged? These vices of youth are varnished over by the saying, that there must be a time for 'sowing the *wild oats*' and that 'the *wildest colts* make the *best horses*'. These figurative oats are, however, generally like the literal ones; they are *never to be eradicated from the soil*; and as to the *colts*, wildness in them is an indication of *high animal spirit*, having nothing at all to do

with the *mind*, which is invariably debilitated and debased by profligate indulgences. Yet this miserable piece of sophistry, the offspring of parental weakness, is in constant use, to the incalculable
injury of the rising generation. What so amiable as a steady, trustworthy boy? He is of *real use* at an early age: he can be trusted far out
of the sight of parent or employer, while the 'pickle', as the poor fond
parents call the profligate, is a great deal worse than useless, because
there must be some one to see that he does no harm. If you have to
choose, choose companions of *your own rank in life*, as nearly as may
be; at any rate, none to whom you acknowledge *inferiority*; for slavery
is too soon learned; and, if the mind be bowed down in the youth, it
will seldom rise up in the man . . .

In your *manners* be neither boorish nor blunt, but even these are
preferable to simpering and crawling. I wish every English youth
could see those of the United States of America; always *civil*, never
servile. Be obedient, where obedience is due; for it is no act of
meanness, and no indication of want of spirit, to yield implicit and
ready obedience to those who have a right to demand it at your hands.
In this respect England has been, and I hope always will be, an
example to the whole world. To this habit of willing and prompt
obedience in apprentices, in servants, in all inferiors in station, she
owes, in a great measure, her multitudes of matchless merchants,
tradesmen, and workmen of every description, and also the achievements of her armies and navies . . .

To obtain respect worth possessing, you must, as I observed
before, do more than the common run of men in your state of life;
and, to be enabled to do this, you must manage well *your time*: and,
to manage it well, you must have as much of the *day-light* and as
little of the *candle-light* as is consistent with the due discharge of your
duties. When people get into the habit of sitting up *merely for the
purpose of talking*, it is no easy matter to break themselves of it: and
if they do not go to bed early, they cannot rise early. Young people
require more sleep than those that are grown up: there must be the
number of hours, and that number cannot well be, on an average, less
than *eight*: and, if it be more in winter time, it is all the better; for an
hour in bed is better than an hour spent over fire and candle in an
idle gossip. People never should sit talking till they do not know what
to talk about. It is said by the country-people that one hour's sleep before midnight is worth more than two are worth after midnight, and
this I believe to be a fact; but it is useless to go to bed early and even

to rise early, if the time be not well employed after rising. In general, half the morning is *loitered* away, the party being in a sort of half-dressed half-naked state; out of bed, indeed, but still in a sort of bedding. Those who first invented *morning-gowns* and *slippers* could have very little else to do. These things are very suitable to those who have had fortunes gained for them by others; very suitable to those who have nothing to do, and who merely live for the purpose of assisting to consume the produce of the earth; but he who has his bread to earn, or who means to be worthy of respect on account of his labours, has no business with morning-gown and slippers. In short, be your business or calling what it may, *dress at once for the day*; and learn to do it as *quickly* as possible. A looking-glass is a piece of furniture a great deal worse than useless. *Looking* at the face will not alter its shape or its colour; and, perhaps, of all wasted time, none is so foolishly wasted as that which is employed in surveying one's own face. Nothing can be of *little* importance, if one be compelled to attend to it *every day of our lives*; if we *shaved* but once a year, or once a month, the execution of the thing would be hardly worth naming: but this is a piece of work that must be done every day; and, as it may cost only about *five* minutes of time, and may be, and frequently is, made to cost *thirty*, or even *fifty minutes*; and, as only fifteen minutes make about a fifty-eighth part of the hours of our average daylight; this being the case, this is a matter of real importance. I once heard Sir John Sinclair ask Mr Cochrane Johnstone, whether he meaned to have a son of his (then a little boy) taught Latin. 'No,' said Mr Johnstone, 'but I mean to do something a great deal better for him.' 'What is that?' said Sir John. 'Why,' said the other, 'to teach him *to shave with cold water and without a glass*.' Which, I dare say, he did; and for which benefit I am sure that son has had good reason to be grateful. Only think of the inconvenience attending the common practice! There must be *hot water*; to have this there must be *a fire*, and, in some cases, a fire for that purpose alone; to have these, there must be a *servant*, or you must light the fire yourself. For the want of these, the job is put off until a later hour: this causes a stripping and *another dressing bout*; or, you go in a slovenly state all that day, and the next day the thing must be done, or cleanliness must be abandoned altogether. If you be on a journey you must wait the pleasure of the servants at the inn before you can dress and set out in the morning; the pleasant time for travelling is gone before you can move from the spot; instead of being at the end of your day's journey in good time, you are benighted, and have to endure all the great inconveniences attendant on tardy movements. And, all this, from the apparently insignificant affair of shaving! How many a piece of important business has failed from a short delay! And how many thousand of such delays daily proceed from this unworthy cause! . . . Do the whole at once for the day, whatever may be your state of life; and then you have a day unbroken by these indispensable performances. Begin thus, in the days of your youth, and, having felt the superiority which this practice will give you over those in all other respects your equals, the practice will stick by you to the end of your life. Till you be shaved and dressed for the day, you cannot set steadily about any business; you know that you must presently quit your labour to return to the dressing affair; you, therefore, put it off until that be over; the interval, the precious interval, is spent in lounging about; and, by the time that you are ready for business, the best part of the day is gone . . .

Money is said to be *power*, which is, in some cases, true; and the same may be said of *knowledge*; but superior *sobriety*, *industry*, and *activity*, are a still more certain source of power; for without these, *knowledge* is of little use; and, as to the power which *money* gives, it is that of *brute force*, it is the power of the bludgeon and the bayonet, and of the bribed press, tongue and pen. Superior sobriety, industry, activity, though accompanied with but a moderate portion of knowledge, command respect, because they have great and visible influence. The drunken, the lazy, and the inert, stand abashed before the sober and the active . . .

Book-learning is by no means to be despised; and it is a thing which may be laudably sought after by persons in all states of life. In those pursuits which are called professions, it is necessary, and also in certain trades; and, in persons in the middle ranks of life, a total absence of such learning is somewhat disgraceful. There is, however, one danger to be carefully guarded against; namely, the opinion that your genius, or your literary acquirements, are such as to warrant you in disregarding the calling in which you are, and by which you gain your bread. Parents must have an uncommon portion of solid sense to counterbalance their natural affection sufficiently to make them competent judges in such a case. Friends are partial; and those who are not, you deem enemies. Stick, therefore, to *the shop*; rely on your mercantile, or mechanical, or professional calling; try your strength in literature, if you like; but *rely* on the shop . . .

Perseverance is a prime quality in every pursuit, and . . . yours is, too, the time of life to acquire this inestimable habit. Men fail much oftener from want of perseverance than from want of talent and of good disposition: as the race was not to the hare but to the tortoise, so the meed of success in study is to him who is not in haste, but to him who proceeds with a steady and even step . . . Five or six triumphs over temptation to indolence or despair lay the foundation of certain success; and, what is of still more importance, fix in you the *habit of perseverance* . . .

The Qualities to Look for in a Wife

Chastity, perfect modesty in word, deed, and even thought, is so essential that, without it, no female is fit to be a wife. It is not enough that a young woman abstain from everything approaching towards indecorum in her behaviour towards men; it is, with me, not enough that she cast down her eyes, or turn aside her head with a smile, when she hears an indelicate allusion: she ought to appear *not to understand* it, and to receive from it no more impression than if she were a post. A loose woman is a disagreeable *acquaintance*: what must she be, then, as a *wife*? Love is so blind, and vanity is so busy in persuading us that our own qualities will be sufficient to ensure fidelity, that we are very apt to think nothing, or, at any rate, very little, of trifling symptoms of levity; but if such symptoms show themselves *now*, we may be well assured, that we shall never possess the power of effecting a cure. If *prudery* mean *false* modesty, it is to be despised; but if it mean modesty pushed to the utmost extent, I confess that I like it. Your 'free and hearty' girls I have liked very well to talk and laugh with; but never, for one moment, did it enter my mind that I could have endured a 'free and hearty' girl for a wife. The thing, I repeat, is to *last for life*; it is to be a counterbalance for troubles and misfortunes; and it must therefore be perfect, or it had better not be at all . . .

Sobriety. By *sobriety* I do not mean merely an absence of *drinking to a state* of intoxication; for, if that be *hateful* in a man, what must it be in a woman! There is a Latin proverb, which says that wine, that is to say, intoxication, *brings forth truth*. Whatever it may do in this way, in men, in women it is sure, unless prevented by age or by salutary ugliness, to produce a moderate, and a *very moderate*, portion of chastity. There never was a drunken woman, a woman who loved strong drink, who was chaste, if the opportunity of being the contrary presented itself to her. There are cases where *health* requires wine, and even small portions of more ardent liquor; but . . . *young* unmarried women can seldom stand in need of these stimulants; and . . . only in cases of well-known definite ailments . . . As soon as have married a girl whom I had thought liable to be persuaded to drink habitually, '*only* a glass or two of wine at dinner, or so'; as soon as have *married* such a girl, I would have taken a strumpet from the streets . . . There are few more things so disgusting as a guzzling woman. A gormandizing one is bad enough; but one who tips off the liquor with an appetite, and exclaims '*good! good!*' by the smack of her lips, is fit for nothing but a brothel . . .

But by the word Sobriety, in a young woman, I mean a great deal more than even a rigid abstinence from that love of *drink*, which I am not to suppose, and which I do not believe, to exist any thing like generally amongst the young women of this country. I mean a great deal more than this; I mean *sobriety of conduct.* The word *sober*, and its derivatives, do not confine themselves to matters of *drink*: they express *steadiness, seriousness, carefulness, scrupulous propriety of conduct*; and they are thus used amongst country people in many parts of England. When a Somersetshire fellow makes too free with a girl, she reproves him with, 'Come! be *sober!*' And when we wish a team, or any thing, to be moved on *steadily* and with *great care*, we cry out to the carter, or other operator, '*Soberly, soberly.*' Now this species of sobriety is a great qualification in the person you mean to make your wife. Skipping, capering, romping, rattling girls are very amusing where all costs and other considerations are out of the question; and they *may* become *sober* in the Somersetshire sense of the word. But while you have *no certainty* of this, you have a presumptive argument on the other side. To be sure, when girls are *mere children*, they are to play and romp like children. But when they arrive at that age which turns their thoughts towards that sort of connexion which is to be theirs for life; when they begin to think of having the command of a house, however small or poor, it is time for them to cast away the levity of the child. It is natural, nor is it very wrong, that I know of, for children to like to gad about and to see all sorts of strange sights, though I do not approve of this even in children; but if I could not have found a *young woman* . . . who I was not *sure* possessed *all* the qualities expressed by the word sobriety, I should have remained a bachelor to the end of that life, which, in that case, would, I am satisfied, have terminated without my having performed a thousandth part of those labours which have been, and are, in spite of all political prejudice, the wonder of all who have seen, or heard of, them . . .

If any young man imagine that this great *sobriety of conduct* in young women must be accompanied with seriousness approaching to *gloom*, he is, according to my experience and observation, very much deceived. The *contrary* is the fact; for I have found that as, amongst men, your jovial companions are, except over the bottle, the dullest and most insipid of souls; so amongst women, the gay, rattling, and laughing are, unless some party of pleasure, or something out of domestic life, is going on, generally in the dumps and blue-devils . . . A greater curse than a wife of this description it would be somewhat difficult to find; and . . . you are to provide against it. I hate a dull, melancholy, moping thing: I could not have existed in the same house with such a thing for a single month. The mopers are, too, all giggle at other times: the gaiety is for others, and the moping for the husband, to comfort him, happy man, when he is alone: plenty of smiles and of badinage for others, . . . but the moping is reserved exclusively for him. One hour she is capering about, as if rehearsing a jig; and the next, sighing to the motion of a lazy needle, or weeping over a novel; and this is called *sentiment*! Music, indeed! Give me a mother singing to her clean and fat and rosy baby, and making the house ring with her extravagant and hyperbolical encomiums on it. That is the music which is 'the food of love'; and not the formal, pedantic noises, an affectation of skill in which is nowadays the ruin of half the young couples in the middle rank of life. Let any man observe, as I so frequently have, with delight, the excessive fondness of the labouring people for their children. Let him observe with what pride they dress them out on a Sunday, with means deducted from their own scanty meals. Let him observe the husband, who has toiled all the week like a horse, nursing the baby, while the wife is preparing the bit of dinner. Let him observe them both abstaining from a sufficiency, lest the children should feel the pinchings of hunger. Let him observe, in short, the whole of their demeanour, the real mutual affection, evinced, not in words, but in unequivocal deeds. Let him observe these things, and having then cast a look at the lives of the great and wealthy, he will say, with me, that, when a man is choosing his partner for life, the dread of poverty ought to be cast to the winds. A labourer's cottage, on a Sunday; the husband or wife having a baby in arms, looking at two or three older ones playing between the flower-borders going from the wicket to the door, is, according to my taste, the most interesting object that eyes ever beheld; and it is an object to be beheld in no country upon earth but England . . . In riding once, about five years ago, from Petworth to Horsham, on Sunday in the afternoon, I came to a solitary cottage which stood at about twenty yards distance from the road. There was a wife with the baby in her arms, the husband teaching another child to walk, while *four* more were at play before them. I stopped and looked at them for some time, and then, turning my horse, rode up to the wicket, getting into talk by asking the distance to Horsham. I found that the man worked chiefly in the woods, and that he was doing pretty well. The wife was then only *twenty-two*, and the man only *twenty-five*. She was a pretty woman, even for *Sussex*, which, not excepting Lancashire, contains the prettiest women in England. He was a very fine and stout young man. 'Why,' said I, 'how many children do you reckon to have at last?' 'I do not care how many,' said the man: 'God never sends mouths without sending meat.' 'Did you ever hear,' said I, 'of one Parson Malthus?' 'No, sir.' 'Why, if he were to hear of your works, he would be outrageous [outraged]; for he wants an act of Parliament to prevent poor people from marrying young, and from having such lots of children.' 'Oh! the brute!' exclaimed the wife; while the husband laughed, thinking that I was joking . . . Now, is it not a shame, is it not a sin of all sins, that people like these should, by acts of government, be reduced to such misery as to be induced to abandon their homes and their country, to seek, in a foreign land, the means of preventing themselves and their children from starving? And this has been, and now is, actually the case with many such families in this same county of Sussex!

An *ardent-minded* young man . . . may fear that this *great sobriety of conduct* in a young woman, for which I have been so strenuously contending, argues a want of that *warmth*, which he naturally so much desires; and, if my observation and experience warranted the entertaining of this fear, I should say, had I to live my life over again, give me the *warmth*, and I will stand my chance as to the rest. But, this observation and this experience tell me the contrary; they tell me that *levity* is, ninety-nine times out of a hundred, the companion of *a want of ardent feeling*. Prostitutes never *love*, and, for the far greater part, never did. Their passion, which is more *mere animal* than any thing else, is easily gratified; they, like rakes, change not only without pain, but with pleasure; that is to say, pleasure as great as they can enjoy. Women of *light minds* have seldom any ardent passion; love is a mere name, unless confined to one object; and young women, in whom levity of conduct is observable, will not be this restricted . . .

Industry. By *industry*, I do not mean merely *laboriousness*, merely labour or activity of body, for purposes of gain or of saving; for there may be industry amongst those who have more money than they know well what to do with: and there may be *lazy ladies*, as well as lazy farmers' and tradesmen's wives. There is no state of life in which industry in the wife is not necessary to the happiness and prosperity of the family, at the head of the household affairs of which she is placed. If she be lazy there will be lazy servants, and, which is a great deal worse, children habitually lazy: every thing, however necessary to be done, will be put off to the last moment. then it will be done badly, and, in many cases, not at all: the dinner will be *too late*; the journey or the visit will be tardy; inconveniences of all sorts will be continually arising: there will always be a heavy *arrear* of things unperformed; and this, even amongst the most wealthy of all, is a great curse; for, if they have no *business* imposed upon them by necessity, they *make business* for themselves; life would be unbearable without it; and therefore a lazy woman must always be a curse, be her rank and station what it may.

But, who is to tell whether a girl will make an industrious woman? How is the purblind lover especially, to be able to ascertain whether she, whose smiles and dimples and bewitching lips have half bereft him of his senses; how is he to be able to judge, from anything that he can see, whether the beloved object will be industrious or lazy? Why, it is very difficult . . . but there are, nevertheless, certain outward and visible signs, from which a man, not wholly deprived of the use of his reason, may form a pretty accurate judgement as to this matter . . .

First, if you find the *tongue* lazy, you may be nearly certain that the hands and feet are the same. By laziness of the tongue I do not mean *silence*; I do not mean an *absence of talk*, for that is, in most cases, very good; but I mean a *slow* and *soft utterance*; a sort of *sighing out* of the words instead of *speaking* them; a sort of letting the sounds fall out, as if the party were *sick at stomach*. The pronunciation of an industrious person is generally *quick*, *distinct*, and the voice, if not strong, *firm* at the least . . . Look a little, also, at the labours of the *teeth*, for these correspond with those of the other members of the body, and with the operations of the mind. 'Quick at *meals*, quick at *work*', is a saying as old as the hills, in this, the most industrious nation upon earth; and never was there a truer saying . . . Another mark of industry is a *quick step*, and a somewhat *heavy tread*, showing that the foot comes down with a *hearty good will*; and if the body lean a little forward, and the eyes keep steadily in the same direction, while the feet are going, so much the better, for these discover *earnestness* to arrive at the intended point. I do not like, and I never liked, your *sauntering*, soft-stepping girls, who move as if they were perfectly indifferent as to the result; and, as to the *love* part of the story, whoever expects ardent and lasting affection from one of these sauntering girls, will, when too late, find his mistake . . .

Early rising is another mark of industry; and though, in the higher situations of life, it may be of no importance in a mere pecuniary point of view, it is, even there, of importance in other respects; for it is, I should imagine, pretty difficult to keep love alive towards a woman who *never sees the dew*, never beholds the *rising* sun, and who constantly comes directly from a reeking bed to the breakfast table, and there chews about, without appetite, the choicest morsels of human food . . .

Frugality . . . means the contrary of *extravagance*. It does not mean *stinginess*; it does not mean a pinching of the belly, nor a stripping of the back; but it means an abstaining from all *unnecessary* expenditure, and all *unnecessary* use, of goods of any and of every sort; and a quality of great importance it is, whether the rank in life be high or low . . . The outward and visible and vulgar signs of extravagance are *rings*, *broaches*, *bracelets*, *buckles*, *necklaces*, *diamonds* (real or mock), and, in short, all the *hard-ware* which women put upon their persons . . . Reason and broaches and bracelets do not go in company: the girl who has not the sense to perceive that her person is disfigured, and not beautified, by parcels of brass and tin (for they are generally little better) and other hard-ware, stuck about her body; the girl that is so foolish as not to perceive that, when silks, and cottons, and cambrics, in their neatest form, have done their best, nothing more is to be done; the girl that cannot perceive this is too great a fool to be trusted with the purse of any man.

Cleanliness . . . is a capital ingredient; for there never yet was, and there never will be, love of long duration, sincere and ardent love, in any man, towards a *filthy mate* . . . The signs of cleanliness are, in the first place, a clean *skin*. An English girl will hardly let her lover see the stale dirt between her fingers, as I have many times seen it between those of French women, and even ladies, of all ages. An English girl will have her *face* clean, to be sure, if there be soap and water within her reach; but get a glance, just a glance, at her *poll*, if you have any doubt upon the subject; and, if you find there, or *behind the ears*, what the Yorkshire people call *grime*, the sooner you cease your visits the better . . .

Good temper . . . is a very difficult thing to ascertain before-hand. Smiles are so cheap; they are easily put on for the occasion; and besides, the frowns are, according to the lover's whim, interpreted into the contrary. By 'good temper' I do not mean *easy temper*, a serenity which nothing disturbs, for that is a mark of laziness. *Sulkiness*, if you be not too blind to perceive it, is a temper to be avoided by all means. A sulky man is bad enough; what, then, must be a sulky woman, and that woman a *wife*; a constant inmate, a companion day and night! . . .

Beauty . . . I by no means think . . . the last in point of importance . . . It is certainly true that pretty girls will have more, and more ardent, admirers than ugly ones; but, as to the *temptation* when in their unmarried state, there are few so very ugly as to be exposed to no temptation at all; and, which is the most likely to resist, she who has a choice of lovers, or she who if she let the occasion slip may never have it again? . . . The great use of female beauty, the great practical advantage of it is, that it naturally and unavoidably tends to *keep the husband in good humour with himself*, to make him, to use the dealer's phrase, *pleased with his bargain*. When old age approaches, and the parties have become endeared to each other by a long series of joint cares and interests, and when children have come and bound them together by the strongest ties that nature has in store; at this stage the features and the person are of less consequence; but, in the *young days* of matrimony, when the roving eye of the bachelor is scarcely become steady in the head of the husband, it is dangerous for him to see, every time he stirs out, a face more captivating than that of the person to whom he is bound for life. Beauty is, in some degree, a matter of *taste*: what one man admires, another does not; and it is fortunate for us that it is thus. But still there are certain things that all men admire; and a husband is always pleased when he perceives that a portion, at least, of these things are in his own possession: he takes this possession as a *compliment to himself*: there must, he will think the world will believe, have been

some merit in him, some charm, seen or unseen, to have caused him
to be blessed with the acquisition . . .

[*Advice to Young Men*, 1829]

Boxing

The public attention having been called to a recent, an extraordinary,
and somewhat alarming decision of a Coroner's jury upon a case
wherein death was the consequence of a boxing-match, I cannot,
consistently with the opinions I have always entertained and frequently expressed upon the subject, omit, upon this occasion, to
submit to my readers, some few of the reflections that press upon my
mind . . .

Upon inquiry I find . . . that the combatants were two journeymen in the same shop who, having quarrelled at their shop-board,
agreed to decide their quarrel by a boxing match. It is said that the
only pecuniary stake, for which they contended, was a bet of half a
guinea, which bet, however, did not take place till the moment before
the fight began. There was so little of what could be truly called
malice between them that the deceased had proposed to make up
their difference without fighting; and, though this was not accepted,
a similar proposition was made by the survivor during the course of
the battle. There was . . . no reason to suppose the death to be
occasioned by any particular blow, but merely by the effect of exertion and the breaking of a bloodvessel, as might have happened in
a race, a rowing-match, a jumping-match, a cricket-match, or in any
other exercise requiring, either constantly or occasionally, any extraordinary exertion of bodily strength. These being the circumstances
of the case one may confidently hope that this will not be the instance
in which the last blow will be struck at that manly, that generous
mode of terminating quarrels between the common people, a mode
by which the common people of England, have, for ages, been distinguished from those of all other countries. But, though we may
safely rely upon the wisdom and justice of the courts, before one of
which this unfortunate boxer must finally take his trial, the occasion
calls for some remark upon those exertions which, of late, have been,
and which yet are, making in every part of the country, with the
obvious, and in many instances, with the declared, intention of utterly
eradicating the practice of boxing; than which, I am thoroughly
persuaded, nothing could be more injurious, whether considered as

to its effects in civil life, or in its higher and more important effects on the people regarded as the members of a state, and, of course, always opposed to some other state, and therefore always liable to be called upon to perform the duties of war.

As few persons will be inclined to believe it possible so far to work, by any human laws, such a change in the hearts and minds of men as shall prevent all quarrelling amongst them, it is not necessary to insist that, in spite of the law and the gospel, in spite of the animadversions of the bench and the admonitions of the pulpit, there will still be practised some mode or other of terminating quarrels, some way in which the party injured or offended will seek for satisfaction, without waiting for the operation of the law, even in those cases where the law affords the means whereby satisfaction is to be obtained. If this be not denied, it will remain with the innovating foes of the pugilistic combat to show that there are other modes of terminating quarrels amongst the common people less offensive to the principles of sound morality, less dangerous in their physical effects, better calculated to produce the restoration of harmony, to shorten the duration, and to prevent the extension of resentment, together with the evils attendant upon a long-harboured spirit of revenge. Without proceeding another step, I am confident that the reflecting reader, though he may, for a moment, have been carried away by the cry of '*brutality*', latterly set up against boxing, will, from our thus simply stating what our opponents have to prove, have clearly perceived that the proof is not within their power. He will have perceived that, of all the ways in which violence can possibly be committed (and violence of some sort there must be in the obtaining of personal satisfaction), none has in it so little hostility to the principles of our religion, and that none is so seldom fatal to the parties, as boxing. He will have perceived, too, that this mode, by excluding the aid of every thing extraneous, by allowing of no weapons, by leaving nothing to deceit, and very little to art of any sort, is, in most cases, decisive as to the powers of the combatants, and proceeds, besides, upon the generous principle that with the battle ceases for ever the cause whence it arose; a principle of such long and steady growth, so deeply rooted in the hearts of Englishmen, that to attempt the revival, or even to allude to, with apparent resentment, the grounds of a quarrel which has been terminated by the fists, is always regarded as a mark of baseness, whether visible in the conduct of the parties themselves, or in that of their relations or friends.

Instead, however, of rejoicing at the existence of a practice which is so well calculated to soften the natural effects of the violent passions, there are but too many amongst us, who seem to be perfect enthusiasts in their efforts to extirpate it. Whether, if they could extirpate those passions themselves, or could so far neutralize them as effectually to prevent their producing acts of violence; whether, in that case, they would leave us any thing whereby, and whereby alone, private injustice, domestic oppression, or foreign hostility is to be resisted, I submit as a question to the doctors in the school of modern philanthropy; but, unless those passions can be *extirpated*, and until that great work be *completed*, I think that every one who listens to reason in preference to an outcry, and who is attached to the substance and not the mere sounds of humanity and gentleness, will readily agree, that to attempt the extirpation of the practice of boxing is to make an attempt which, if successful, would lead to the frequent commission of all those sanguinary and horrible acts by which the common people of but too many other countries are disgraced, and which, amongst the people of England, have, till of late, been almost unknown. In support of this opinion, I may, as to an argument of experience, surely appeal to the law, recently passed . . .; and that such a law should have become necessary I am sure the reader, if he has an English heart in his bosom, will reflect with sorrow and with shame.* What is now become of those manners which authorized the honest exultation of so many of our eminent writers, that, from the generous spirit of Englishmen, acts of cruelty were rendered so rare in their country? Our travellers must now hold their tongues; for the world is told, and that too by the legislature itself, who have placed the disgraceful truth upon the records of Parliament, that the laws and statutes of the land, heretofore in force, are *no longer sufficient* to prevent us from committing 'cruel and barbarous outrages, with intent to murder, maim, disfigure, or disable one another'. It is not till 'of late', certainly, that such a law has been necessary, and, it is not till of late, that such a general desire to suppress the practice of boxing has prevailed. The mere co-existence of this desire (and of the measures proceeding from it), with the frequency of the commission of cruel and barbarous acts, may not, indeed, be regarded as a conclusive argument in favour of the practice of boxing; but, no

* Cobbett is referring to Lord Ellenborough's Act, passed in 1803, laying down more severe punishments for offences involving grievous bodily harm, maiming, and disfigurement.

one can deny, that it strongly corroborates the conclusion which reason, without the aid of experience, has taught us to draw; and, if this conclusion, thus fortified, be legitimate, it follows, of course, that we must either have *cuttings and stabbings* or *boxing*; the former of which, as being perfectly compatible with 'a godly *conversation*' and with the cant of humanity, it is more than probable that the saints and philanthropists would not hesitate to prefer.

But it is the political view of this subject which appears to me to be the most worthy of attention; the view of the effect which may, by the contemplated change of manners, be produced upon the people, considered as the members of a state, always opposed to some other state; for, much as I abhor cuttings and stabbings, I have, as I hope most others of my countrymen have, a still greater abhorrence of submission to a foreign yoke. Commerce, Opulence, Luxury, Effeminacy, Cowardice, Slavery: these are the stages of national degradation. We are in the fourth; and I beg the reader to consider, to look into history, to trace states in their fall, and then say how rapid is the latter part of the progress! Of the symptoms of *effeminacy* none is so certain as a change from athletic and hardy sports or exercises to those requiring less bodily strength, and exposing the persons engaged in them to less bodily suffering; and when this change takes place, be assured that national cowardice is at no great distance, the general admiration of deeds of hardihood having already been considerably lessened. Bravery, as indeed the word imports, consists not in a readiness or capacity to kill or to hurt, but in a readiness and a capacity to venture, and to bear the consequences. As sports or exercises approach nearer and nearer to real combats, the greater, in spite of all we can say, is our admiration of those who therein excel. Belcher* has, by the sons of cant, in every class of life, been held up to us as a monster, a perfect ruffian; yet there are very few persons who would not wish to see Belcher; few from whom marks of admiration have not, at some time, been extorted by his combats; and scarcely a female saint, perhaps, who would not, in her way to the conventicle, or even during the snuffling there to be heard, take a peep at him from beneath her hood. Can as much be said by any one of those noblemen and gentlemen who have been spending the best years of their lives in dancing by night and playing at cricket by day? The reason is, not that Belcher strikes hard; not that he is strong; not that

* The famous contemporary prize-fighter.

he is an adept at his art; but that he exposes himself voluntarily to so much danger and that he bears so many heavy blows. We are apt to laugh at the preference which women openly give to soldiers (including, of course, all men of the military profession), a preference which is always found, too, to be given by young persons of both sexes. But if we take time to consider, we shall find this partiality to be no fit subject for ridicule or blame. It is a partiality naturally arising from the strongest of all feelings, *the love of life*. The profession of arms is always the most honourable. All kings and princes were soldiers. Renowned soldiers are never forgotten. We all talk of Alexander the Great and of Julius Caesar; but very few of us ever heard, or ever thought of inquiring, who were the statesmen of those days. There is not, perhaps, a ploughman in England, who has not a hundred times repeated the names of Drake and of Marlborough; and of the hundreds of thousands of them, there is not one, perhaps, who ever heard, or ever will hear pronounced the name of Cecil or of Godolphin. When princes are not renowned military commanders, they themselves, though they leave so many and such various traces behind them, are, amongst the mass of the people, soon forgotten, except as having reigned during the victories of such or such a commander. Literary men have, almost uniformly, spoken with more or less contempt of military fame; but, notwithstanding the singular advantages which they have over soldiers, in perpetuating a knowledge of their famous deeds, within how narrow a sphere, comparatively speaking, is their fame confined! Where is the man, woman, or child, in this kingdom, who has not heard and talked of Nelson? And does not the reader believe that there are many parishes in either of which the knowledge of Pope or of Johnson's having existed is confined to two or three persons? Such, too, is the nature of military fame that it obliterates all the folly and all the crimes of the possessor. The discriminating few, the criticizers of character, will, indeed, take these into account; but with the people in general, and particularly those of the nation to which the renowned soldier belongs, his deeds of valour only are remembered.

Whence, then, arises this universal suffrage of mankind in favour of military heroes? Why are their deeds prized above those of all other men? Not because their profession demands more skill than that of others; not because it supposes hard study or great labour of any sort; not because it is thought to require an extraordinary degree of genius or of wisdom. Some have ascribed it to the terror inspired by military combats; but we often admire those heroes most at whose deeds it is impossible we can have felt any terror. Others have ascribed it to the signal and extensive consequences produced in the world by the deeds of military commanders; but the deeds of statesmen produce much more signal and more extensive consequences, and yet these latter sink silently to the grave and rot there, without ever being named by the common folk of only the next generation. To what, therefore, can we ascribe this universal preference of military fame before all other fame, but to that all-pervading and ever-predominating principle, the love of life, and the consequent admiration of those who voluntarily place their lives in the most frequent and most imminent danger? This principle exists, naturally, in the same degree in every human breast; and bravery consists, as was before said, simply in the capacity of subduing the love of life so far as knowingly, deliberately, and voluntarily to put it to risk. Hence it is that we cannot refrain from admiring the hardihood of miners, well-sinkers and the like; but in them we justly ascribe a good deal to habit, to hard necessity, and besides we do not, in their case, see where and what is the immediate cause of their danger; but in the case of the soldier we clearly perceive this cause; we see him voluntarily going forth and marching on till he comes within reach of those who, on their side, are advancing for the sole purpose of taking his life. In proportion as the readiness to hazard life exists in a country, that country is brave, and consequently, in proportion to its numbers, powerful. How deeply sensible of this does our rival and enemy appear to have been! Amongst all the changes and chances of the French Revolution there had never been a single day when the rulers were not careful to reward and honour those who had distinguished themselves by putting their lives to risk. The consequences we have seen and now but too sensibly feel. We, on the contrary, seem to be using our utmost endeavours to extirpate every habit that tended to prepare the minds of the common people for deeds of military bravery. Am I told that there are no boxers in France? I answer that there never were; that their exercises and their combats were of another description; I have seen peasants in France turn out into a field, and cut one another with their sabres. But, if you extirpate boxing in England, can you substitute any other mode of exercise or combat in its stead? No: and that is not the object; the professed object is to cry down and put an end to every species of exercise or of combat in which life shall at all be put to the risk, or, indeed, in which bodily opposition and great bodily strength and a great capacity of bearing bodily pain are acquired.

Not only boxing, but wrestling, quarter-staff, single-stick, bull-baiting, every exercise of the common people that supposes the possible risk of life or limb, and, of course, that tends to prepare them for deeds of bravery of a higher order, and, by the means of those deeds and of the character and consequence naturally growing out of them, to preserve the independence and the liberties of their country; every such exercise seems to be doomed to extirpation. Even the very animals, for the bravery of which the nation has long been renowned, are to be destroyed, as men would destroy savage and ferocious beasts. Everything calculated to keep alive the admiration, and even the idea, of hardihood, seems to have become offensive and odious in the sight of but too many of those whose duty it is to endeavour to arrest, and not to accelerate, the fatal progress of effeminacy. That many of the persons so zealously engaged in supporting the system of effeminacy (for such it may be properly called) are actuated by motives of tenderness for the common people there can be no doubt; but while I must think that such persons act without due reflection, I hesitate not to declare my belief that those with whom the system originated, and who are the principal instigators of all the measures adopted for affecting the extirpation of boxing and other hardy exercises, are actuated by motives far other than those of compassion for the persons who are in the habit of being therein engaged. Let, however, what will be the motives, the consequences are, some of them, already obvious, and others it is by no means difficult to foresee. That cuttings and stabbings are more fatal than boxing, to say nothing of the disgrace, every one must agree; and it cannot be denied that the former have increased in proportion as the latter has been driven from amongst the people. But boxing matches give rise to assemblages of the people; they tend to make the people bold: they produce a communication of notions of hardihood; they serve to remind men of the importance of bodily strength; they, each in its sphere, occasion a transient relaxation from labour; they tend, in short, to keep alive, even amongst the lowest of the people, some idea of independence; whereas amongst cutters and stabbers and poisoners (for the law above-mentioned includes *English poisoners*) there is necessarily a rivalship for quietness and secrecy; they generally perform their work single-handed; their operations have nothing of riot or commotion in them; as to labour they lose little of the time for that, seeing that their mode of seeking satisfaction is with the greatest chance of success pursued in the dark; and there is not the least fear, that their practices will ever render them politically turbulent or bold. In fact the system of effeminacy as it has grown out of, so it is perfectly adapted to, the Pitt system of internal politics, which, by making in a greater or less degree, almost every man who has property a sort of pensioner, or at least an annuitant of the state, aims at ruling the nation by its base, instead of its honourable, feelings. On the selfishness of the common people, particularly the labouring part of them, the Pitt system of finance and taxation has, directly at least, no hold; and, therefore, it required the aid of the system of effeminacy, which includes the suppression of mirth as well as of hardy exercises, and, indeed, of everything that tends to produce relaxations from labour and a communication of ideas of independence amongst the common people. Systems better calculated for preventing internal opposition to the government never were invented; but, this is not *all* that a wise statesman and one that loves his country will look to. Such a statesman will perceive that if he destroy the feelings, from the operation of which the government might occasionally have something to apprehend, he thereby destroys the means by which alone the government can be permanently preserved. Render the whole nation effeminate; suffer no relaxation from labour or from care; shut all the paupers up in workhouses, and those that are not so shut up, work in gangs, each with its driver; this do, and it is evident that you will have no internal commotion; it is evident that you will hold the people in complete subjection to your will; but then recollect that they will be like the ass in the fable, that they will stir neither hand nor foot to prevent the transfer of their subjection to another master.

Thank God we are yet at a great distance from a state so full of wretchedness and of infamy, and, I trust, that we shall long be so preserved. In speaking of the system of effeminacy as adapted to a co-operation with the Pitt system of internal policy, I by no means would be understood as supposing that it has been contrived, or at all encouraged, at least wilfully, by Mr Pitt, or by any other minister. It is, indeed, one of the many evils that have naturally grown out of the Pitt system; but whatever other faults I may impute to Mr Pitt as a minister, justice to him obliges me to confess that I have heard of his directly favouring the endeavours of those weak, meddling, and, in many instances, fanatical persons who are the chief instruments in the persecution of all manly and mirthful exercises; and I confidently hope that, if any further attempts are made at legislative innovation upon these subjects he will be found amongst their determined opponents.

[*Boxing*, AUGUST 1805, *Political Works* II, 11–17]

Education

[*i*] *The True Nature of Education*

That children may be a blessing and not a curse, care must be taken of their *education*. This word has, of late years, been so perverted, so corrupted, so abused, in its application, that I am almost afraid to use it here. Yet I must not suffer it to be usurped by cant and tyranny ...

Education means *breeding up*, *bringing up*, or *rearing up*; and nothing more. This includes everything with regard to the *mind* as well as to the *body* of a child; but of late years it has been so used as to have no sense applied to it but that of *book-learning*, with which, nine times out of ten, it has nothing at all to do. It is, indeed, proper, and it is the duty of all parents to teach, or cause to be taught, their children as much as they can of books, *after*, and not before, all the measures are safely taken for enabling them to get their living by labour, or for *providing them a living without labour*, and that, too, out of the means obtained and secured by the parents out of their own income. The taste of the times is, unhappily, to give to children something of *book-learning*, with a view of placing them to live, in some way or other, *upon the labour of other people* . . . When the project has failed, what disappointment, mortification, and misery, to both parent and child! The latter is spoiled as a labourer, his book-learning has only made him conceited: into some course of desperation he falls; and the end is but too often not only wretched but ignominious.

[*Cottage Economy* (1821), p. 10]

[*ii*] *The Dangers and Delusions of Education*

It is the lot of man, and most wisely has it so been ordained, that he shall live by the sweat of his brow. In one way or another every man must labour, or he must suffer for the failure in health or in estate. Some are to labour with the mind, others with the limbs; and to suppose what is, by Mr Whitbread, called education, necessary to those who labour with their limbs is, in my opinion, as absurd as it would be to suppose that the being able to mow and to reap are necessary to a minister of state or an astronomer. The word *ignorance* is as much abused by some persons as the word *learning*; but those who regard the latter as consisting *solely* in the acquirement of the knowledge of the meaning of words in various languages, which knowledge is to be derived only from books, will naturally regard the former as consisting *solely* of a want of the capacity to deprive any knowledge at all from books. If the farmer understands well how to conduct the business of his farm, and if, from observation of the seasons and the soil, he knows how to draw from the latter as much profit as therefrom can be drawn; if the labourer be expert at ploughing, sowing, reaping, mowing, making of ricks and of fences, loading the waggon, threshing and winnowing the corn, and bestowing upon the cattle the various necessary cares; if this be the case, though neither of them can write or read, I call neither *an ignorant* man. The *education* of these men is a finished one, though neither may have looked into a book; and, I believe, Mr Whitbread would be greatly puzzled to suggest even the most trifling benefit that either could derive from an acquaintance with the use of letters.

'But men, thus naturally gifted and disposed, might have *risen* in life, if they had been taught reading and writing.' It is very likely that they might have been, by such means, removed from the fields to the city; but without allowing that that remove would have *raised* them in life, and positively denying that it would have added to their happiness, I think I may anticipate that Mr Whitbread will concede that *all* men cannot be so removed; and then, let it be observed, that his system of education is intended for *general* effect. Would I, then, advise every parent to prevent his children from learning to read and write? No: but I would leave each parent to his own taste and his own means co-operating with the disposition and capacity of the child. The general taste of parents, and their naturally high opinion of their children's capacities, are quite sufficient to furnish the schools, without the aid of another Act of Parliament *and another cursed tax*. It is natural to the fondness of parents, it is laudable emulation in them, to endeavour to raise their children in the consideration of the world; and, as no great degree of eminence is to be attained without the use of letters, it is laudable in them to make use thereof when they can. But some people must remain to labour; all men cannot attain to eminence in the world; and, therefore, that which is laudable in individuals is, to say the best of it, foolish upon a national scale.

It is contended that learning to read and write would *mend the morals* of the people. I have before observed that the assumed increase of vice has taken place while schools and newspapers have been increasing tenfold. By the help of Mr Wilberforce, indeed, the word *religious* was to have been placed, in the Bill,* before *education*; and great care was to be taken to give the parson of the parish sufficient authority in the superintending of the school, without, however, making any provision to ensure even a tolerable chance of there being a parson in the parish, except, perhaps, for a couple of hours of a Sunday. But, though Mr Wilberforce would easily believe that, with the help of a little new light, the scholars would have no difficulty in solving those knotty points, arising from the text of the Scriptures, about which so many doctors have been quarrelling for so many centuries, each doctor condemning the other doctor to flames eternal and that, too, not *ignorantly*, but in good decent Latin and Greek; yet it does not appear to have occurred to him that, when they had learnt to read the Bible, they might possibly read something else, and that Grub Street and the novel shops might furnish them with ideas exceedingly well calculated to add to, instead of diminishing, the fearful stock of vice assumed to be already existing. Is it, however, seriously urged; is there a man who will soberly assert that the people of England, in any considerable number, can *possibly* be ignorant of their moral duties? Go to the top of any hill in the kingdom, and see how thickly the spires are scattered; consider how easy and how constant is the communication between all ranks of men; how scrupulous men are as to all matters relating to property; how frequent and how regular, and, generally speaking, how impartial, the administration of justice. Do this, Mr Whitbread, and then say, if you can, that the people of England are *ignorant*, or can *possibly* be ignorant, of their moral duties; and that they want *reading* to teach them those duties.

'But, the *political* effects of this education!' Mr Whitbread did not, that I know of, promise any benefit of this sort from his plan; but the editor of the *Morning Chronicle* and others have affected to see a

* Cobbett is here referring to an amendment which Samuel Whitbread, the brewer and Whig M.P., was attempting to make to the Poor Laws, by which rates were to be levied for the establishment of schools for the poor in each parish.

prospect of great advantage in 'enlightening' the people in this way.
I, however, can see none. For what would the teaching of the people
to read do? Enable them to read newspapers, those vehicles of falsehood, and of bad principles. That the press, *left to itself*, would
enlighten men I allow; that discussion, if *free*, would end in favour of
truth I well know. But of the newspapers and other periodical
publications, and all books, or printed works, treating of politics, five
sixths, at least, are, by one means or other, *bought*. The writers are,
in fact, hired; and hired, too, to deceive the people; to spread falsehood instead of truth; darkness instead of light. Truth is a libel; and
what is the worst of it fine and imprisonment are constantly dreaded
on the one side, and perfect impunity as constantly relied on on the
other side. What information, what light are the people to receive
from such a press? Do the people benefit from their reading of
politics in France? Did they profit from it at Berlin? Do they profit
from it in Russia or in Austria or in Holland? Yet there are newspapers in abundance there; and full as free, too, in fact, as the far
greater part, as nine-tenths even, of our newspapers. Of public men
and measures, if you disapprove, you must speak very cautiously;
but if you please to praise them, no matter how bold, how exaggera-
ted, how false your statements! There is no gainsaying this: that
where to publish what is true may subject a man to fine and imprisonment and pillory, the press must be an injury to political freedom.
Some truths, and valuable truths, get abroad through the means of
the press; but these are infinitely outnumbered by the falsehoods;
and if the people were left without any press at all matters would be
much better because they would then judge and act from what they
saw and what they *felt*, and not from what they *read*. The operations
of the press have, every one must allow, increased greatly in their
extent within the last twenty-three years. Has political freedom
gained much in that time? . . .

There was one argument of experience, brought forward in
support of this project, which, by way of conclusion I must take a
little notice of – *the example of the people of Scotland*. The Scotch are
never backward in putting forward their claims of any sort and many
just claims they have; but I am not amongst those who are ready to
allow them a *monopoly* either of virtue or of talent; and I deny that
their lower classes afford any example worthy of the imitation of ours.
I deny that they are more industrious, more moral, more virtuous in
any respect, than the people of England are. I have seen colonies that

have been settled by Englishmen, and some by Irishmen, where industry alone could possibly have succeeded; but I never yet saw a country settled and cleared by the labour of Scotchmen. The boastings which have been heard about the wondrous improvements in Scotland are infinite; but will any man pretend to say that the labourers of that country are more moral, more orderly, their habitation more cleanly, their struggles against poverty more un-remitted, their labour and their industry greater, than are those of the English labourers? This notion about Scotch example seems to have come up amongst us with the juvenile economists, whom the late ministers drafted from the office of the *Edinburgh Review*, which is a port of depot for speculators in politics, who go off, each in his turn, as he can make shift to write himself into place . . .

We are a people that delight in quacks and pretenders of all sorts, otherwise it would have been impossible that the Parliament, how-ever constituted, supposing a majority to be English, should for a moment . . . have tolerated in any shape such an outrage upon the orderly and honest and laborious and ingenious and persevering and patient people of England. Where did any man, however far he may have travelled, see such cleanliness, such neatness, such attention to ornament as well as conveniences, such care of their animals, such affection and tenderness for their parents and children amongst the labouring part of the community, as are visible in the dress, in the houses, in the gardens, and in the domestic life and manners of English labourers? . . . And can I see and admire the dispositions of men who, though pressed down with poverty, can, at their return from their daily labour, spend the twilight in works of neatness round their cottages; can I, when I see this, refrain from feeling indignation at a set of upstart politicians who know nothing of England but what they have seen from the deck of a smack or through the pane of a stage-coach window and who have the audacity to bid these English labourers to look for an example to the garden-less and floor-less and chimney-less cabins of Scotland, where the master of the mansion nestles in at night in company with his pig or his cow? . . .

Go! Go! thou Scotch Philosopher! Keep thy pimping books, thy primers of debauchery and blasphemy amongst the lads and lasses of thy own country; fortify them against the deceiver by giving them a foretaste of vice; but come not, I pray, on this side the Tweed! . . .

The principle that all *animal* amusements are *necessarily vicious* . . . is a little doubtful with me; and . . . I should think that animal amusements, generally speaking, are the least likely . . . to engender vice. And as to the ploughman, sitting down to read his good book after his labour is done, the idea never could have found its way into the mind of any one who knew what a ploughman was. Take a thousand ploughmen, set them down to their good books after their day's work is done, and in less than ten minutes the whole thousand will be asleep. Animal amusement is the only amusement that such men *can* enjoy. They are up long before the sun; and in the evening of the day, if they are not engaged in bodily exercise, they must be asleep, and asleep they would be though a torrent of . . . philosophy . . . were pouring down upon their devoted heads . . .

But if I doubt of the advantage of reading and writing amongst those of the common people who are destined to labour in the fields, on the shop-board, or in the manufactory, I am quite certain that generally speaking they are worse than useless in the army and the navy. Some persons have a bright idea about the 'Sons of Mars and of Neptune' rising, in virtue of their schooling, from the lowest to the highest ranks; but, besides the notoriety of the fact that this is not the case now, is it not evident that *all* men cannot so rise, that *all* soldiers and sailors cannot become officers, either commissioned or non-commissioned? And, this being the case, would not the 'education', as it is called, of nine-tenths of them tend to create discontent rather than a cheerful obedience? Upon this part of the subject I can speak with some little experience; and I appeal to any commanding officer who has continued long settled with his regiment, or to any captain of a man-of-war, whether your 'scholars', as they are called, are not in general the worst of soldiers and sailors. The conceit makes them saucy; they take the lead in all matters of mischief; they are generally dirty and drunkards; and the lash drives them to desert. So true it is, that 'scholars' are not the best soldiers, that, though one third part at least of the men of every regiment can read and write, yet you will find in every regiment men chosen for non-commissioned officers who can neither read nor write. Reading and writing and honesty and good behaviour are all wanted in a non-commissioned officer; but, as the two latter are absolutely necessary, the commander is frequently compelled to appoint men who can neither write nor read; though he has hundreds of 'scholars' in his regiment or his ship; and, it is curious to observe, that the 'scholars' become the clerks of the 'ignorant' non-commissioned officers, make out their reports and accounts for them, leaving them the trouble of merely scrawling their name. This practice is universal thoughout the army and the navy, and it is a striking instance of the superiority of intrinsic worth over acquired talent. The man of reading and writing is to be preferred, if he be equally good with his comrade in other respects; and the great convenience of his talents generally procures him a trial, before his comrade be thought of for promotion; but, in the end, the sober, cleanly, punctual, early-rising, vigilant, honest and unassuming man is sure to be preferred, because these qualities are indispensable, and because reading and writing can be dispensed with. 'But *somebody* must read and write.' Granted; and what I contend for is that the number will be quite large enough if you leave the parents to their own taste and their own means. There will then be as many readers and writers as the state of things calls for; but, if you make *all* men readers and writers, you must produce an unnatural and disjointed state of things.

The word ignorance is misapplied in using it as the opposite of book-learning . . . What reading could possibly render the labourer more skilled in his profession? The old story about the judge and the sailor is quite apt to our purpose here. 'Not know the meaning of the *implication*,' said the judge, 'what an *ignorant* fellow you must be!' 'Well,' continued the sailor after the interruption, 'as I was saying he took hold of the *painter*—' 'The *painter*!' interrupted the judge, 'what's the painter?' 'Oh, Lord!' exclaimed the sailor. 'Not know what the *painter* is? What an *ignorant* man you must be!' If this story be true, the sailor, doubtless, was committed to jail; but that did not make his conclusion more erroneous than that of the judge. According to the notion of my Scotch critic a man may first become completely skilled in all the business of husbandry; he may next learn to fell and hew timber and convert the several woods of the coppices into hoops, staves and shingles; then he may take the corn into the mill and go through the several stages of making it into flour; next he may become a soldier, may learn all the laborious duties of that profession, marching, shooting, riding, sapping, and mining; transferred from the army to the fleet, he may learn to hand, reef, and steer, to sound the sea, and to man the guns in battle; in the course of his life he may see all the quarters and countries of the world, the manners of all the different nations, and may feel the effects of all climates; and yet, when he comes home, with his mind necessarily stored with ideas, of which that of his neighbour must be totally destitute, he is to be called *ignorant*, in comparison with that neighbour, if he cannot read in a book and if that neighbour can read in a book. Such a notion never, surely could have entered the mind of a man, whose trade it was not to teach reading, and who did not view what he calls education through the deceitful medium of self-interest . . .

[*On the Poor Laws*, AUGUST AND SEPTEMBER 1807, *Political Works* 11, 289–300]

[*iii*] *On Teaching the Children of the Poor to Read*

The subject naturally divides itself into two parts; or rather presents two subjects for discussion: 1st. Whether, under the present circumstances in this country, the teaching of poor children *to read generally* be likely to do good; and 2nd. Whether it be likely to do good to teach them *to read the Bible*.

Whatever men may think about reading the Bible; however their opinions may differ as to the utility of reading this particular Book, the number is very small indeed who think that the teaching of poor children to read generally is not a good past all dispute. To that very small number, however, I belong; and my opinion decidedly is that, under the present circumstances of this country, the teaching of poor children to read generally is calculated to produce *evil* rather than *good*; for which opinion I will now proceed to offer you my reasons, and not without some hope of being able to convince you that your money, laid out in pots of beer to the parents, would be full as likely to benefit the community.

The *utility* of reading consists in imparting knowledge to those who read; knowledge dispels ignorance. Reading, therefore, naturally tends to enlighten mankind. As mankind became enlightened they became less exposed to the arts of those who would enslave them. Whence reading naturally tends to promote and ensure the liberties of mankind. 'How, then,' you will ask, 'can you object to the teaching of the children of the ignorant to read?' But, Sir, when we thus describe the effects of reading, we must always be understood as meaning the reading of works which convey *truth* to the mind; for, I am sure, that you will not deny that it is possible for a person to become by reading more ignorant than he was before. For instance, a child has *no knowledge* of the source whence coals are drawn; but if in consequence of what he reads he believes coals to be made out of clay he is more ignorant than he was before he read; because falsehood is farther from truth than is the absence of knowledge. A child in the neighbourhood of Loretto, who had been happy enough to escape the lies of the priests, would know nothing at all of the origin of the Virgin Mary's House at that famous resort of pilgrims; but if he had read the history of the Bees' House he would believe that it came thither, flying across the sea from Palestine; and he would, of course, be a great deal *more ignorant* than if he had never read the said history.

Thus, then, reading does not tend to enlighten men unless what they read convey *truth* to their minds. The next question is, therefore, whether, under the present circumstances of the country the children of the poor are likely to come at truth by reading; which question, I think, we must decide in the negative.

You will please to observe that I am not now speaking of the Bible, or of works upon religion. Those I shall notice by-and-by. I am now speaking of *reading in general*. To those who object to the teaching of children to read the Bible, as being above their capacity to comprehend, it is usually answered that if children learn to read the Bible, they will inevitably read *other things*; and that out of reading will proceed *light*, and the means of giving the people true notions of their *rights* in society. But here again it is taken for granted that what they will read, after they have been taught to read the Bible, will be calculated to give them *true notions*, and will inculcate the principles upon which men ought to be governed.

Now . . . is this a fact? Does the press in this country send forth works calculated to produce such an effect? That is to say, are its productions *generally* of this description? Or, to put the question more closely, is the *major part* of its productions of this description? Because if it send forth more productions which are calculated to give *false* notions, than of productions which are calculated to give *true* notions, it follows, of course, that reading generally must tend to the increase of a belief in falsehood, which no one will deny to be the worst species of ignorance . . .

Very well; but if this be the case can the reading of the productions of this press tend to dispel ignorance; can it tend to enlighten the people? Can it be any public benefit, can it further the cause of public liberty, to teach the children of the poor to *read*?

Let us, if you please, trace one of these poor boys in his progress of reading, after he has been taught, at your Lancaster school, to read in the Bible. He is, you will please to observe, not going to live in the house of a father or a master, who has the means or the capacity to direct his studies in any particular channel. He has no one to tell him what publications he ought to look upon as good and what as bad. He has no one to point out to him what is the production of venality and what is not. He must take things promiscuously as they come before him. He has no guide; no criterion of truth; nothing to excite his doubts of the veracity of his author; but he must swallow everything which chance sends into his hands. What, then, will be the probable course of his reading? 'Children's Books' as they are called he will naturally begin with. As far as these consist of *sheer nonsense* they may do his mind little harm; but, past all dispute, it is impossible for them to have the smallest tendency towards *enlightening* that mind. If they rise only a little above the nonsensical, look at them, and you will find, that from one end to the other their tendency is to inculcate *abject submission*. His next series are ballads and songs, which, if they step out of nonsense, go at once into the national braggings which, while they are applauded as the means of keeping up the spirit of the people, have been one cause of plunging us into, and of prolonging those wars which have occasioned our enormous debts and taxes, and have led to the filling of the country with all those military establish-ments, heretofore regarded as so dangerous to the liberties of England. Addison, who was a very vile politician, approved of these means of keeping alive what is called 'the honest prejudices of Englishmen'. What a base idea! To inculcate undisguisedly the praiseworthiness of *keeping the people in ignorance*; and that, too, for the *good of the country*, and by the means of the press! Honest prejudices! That is to say, an honest *belief in falsehoods*; an *honest belief that falsehood is truth*! One cannot help hating the man who could avow such an idea.

If your pupil live in the country his standard book will, in all likelihood, be MOORE'S ALMANACK, that universal com-panion of the farmers and labourers of England. Here he will find a perpetual spring of knowledge; a *daily supply*, besides an extra por-tion monthly. Here are *signs* and *wonders* and *prophecies*, in all which he will believe as implicitly as he does in the first chapter of Genesis. Nor will he want a due portion of politics. To keep a people in a state of profound ignorance; to make them superstitious and slavish, there needs little more than the general reading of this single book. The poor creature, who reads this book, and who believes that the com-piler of it is able to foretell when it will rain and when it will snow, is very little more enlightened than those men who believed most firmly that St Dunstan took the Devil by the nose; and there is no doubt in my mind that if that legend were now published they would believe it. You will say, perhaps, that it is only the very lowest of the people who believe in the prophecies of Moore's Almanack; but is it not the very lowest description of people whom you are attempting to teach? And when they get out of your hands, must they not be left to themselves? You certainly do not mean to follow them to their hovels to superintend their reading.

But the great source of your pupil's knowledge, the great source of that *light*, which he is to acquire, will be the NEWSPAPERS. Here he will find a constant and copious supply. And of *what*? Of *truth*? Will he here find bold and impartial statements of facts? Will he here find plain and fearless censure of public wrong-doers? Will he here see the cause of the oppressed manfully espoused and the oppressor painted in colours calculated to rouse against him the hatred of mankind? You know, Sir, that he will not. You know that he will find the reverse of all this. You know that he will find falsehoods upon every subject of a public nature; praises of all those who have power to hurt or to reward, and base calumnies on all those who, in any degree, make themselves obnoxious to power . . .

We often hear it said, 'Let us have *discussion*, discussion will *do good*'. But . . . what does discussion mean? It means the arraying by one person, of *all* the facts and *all* the arguments that he can muster up, against the facts and arguments of another. It does not mean open-mouthed statement and argument on one side, while, on the other, the combatant is muzzled, is compelled, for his safety, to suppress his facts, and is only permitted tremblingly to state in parables and argue by hypothesis. In short, discussion demands a perfectly unshackled use of all that the mind suggests; and, if this be denied, there is no discussion . . . Why, then, talk of discussion? Discuss, indeed, we may, and freely too, all questions relating to the qualities of trees and herbs. There is no danger in writing about dung or potatoes or cabbage. Here your pupils will have a large field; but, as to politics, law and religion, the army or the navy, peace or war; as to all those subjects interesting to man as a member of society, they will assuredly meet with nothing, issuing from the press of this country, worthy of the name of discussion.

Why, then, teach the children of the poor to read? Why waste in this pursuit either money or time; seeing that, if you succeed, your success must necessarily tend to the increase of error and to the debasement of the people ? It is not the mere *capability of reading* that can raise man in the scale of nature. It is the *enlightening* of his mind; and, if the capability of distinguishing words upon paper does not tend to enlighten him that acquirement is to be considered as nothing of any value.

[*Letter to Mr Alderman Wood*, 8 DECEMBER 1813, *Political Works* IV, 277–82]

COBBETT AND CONTEMPORARY SOCIAL PROBLEMS

The Evils of the Factories

For many years past it has been matter of boast with our Government, and, indeed, with the people in general, that our manufacturers are the most numerous in the world. It is not long since Mr Canning said, and exultingly said, that the time appeared to be arrived, when we were to depend chiefly upon the profit of supplying goods to our neighbours. In short, it is matter of perfect notoriety that it has been, with all the people in power, with the talkers in Parliament, and, in short, with the people, the subject of boast, that there are now so many great manufactories, so many thousands employed on this spot, so many thousands on that spot.

It was no great while ago matter of boast that our population was increasing so fast. That increase is, to the very same boasters, now become matter of alarm. I can remember the time when potatoes were such favourites with the collective wisdom that a proposition was made in the House to enact a premium for the raising of the greatest quantity of potatoes. I have lived to hear, in the same House of Commons, potatoes represented as one of the great causes of the misery and degradation of the people of Ireland.

So that our having boasted of a thing, by no means proves that that thing is good; and we are beginning to doubt pretty seriously whether great manufactories be so good a thing as we thought them. For my own part I have long been satisfied of their mischievous consequences. I have long regarded them as a very great evil; and I now address myself to you, who are so deeply interested in the matter, on the subject; not with any hope that you will be able to remove this evil; but in order that you may see how you are affected by these establishments.

It is the natural tendency of a system of loans and funds to draw money into great masses; to rob the most numerous class, and still to keep heaping riches upon the few. The devil of funding covers the country with his imps, the tax-gatherers. These latter draw away the substance of the people, and bring it to be deposited in great parcels. Thus collected into great parcels, it is made the means of commanding the common people to stoop in abject submission to the few.

Before this infernal system was known in England; before this system, which has corrupted everything, was known in this country, there were none of those places *called manufactories*. To speak of these places with any degree of patience is impossible. It is to be a despicable hypocrite to pretend to believe that the slaves in the West Indies are not better off than the slaves in these manufactories. However, I have first to speak of the great injury which these factories, as they are called, have done to *the land*.

The occupations of the people of a country should consist, in a great part, of the rearing of food and of raiment. Everything of which food and raiment are composed is produced by *agriculture*. To the carrying on of agriculture a great part of the labour of the whole of the people is necessary. The men and the stout boys are, and must be, the principal workers upon the land. At particular seasons, women and girls do something in the fields, and also the little boys. But, during the far greater part of the year, there is no work in the fields for the women and girls. When things are in their proper state, they are employed, at these times of the year, in preparing materials for the making of raiment; and, in some cases, actually making articles of raiment. In the 'dark ages' when I was a boy, country labourers' wives used to spin the wool, and knit the stockings and gloves that were wanted in the family. My grandmother knit stockings for me after she was blind. In those 'dark ages' the farmers' wives and daughters and servant maids were spinning, reeling, carding, knitting or at something or other of that sort, whenever the work of the farmhouse did not demand them.

The manufacturing which was thus divided amongst the millions of labourers' wives and children, while it was a great blessing to the labouring people themselves, was also a great benefit to the landowner. Agriculture cannot be carried on without men and boys. But to have these men and boys, you must have women and girls; and if you have these without their having profitable employment you must have them a burden upon the land. They must be kept by the parish-rates, instead of being kept by their own labour.

The lords of the loom enabled by the funding system, and encouraged and assisted by this foolish Government in all sorts of ways, have drawn away from the land all this profitable and suitable employment for the women and girls. Some will say that the women and girls may follow the employment to the factories. That is impossible. They cannot do that. They must remain with the men and boys, or there will be nobody at all to carry on the labours of agriculture.

This change, as to the mode of making the raiment of the people, has been attended with consequences extremely injurious. The girls have had nothing to do, or, at least, nothing suitable to their sex and their age. They have contracted habits of carelessness and idleness. It used to be the pride of a country girl to say that she had made, with her own hands, all the clothes upon her back. Now the poor creatures, drawn off now and then in tawdry cottons, hardly know whence their clothing comes: hardly know that linen is made of flax, and cloth of wool. In all my hundreds of miles of rides about England I have seen but one single instance of a piece of linen made in a cottage. That was in Sussex, between Horsham and Petworth.

This is one great cause of pauperism, and of the degradation of the people. The women and girls must be where the men and boys are; and a wise Government would have taken care that they should not lose their employment. This is, however, only to say that a wise Government would not have made a funding system, and that it would have done none of those things by which the country has been brought into its present state. The man who invented the funding system should have been burnt alive the moment he opened his lips upon the subject. It has totally eradicated happiness in this country; and it must, at last, bring dreadful punishment upon somebody; upon some of its upholders and abettors.

When Malthus and his crew are talking of an increase in the population, they have their eye upon the masses which their greedy upstart lords of the loom have drawn together; and the horrible condition of which masses I shall more particularly mention by and by. They overlook the depopulation which has taken place in order to create this abominable crew of upstarts, who, in order to support their injustice and tyranny, which are wholly without a parallel, except, perhaps, in the cases connected with the game, procured laws to be passed, called *combination laws*, such as never were heard of before in any country in the world.

Malthus and his crew of hard-hearted ruffians; those cool calculators of how much 'national wealth' can be made to arise out of the misery of millions, wholly overlook the frightful depopulation which has taken place in consequence of the destruction of seven-eighths, at least, of the farmhouses, and a similar destruction of cottages, in consequence of the enclosure of wastes. This destruction has, in part, arisen from the total ruin of the agricultural manufactories. These profitable labours having been taken from the women, girls, and little boys, it became hardly possible for a large family to live upon a small farm. The profit of the small farm received a great addition from the fruit of the labours of spinning, knitting, and the like; but, when these were taken away by the lords of the loom; when flagrant impolicy had thrown all these profits into the hands of a very few persons, who had converted the manufacturing labourers into the slaves that we shall presently see them, the little farm itself did not afford a sufficiency of means to maintain a considerable family. The occupiers of such farms were poor; became unable to pay their rents, and, in a short time, were driven from their healthy habitations; were huddled into sheds and holes, became mere labourers, and a large part of them paupers. Malthus and his crew never look at this cause of depopulation. The landowner naturally sought to get rent for his land and he could now get it from nobody but one who had made money sufficient to hold nine or ten farms. The women, girls and little children having now lost their natural employment for the greater part of the year, became a mere burden upon the land; and the farmer and the landowner resorted to all sorts of expedients to diminish that burden. To diminish the burden, there were no means but that of reducing the number of the labouring class of country people as much as possible. The man and the boy were necessary to agriculture, agriculture could not have them without the women and the girls; it became necessary therefore to do without the men and the boys as much as possible.

To do without them all sorts of schemes were resorted to. To make horses perform that which was before performed by men was one of the methods pursued, and with most destructive success. So that, at last, the agricultural parts of the country have been stripped of a very large part of their population. Every scheme that the ingenuity of greediness could devise has been put into practice; but, after all, there remains a mass of pauperism and of misery which the law-makers themselves declare is frightful to behold; and, whatever else their reports may contain, however widely they may differ from one another, and however completely each may be at variance with itself, every one declares that the *evil is constantly increasing*.

While this is the case, and while the country is going on becoming more and more depopulated, and more and more miserable, the great towns, and particularly the manufacturing districts, are daily increasing in numbers. If the people, thus drawn together in masses, were happily situated, there might be less ground for lamentation; but, so far from this being the case, these masses are still more miserable than the wretches left behind them in the agricultural districts.

Some of these lords of the loom have in their employ thousands of miserable creatures. In the cotton-spinning work these creatures are kept, fourteen hours in each day, locked up, summer and winter, in a heat of from EIGHTY TO EIGHTY-FOUR DEGREES. The rules which they are subjected to are such as no negroes were ever subjected to. I once before noticed a statement made on the part of these poor creatures, relative to their treatment in the factories of Lancashire. This statement is dated on 15th of February 1823, and was published at Manchester by J. Phenix, No 12 Bow Street, in that blood-stained town. This statement says that the heat of the factories is from *eighty to eighty-four degrees*. A base agent of the Cotton Lords, who publishes a newspaper at Stockport, has lately accused me of exaggeration in having stated the heat at eighty-four degrees.

Now, the statement of which I am speaking was published at Manchester; and does any man believe that such a statement would have been published there if it had not been founded on fact? There was a controversy going on at the time of the publishing of this statement. I read very carefully the answer to this statement; but this answer contained no denial of the heat being from eighty to eighty-four degrees.

Now, then, do you duly consider what a heat of eighty-two is? Very seldom do we feel such a heat as this in England. The 31st of last August, and the 1st, 2nd, and 3rd of last September, were very hot days. The newspapers told us that men had dropped down dead in the harvest fields and that many horses had fallen dead upon the road; and yet the heat during those days never exceeded eighty-four degrees in the *hottest part of the day*. We were retreating to the coolest rooms in our houses; we were pulling off our coats, wiping the sweat off our faces, puffing, blowing, and panting; and yet we were living in a heat nothing like eighty degrees. What, then, must be the situation of the poor creatures who are doomed to toil, day after day, for three hundred and thirteen days in the year, fourteen hours in each day, in an average heat of eighty-two degrees? Can any man, with a heart in his body, and a tongue in his head, refrain from cursing a system that produces such slavery and such cruelty?

Observe, too, that these poor creatures have no cool room to retreat to, not a moment to wipe off the sweat, and not a breath of air to come and interpose itself between them and infection. The 'door of the place wherein they work, is *locked*, except *half an hour*, at tea-time; the workpeople are not allowed to send for water to drink, in the hot factory; even the *rain-water is locked up*, by the master's order, otherwise they would be happy to drink even that. If any spinner be found with his *window open*, he is to pay a fine of a shilling'! Mr Martin of Galway has procured Acts of Parliament to be passed to prevent *cruelty to animals*. If horses or dogs were shut up in a place like this they would certainly be thought worthy of Mr Martin's attention.

Not only is there not a breath of sweet air in these truly infernal scenes; but, for a large part of the time, there is the abominable and pernicious stink of the GAS to assist in the murderous effects of the heat. In addition to the heat and the gas; in addition to the noxious effluvia of the gas, mixed with the steam, there are the *dust*, and what is called the *cotton-flyings* or *fuz*, which the unfortunate creatures have to inhale: and the fact is, the notorious fact is, that well-constitutioned men are rendered old and past labour at forty years of age, and that children are rendered decrepit and deformed, and thousands upon thousands of them slaughtered by consumptions, before they arrive at the age of sixteen. And are these establishments to boast of? If we were to admit the fact that they compose an addition to the population of the country; if we were further to admit that they caused an addition to the pecuniary resources of the Government, ought not a government to be ashamed to derive resources from such means?

If we wanted any proof of the *abject slavery* of these poor creatures, what proof do we want more than the following list of fines?

Any Spinner found with his window open	1s.
Any Spinner found washing himself	1s.
Any Spinner leaving his oil-can out of its place	6d.
Any Spinner putting his gas out too soon	1s.
Any Spinner spinning with his gas-light too long in the morning	2s.
Any Spinner *heard whistling*	1s.
Any Spinner being five minutes after the last bell rings ...	2s.
Any Spinner being sick and cannot find another Spinner to give satisfaction, to *pay for steam*, per day	6d.

There are many other of these pecuniary punishments, one of which I shall mention by-and-by; and, observe the canting scoundrels of Methodists, who are making such a clamour about the slavery of the blacks, are amongst the most efficient tools of the Cotton Lords in the upholding of this abominable slavery. They preach content and patience to these suffering mortals; they bid them be *grateful* that they have the comforts of what these rascals call the Gospel. They tell them they will be damned to all eternity if they listen to those who would take them out of eighty-four degrees of heat and the cotton fuz.

When the pay, the miserable pittance of pay, gets into the hands of these poor creatures, it has to be laid out at a SHOP. That shop is, generally, directly or indirectly, the master's. At this shop the poor creatures must lay out their money, or they are very soon turned off. The statement that I have just mentioned relates an instance where 'If any workman's wife purchase but a trifling matter at another shop, the shopkeeper tells the book-keeper and the latter says to the workmen that the master will not allow of such work, and that they must tell their wives neither to go to another shop nor give saucy language to the shopkeeper'!

It must be manifest to every one that, under such circumstances, the *pay* is nearly nominal. The greedy master takes back again as much of it as he pleases. Another mode of despoiling the poor creatures is this: the master is the owner of cottages, or, rather, holes which the workpeople have to rent. The statement says, 'That cottages of exceedingly small dimensions are let to the workmen at NINE POUNDS A YEAR. But, though the rent is by the year, it is stopped from them at the end of every fortnight. A cellar is two shillings and sixpence a week; and if a house or cellar be empty and a workman come to work and have another house or cellar already, he must pay rent for the empty one, whether he occupy it or not.'

Nine hundred and ninety-nine thousandths of the people of England have not the most distant idea that such things are carried on in a country calling itself free; in a country whose Minister for Foreign Affairs is everlastingly teasing and bothering other Powers to emulate England in 'her humanity' in abolishing the slave trade in the blacks. The blacks, when carried to the West Indies, are put into a paradise compared with the situation of these poor white creatures in Lancashire, and other factories of the north. And yet the editor of the *Morning Chronicle* is incessantly singing forth the blessings of the manufacturing districts. Bad as is the situation of the labourers in the agricultural counties it is heaven itself compared with that of these poor creatures . . .

Then, the immoralities engendered in these pestiferous scenes are notorious. They were very well described by TIMOTHEUS in a letter first published in a Manchester paper, and republished in the *Register* in August last. 'Here,' as that writer observes, 'the sexes are huddled together, while man is separated from wife, and child from father, for full three-fifths of the waking hours of their lives.' All experience proves that the congregating of people together in great masses is sure to be productive of impurity of thought and of manners. The country lad, who becomes a soldier, has a new soul in him by the time that he has passed a year in a barrack-room. Even in great schools all experience tells us how difficult it is to prevent contagious immoralities. This is universally acknowledged. What, then, must be the consequences of heaping these poor creatures together in the cotton factories? But what more do we want; what other proof of the corrupting influence of these assemblages; what more than the following regulation, which I take from the list of fines imposed at the factory of Tyldesley, in Lancashire?

Any two Spinners, *found together* in the *necessary*, each man...1s.

I challenge the world to produce me so complete a proof of familiarity with the most shocking immorality. One is almost ashamed to put this thing upon paper, though for the necessary purpose of exposing it to just indignation. To what a pitch must things have come; how familiar people must have become with infamy, before a master manufacturer could put such a thing into writing and stick it up in his factory! What hotbeds of vice and corruption! Here we have, in the heart of England, hatched the heat of the East, and hatched all its loathsome and infamous vices along with it: and yet those manufactories are to be our boast, and we are to applaud the Government for having upheld and cherished them!

The Reverend Anthony Collett, and several other persons of the same *trampe*, as the French call it, who have appeared before Committees of the House of Commons, when those Committees have been sitting upon the subject of agricultural distress, seem to have taken particular pains to describe the immoralities of the country people, or peasantry as the Scotch Economists call them. It is very curious that not a man of them all has ever dropped a word about these abominations in Lancashire; about this intolerable tyranny and these most shameful immoralities. These perverse fellows complain of the surplus population of the fields and woods, where human beings have been growing thinner and thinner for the last hundred years; but say not a word about surplus population in these hellish stews of eighty-four degrees of heat, crammed with wretched creatures, from whom even the rain water is locked up; who, in gaping for air, swallow cotton-fuz; and who are visibly perishing by inches under the eye of the slave-holder, who has no interest in the life of the poor creatures, who cares not how soon they die, so that he profit by their labour to the end of their lives.

Not a word do we ever hear from all these famous witnesses brought before Committees about the immoralities of those monstrous heaps of human bodies. Nay, the Scotch Economists are everlastingly singing forth the praises of these horrible establishments, which they are pleased to look upon as so many proofs of 'national wealth'. Ricardo, who got half a million of money by 'watching the turn of the market', very frequently had the impudence to say, even in the House of Commons, that it was no matter to the country how small a portion of its food it raised from its own land, and that if it could buy all its food from foreign countries, and give them manufactures in exchange, it would be as well for England. So say all the Scotch Economists. They seem to care about nothing but the *money*. Their vulgar, huckstering notion is that *money is to be got from other nations*. They care nothing about the means. They always look upon the labouring classes as they do upon sheep, or pigs, or any other 'useful animals'.

The poor cotton slave is held in bondage as complete as that of the negro. Our histories contain accounts of vassals and villeins of old times and affect to pity them. Nothing but the basest hypocrisy, or the grossest ignorance, can place those villeins beneath the miserable creatures in the North. The villeins belonged to the estate on which they were born. If the estate were transferred they were transferred along with it. They could not go away and live where they liked. The fruit of their labour belonged to their lords. Their lords could do almost what they liked with them. Now, supposing all this to be literally true, are not the cotton slaves fast bound to the spot where they are? Can they quit that spot to go and live where they like? Are they not transferred with the factory? Do not their lords take to themselves the fruit of their labour, leaving them the bare means of the most sorry existence? The villeins were not, at any rate, shut up in a heat of eighty-four degrees. If they were ill, or crippled, the interest of their lords necessarily induced them to take care of them; and they were not packed off to be dealt with by an 'Overseer', to be lugged away in a cart, upon a bundle of straw, and frequently dying in the road . . .

[*To the Landowners on the Evils of Collecting Manufacturers into Great Masses* 17 NOVEMBER 1824, *Political Works* VI, 430–42]

The Popularity of Emigration

Another respect in which our situation so exactly resembles that of France on the eve of the Revolution is the *fleeing from the country* in every direction. When I was in Norfolk there were four hundred persons, generally young men, labourers, carpenters, wheelwrights, millwrights, smiths, and bricklayers; most of them with some money, and some farmers and others with good round sums. These people were going to Quebec, in timber-ships, and from Quebec by land into the United States. They had been told that they would not be suffered to land in the United States from on board of a ship. The roguish villains had deceived them: but no matter; they will get into the United States; and going through Canada will do them good, for it will teach them to detest everything belonging to it. From Boston two great barge loads had just gone off by canal to Liverpool, most of them farmers; all carrying some money, and some as much as two thousand pounds each. From the North and West Riding of Yorkshire numerous waggons have gone, carrying people to the canals leading to Liverpool; and a gentleman whom I saw at Peterboro' told me that he saw some of them; and that the men all appeared to be respectable farmers. At Hull the scene would delight the eyes of the wise Burdett; for here the emigration is going on in the 'old Roman plan'.* Ten large ships have gone this spring, laden with these fugitives from the fangs of taxation; some bound direct to the ports of the United States; others, like those at Yarmouth, for Quebec. Those that have most money go direct to the United States. The single men, who are taken for a mere trifle in the Canada ships, go that way, have nothing but their carcasses to carry over the rocks and swamps, and through the myriads of place-men and pensioners in that miserable region; there are about fifteen more ships going from this one port this spring. The ships are fitted up with berths as transports for the carrying of troops. I went on board one morning, and saw the people putting their things on board and stowing them away. Seeing a nice young woman, with a little baby in her arms, I told her that she was going to a country where she would be sure that her children would never want victuals; where she might make her own malt, soap, and candles, without being half put to death for it, and where blaspheming Jews would not have a mortgage on the life's labour of her children.

There is at Hull one farmer going who is seventy years of age, but who takes out five sons and fifteen hundred pounds! Brave and sensible old man! and good and affectionate father! He is performing a truly parental and sacred duty; and he will die with the blessing of his sons on his head, for having rescued them from this scene of slavery, misery, cruelty, and crime. Come, then, . . . come into Lincolnshire, Norfolk, and Yorkshire; come and bring Parson Malthus along with you; regale your sight with this delightful 'stream of emigration'; congratulate the 'greatest captain of the age', and your brethren of the Collective; congratulate the 'noblest assembly of free men' on these happy effects of their measures . . . Oh! no, generous and sensible Burdett, it is not the aged, the infirm, the halt, the blind, and the idiots that go: it is the youth, the strength, the wealth, and the spirit that will no longer brook hunger and thirst, in order that the maws of tax-eaters and Jews may be crammed. You want the Irish to go, and so they will *at our expense*, and all the bad of them, to be kept at our expense on the rocks and swamps of Nova Scotia and Canada. You have no money to send them away with:

* Cobbett is thinking of the ancient Roman practice of deliberately planting colonies overseas composed of ex-servicemen.

the tax-eaters want it all; and thanks to the 'improvements of the age', the steam-boats will continue to bring them in shoals in pursuit of the sorts of food that their taskmasters have taken away from them.

After evening lecture, at Horncastle, a very decent farmer came to me and asked me about America, telling me that he was resolved to go, for that if he stayed much longer, he should not have a shilling to go with. I promised to send him a letter from Louth to a friend at New York, who might be useful to him there, and give him good advice. I forgot it at Louth; but I will do it before I go to bed. From the Thames, and from the several ports down the Channel, about two thousand have gone this spring. All the flower of the labourers of the east of Sussex and west of Kent will be culled out and sent off in a short time. From Glasgow the sensible Scotch are pouring out amain. Those that are poor and cannot pay their passages, or can rake together only a trifle, are going to a rascally heap of sand and rock and swamp, called Prince Edward's Island, in the horrible Gulf of St Lawrence; but when the American vessels come over with Indian corn and flour and pork and beef and poultry and eggs and butter and cabbages and green pease and asparagus for the soldier-officers and other tax-eaters that we support upon that lump of worthlessness; for the lump itself bears nothing but potatoes; when these vessels come, which they are continually doing, winter and summer; towards the fall, with apples and pears and melons and cucumbers; and, in short, everlastingly coming and taking away the amount of taxes raised in England; when these vessels return, the sensible Scotch will go back in them for a dollar a head, till at last not a man of them will be left but the bed-ridden. Those villainous colonies are held for no earthly purpose but that of furnishing a pretence of giving money to the relations and dependants of the aristocracy; and they are the nicest channels in the world through which to send English taxes to enrich and strengthen the United States. Withdraw the English taxes, and, except in a small part in Canada, the whole of those horrible regions would be left to the bears and the savages in the course of a year.

This emigration is a famous blow given to the boroughmongers. The way to New York is now as well known and as little expensive as from old York to London. First the Sussex parishes sent their paupers; they invited over others that were not paupers; they invited over people of some property; then persons of greater property; now substantial farmers are going; men of considerable fortune will follow. It is the letters written across the Atlantic that do the business. Men of fortune will soon discover that, to secure to their families their fortunes, and to take these out of the grasp of the inexorable tax-gatherer, they must get away. Every one that goes will take twenty after him; and thus it will go on. There can be no interruption but *war*: and war the Thing dares not have. As to France or the Netherlands, or any part of that hell called Germany, Englishmen can never settle there. The United States form another England without its unbearable taxes, its insolent game laws, its intolerable dead-weight, and its treadmills.

[19 APRIL 1830, *Rural Rides* II, 257–9]

The Corn Laws

The Corn Law of 1815 prohibited the import of foreign grain until the price of English corn reached 80s. a quarter. This attempt to give security to the English farmer never really worked, but many small farmers believed that it was their only protection against foreign competition.

I am decidedly of opinion . . . that a Corn Bill of no description, no matter what its principles or provisions, can do either tenant or landlord any good; and I am not less decidedly of opinion that though prices are now low they must, all the present train of public measures continuing, be yet lower, and continue lower upon an average of years and of seasons. As to a Corn Bill; a law to prohibit or check the importation of human food is a perfect novelty in our history, and ought, therefore, independent of the reason and the recent experience of the case, to be received and entertained with great suspicion. Heretofore, *premiums* have been given for the exportation, and at other times for the importation, of corn; but of laws to prevent the importation of human food our ancestors knew nothing. And what says recent experience? When the present Corn Bill was passed I, then a farmer, unable to get my brother farmers to join me, *petitioned singly* against this Bill; and I stated to my brother farmers that such a Bill could do us no good, while it would not fail to excite against us the ill-will of the other classes of the community; a thought by no means pleasant. Thus has it been. The distress of agriculture was considerable in magnitude then; but what is it now? And yet the

Bill was passed; that Bill which was to remunerate and protect is still in force; the farmers got what they prayed to have granted them; and their distress, with a short interval of tardy pace, has proceeded rapidly, increasing from that day to this. What, in the way of Corn Bill, can you have, gentlemen, beyond absolute prohibition? And have you not, since about April, 1819, had absolute prohibition? Since that time no corn has been imported, and then only thirty millions of bushels, which, supposing it all to have been wheat, was a quantity much too insignificant to produce any sensible depression in the price of the immense quantity of corn raised in this kingdom since the last bushel was imported. If your produce had fallen in this manner, if your prices had come down very low, immediately after the importation had taken place, there might have been some colour of reason to impute the fall to the importation; but it so happens . . . that your produce has fallen in price at a greater rate in proportion as time has removed you from the point of importation; and as to the circumstance . . . that there is still some of the imported corn *unsold*, what does it prove but the converse . . . that is to say that the holders *cannot afford* to sell it at present prices; for if they could gain but ever so little by the sale would they keep it wasting and costing money in warehouses? There appears with some persons to be a notion that the importation of corn is a *new thing*. They seem to forget that, during the last war, when agriculture was so *prosperous*, the *ports were always open*; that prodigious quantities of corn were imported during the war; that so far from importation being prohibited, high *premiums* were given, paid out of the taxes, partly raised upon English farmers, to induce men to import corn. All this seems to be forgotten as much as if it had never taken place; and now the distress of the English farmer is imputed to a cause which was never before an object of his attention, and a desire is expressed to put an end to a branch of commerce which the nation has always freely carried on. I think . . . that here are reasons quite sufficient to make any man . . . slow to impute the present distress to the importation of corn; but at any rate what can you have beyond absolute efficient prohibition? No law, no duty, however high; nothing that the Parliament can do can go beyond this; and this you now have, in effect, as completely as if this were the only country beneath the sky. For these reasons . . . I am convinced that, in the way of Corn Bill, it is impossible for the Parliament to afford you any, even the smallest, portion of relief. As to . . . the tendency which the present measures and course of things have to carry prices *lower*, and considerably lower than they now are, and to keep them for a permanency at that low rate, this is a matter worthy of the serious attention of all connected with the land, and particularly of that of the renting farmer. During the *war* no importations distressed the farmer. It was not till peace came that the cry of distress was heard. But during the war there was a boundless issue of paper money. Those issues were instantly narrowed by the peace, the law being that the bank should pay in cash six months after the peace should take place. This was the cause of that distress which led to the present Corn Bill. The disease occasioned by the preparations for cash-payments has been brought to a crisis by Mr Peel's Bill, which has, in effect, doubled, if not tripled, the real amount of the taxes and violated all contracts for time; given triple gains to every lender, and placed every borrower in jeopardy.

[*Speech at Battle*, SUSSEX, 3 JANUARY 1822, *Rural Rides* I, 60–62]

The Scandal of Enclosures

I am at all times ready to take the side of the public interest, when opposed to the interests of a few individuals in office; but, whether I view this matter as a Briton, as a farmer, as a man, as a friend of the hungry poor, or of the industrious, and of the enterprising rich; in whichever of these capacities I view this matter, I cannot bring my-self to believe that any act of Parliament or any other measure, tend-ing to produce a general enclosure of the waste lands, would be a benefit to the country.

I do not say that the expenses in passing particular Enclosure Bills might not be with justice reduced; and I think that fees on the pass-ing of Bills is not the proper way of paying the officers belonging to the Houses of Parliament. It is certain that those officers ought to be very highly paid, seeing that the business which they have to transact is of such very great importance; but I would wish to see them re-lieved from all anxiety about the amount of their incomes, and, at any rate, would not suffer to exist amongst them anything like a scramble for fees.

But this has nothing to do with the utility of enclosures. My cor-respondent 'Rusticus', like all those who have written on the same side of the subject, is of opinion that the more new enclosures take place, the greater will be the quantity of corn produced in the country, and that that quantity, too, will be greater than it is now in proportion to the number of the people.

Here are two propositions, the one relating to the *positive* quantity of corn, and the other to the *relative* quantity of corn.

Let us dismiss the latter first, because the former is that which is most generally believed to be true.

It is a principle in nature, and will admit of no more doubt than will the fact of the sun's giving light, that the number of mouths, in any country, which has for ages been inhabited, will always bear an exact proportion to the quantity of food to be got at in that country. If England were to produce ten times as much food as it now produces, the consequence would be, that there would be ten times as many mouths as there are now to consume it.

Do we not constantly see that upon every farm all the cattle food is annually consumed? Do we not see that every farmer proportions the number of his stock to the quantity of his food? Do we not see that in years when cattle food is abundant, there is more of preservation of stock and less of slaughter?

In this case, indeed, causes and effects are more immediately within the power of man, and are of shorter duration; but in the cases of nations, do we not see, that in China, Japan, and several other countries, where the whole earth groans under its produce of two or three crops in a year, that, so far from there being a superabundance of food, the inhabitants have much less to eat than in any of the countries of Europe?

Populousness follows close upon the heels of the production of food; all is eaten; nothing is left, though not a single inch of the ground be suffered to remain unproductive.

It therefore appears very clear to me that an increase of the positive quantity of food raised in England would not have a tendency to augment the quantity which would fall to the lot of each individual poor person; that it would not tend at all to lessen the sufferings of the poor, whose increasing miseries are, in my opinion, to be ascribed to causes wholly different from that of a want of sufficient produce in the country.

To illustrate this, what need we more than the fact that the poor man has just as much food when corn is dear as when it is cheap, his wages, or his additional parish allowance, being proportioned to the price of the loaf? When I first came to Botley the common wages of a day-labourer was twelve shillings a week; it is now fifteen shillings a week; and thus his wages must go on augmenting with the price of the loaf.

Thus, I think, it appears pretty clear that if enclosures of wastes were to add to the positive quantity of food raised in England, they could not add to its quantity, relatively considered with the number of mouths; and that, of course, they could have no tendency to better the lot of the poor.

Now, then, in returning to the first proposition, namely that a general enclosure of the waste lands, that is to say, all lands not now in cultivation, would add to the positive quantity of food in England, this is a proposition from which I wholly dissent.

'Rusticus' will please to observe that I do not mean to deny that there are particular spots, so situated with regard to surrounding circumstances, and also with regard to the nature of the soil itself, that the enclosure of them may be very beneficial, not only to the owners themselves, but to the public also. Hounslow Heath, for instance, and other spots in the neighbourhood of great towns and of increasing population. But these are trifling exceptions. What I mean to contend is this; that, *in general*, new enclosures could not possibly add to the positive quantity of food raised in the country.

There seems to be an opinion prevailing among some persons that the quantity of corn, for we will now speak of corn only, must ever be in proportion to the quantity of land in cultivation.

How any one can seriously entertain such an opinion is very surprising, seeing that it is so notorious that one acre of land, well cultivated, will produce an infinitely larger crop than an acre of land badly cultivated, though both of them be in the very same field and of precisely the same natural quality.

This notion, therefore, is erroneous. It is a fact, not to be doubted, that produce will be proportioned to the sort of cultivation as well as to the quantity of land.

It is also a fact very notorious that the waste lands in general are the worst lands in the country.

Those who think that an augmentation of the quantity of corn is a *necessary* consequence of new enclosures seem never to have reflected that new enclosures will not, any more than the old enclosures, produce corn *without cultivation*, that is to say, *without labour being bestowed upon them*.

They seem to think that these new enclosures would cultivate themselves and that manure would drop down upon them from the clouds. Those who have had experience of them know, I believe to their cost, that waste lands are not thus distinguished from other lands; and that they require pretty nearly the current price of the old lands to be laid out upon them, acre for acre, before they will produce anything at all.

WHENCE, then, let me ask 'Rusticus', are the labour and manure to come to put these waste lands into a productive state?

WHENCE; from what part of this kingdom are this labour and this manure to come? I beg 'Rusticus' to attend to this question. I wish to know from him what is the source from which he would draw the labour and the manure necessary to bring these new lands into a productive state.

It is very easy, in riding across commons and forests and downs to exclaim: 'What a pity that all this land should lie uncultivated, while so many poor creatures are in want of bread!' This is very easy, requiring nothing more than a slight exertion of the lungs, unloaded with any particle of thought. But to show how the cultivation of these lands would add to the quantity of bread, demands much greater powers of argument than I have ever met with in any person who took that side of the subject.

'Rusticus' will observe, that I am always speaking of wastes *in general*, and not of wastes in the neighbourhood of which local circumstances present artificial aid. These particular and partial instances have nothing to do with the general question.

I return, therefore, to the charge, and again ask him from *what source* he would draw the means of putting the wastes of the kingdom into a state to make them produce corn? These means consist of *labour and manure*, or rather they consist simply of labour, for every one must perceive that manure itself is the consequence of labour.

Whence, then, is the labour to come to dig ditches, to make banks and fences round waste lands, to make roads through them, to pare and burn, and plough, and drag, and harrow, and cart chalk, and lime, and marl, and clay, and dung, and, at last, to sow these waste lands? WHENCE, I once more ask, is this labour to come?

He will allow, I suppose, that the labourers in England are all employed now. He must allow this, or else he will have to find out a reason why the lands already enclosed are not better cultivated than they are. Let him travel through the country, and he will see the fields smoking from the fire of *couch grass*. Out of ten fields he will not see above two that are sown with wheat, that most valuable of all corn crops. Let him look closely at the land where even that wheat is, and he will see that the weeds and the couch grass are, in general, enjoying, at least, one-half of the benefit of the last year's dung and tillage.

There are some few exceptions to this, but this is the general state of the lands in England.

Let 'Rusticus' ask the farmer why he suffers his land to get into such a foul state, and why he has not five fields of wheat in place of two. The farmer will tell him that all his capital, all his labour, and all his manure, are employed upon his farm, and that he gets as much out of it as he is able, and keeps it as clean as he is able.

Would it not be a pretty proposition to make such a man, to enclose an additional piece of ground and add it to this farm? It is very likely that greediness might make him grasp at the proposition, nothing appearing to be more natural to the taste of man than the love of extent of landed possessions. But does 'Rusticus' really believe that by adding a piece of waste land to this man's farm (worse of course in its nature than that which he has already enclosed); does 'Rusticus' really believe that such an addition to the extent of the farm, would make an augmentation in this man's crops?

To enclose the piece of waste, even before he begin his process of cultivation, this farmer must take from his present farm a considerable portion of the labour which he now there employs; and before he can make the piece of waste produce him anything at all he must take from his present farm a great deal more of the labour that he now employs upon it. If he does this, his present fields must have less labour than they now have; must be still fuller of weeds and couch grass than they are; must be still poorer; and, of course, must produce less than they now produce and that, too, observe, in a proportion exceeding the produce of the new enclosure because on the new enclosed land there are fencing and other labours to be performed, which are not necessary upon the land already enclosed, to say nothing about the nature of the soil being worse in the new enclosure than in the old, which, however, in general must necessarily be the case.

Thus, then, we see that this augmentation of extent of culture, could not produce an augmentation of corn in this instance.

Perhaps 'Rusticus' will say that this farmer might get more labourers, more horses, more implements than he now has, and might thus avoid robbing his old farm to bring into tillage the new

enclosure. But WHERE, my good friend, is he to find them? Are
not all the labourers, all the horses, all the wheelwrights, all the
blacksmiths, and all the collar-makers employed now? And if they
are not all employed now, why, I ask again, are not the present
enclosed lands better cultivated than they are? But it is a monstrous
proposition to assert that they are not all employed. This being the
case, then, WHERE is this farmer (supposing him to have more
capital than he employs) to find these additional labourers, horses,
and implements? It is obvious that he can find them nowhere but
upon other people's farms, and if he draws them thence he must, of
course, cause a diminution of the crops upon those farms; and then
how is the general quantity of corn to be augmented by this new
enclosure?

Besides, we are talking of a general enclosure, and then we are to
suppose, of course, that all the other farmers are enclosing as well as
this one; so that the labourers, the horses, and the implements, to
bring these new enclosures into a bearing state, must come from
abroad, or from the clouds, or it is impossible that new enclosures
can make any addition to the positive quantity of corn grown in the
country.

If, indeed, the enclosed lands were now cultivated in the best
possible manner; that is to say, if they were now made to produce as
much food as it is possible to make them produce, then there might
be some reason in supposing that there was in the country labour to
spare for the cultivation of new lands; but while we see, all over the
country, the contrary of this; while we see nearly one-half of the land
which is already enclosed lying in an unproductive state, or producing
corn but once in two or three years, and then in very scanty quantity;
while we see these enclosed lands in general overrun with weeds and
couch grass, and stifled with hedgerows, many of which are a pole
or two in breadth, and which in general serve no useful purpose,
while they are a harbour for mice, moles, rabbits, and destructive birds;
while we have this spectacle before our eyes over the far greater part
of the kingdom, can any man in his senses believe that there are
labourers, horses, and implements to spare for the enclosure and
cultivation of *worse* lands than those which are already enclosed?

Let me not be told that these hedgerows, weeds, couch grass, and
scanty crops, arise out of the slovenliness and obstinacy of the
farmers: for though they may be, in general, slovenly and obstinate,
they take pretty good care to have their pennyworth for a penny. Few

of them let either men or horses eat at their expense without working for it. In short, all the labour that there is in the kingdom is employed upon the lands already enclosed, and it necessarily follows that, as those lands are not made to produce so much as they might be made to produce, there is not, as yet, any labour to spare for the cultivation of *worse* lands, and for making a fence round them into the bargain.

Perhaps I shall be told that by an improvement in the mode of cultivating the lands more produce might be raised from the same quantity of labour that is now employed. I accede to this proposition. I believe that even with the present quantity of labour, distributed judiciously, and applied industriously, with great care and skill, upon true principles, all the enclosed lands in England might be made like a garden; that the weeds and the couch . . . grass might be nearly extirpated; and that the crops might be trebled. But we are talking of enclosures in the present state of agriculture; we are not talking of enclosures under a state of agriculture like that of China; a specimen of which may be seen at this moment on a piece of ground, which was recently waste, on the side of the turnpike road between Esher and Kingston in Surrey, where, on a bed of as sour a clay as I ever saw, Mr Braddick will, in my opinion, have, at least, forty bushels of wheat upon three quarters of an acre of ground, the seed being somewhat less than two quarts, or half a Winchester gallon; we are not talking of new enclosures under a state of agriculture like this, the effect of an ingenious mind attentively applied to the object; I am not talking of new enclosures under a state of agriculture like this, but under a state of agriculture such as that now existing in England, and this is the way, of course, in which we must talk upon the subject.

Those who are so eager for new enclosures always seem to argue as if the *waste land*, in its present state, *produced nothing at all*. But is this the fact? Can any one point me out a single inch of it which does not produce something, and the produce of which is not made use of? It goes to the feeding of sheep, of cows, of cattle of all descriptions; and what is of great consequence in my view of the matter, it helps to rear, in health and vigour, numerous families of the children of labourers, which children, were it not for these wastes, must be crammed into the stinking suburbs of towns, amidst filth of all sorts, and congregating together in the practice of every species of idleness and vice. A family reared by the side of a common or a forest is as clearly distinguishable from a family bred in the pestiferous stench of the dark alleys of a town, as one of the plants of Mr

Braddick's wheat is distinguishable from the feeble-stemmed, single-eared, stunted stuff that makes shift to rear its head above the cockle, and poppies and couch grass, in nine-tenths of the broad-cast fields in the kingdom.

This is with me a consideration of great importance. In the beggarly stinking houses of towns, the labourers' children cannot have health. If they have not health, the greatest of all blessings, they must be miserable in themselves, and a burden to the parish. It has been observed that when bred on the side of the commons and forests, they are more saucy and more daring. There may be some inconvenience in this, perhaps, but for my part give me the saucy daring fellow in preference to the poor, crawling, feeble wretch, who is not saucy, only, perhaps, because he feels that he has not the power to maintain himself. I am not in love with saucy servants any more than other people. But I know how to tackle them. A poor, feeble, heartless, humble, crawling creature I can do nothing with; and of this description I have observed are almost all those who are bred up, under a gossiping mother, in the stinking holes, called houses, in country-towns or large villages.

If this scheme of a general enclosure were to take place (the scheme is a mad one and physically impracticable), the whole race of those whom we in Hampshire call foresters would be extirpated in a few years; and my sons, I dare say, would live to see the day when there would be scarcely a man to be found capable of wielding a felling axe. 'Rusticus' appeals to me, as a farmer. If he had known all he might have appealed to me in a character still more closely connected with the subject; that is to say as a person entitled, in the case of a general enclosure, to perhaps fifty, sixty, or a hundred acres of waste land, and that, as it happens, very good land, too. But though I make no use of this waste, and it is very likely that I never shall, I will never give my consent to the enclosure of it, or any part of it, except for the purposes of the labourers. All round this great tract of land, which is called waste, the borders are studded with cottages of various dimensions and forms, but the more beautiful for this diversity. The greater part of these are encroachments, as they are called; but the Bishop of Winchester, who is the Lord of the Manors, has never had a very harsh Steward, and the tenants have had too much compassion to attempt to pull down and lay open any of these numerous dwellings. For my part, rather than see them destroyed and their inhabitants driven into towns, I would freely resign all the claim that I have either to the land or to the herbage. These wastes, as they are called, are the blessing and the ornament of this part of the kingdom; and I dare say that they are the same in every other part of the kingdom where they are to be found.

These are my reasons for being glad that the general Enclosure Bill has failed; and until I see them satisfactorily confuted I shall, of course, retain my present opinion upon the subject.

[*The General Enclosure Bill*, 28 JULY 1813, *Political Works* IV, 257–63]

COBBETT AND THE CHANGING FACE OF ENGLAND

Out and About in England

[i] *From Kensington to Worth, in Sussex*

Monday, May 5 1823.
From London to Reigate, through Sutton, is about as villainous a tract as England contains. The soil is a mixture of gravel and clay, with big yellow stones in it, sure sign of really bad land. Before you descend the hill to go into Reigate, you pass *Gatton* ('Gatton and Old Sarum'), which is a very rascally spot of earth. The trees are here a week later than they are at Tooting. At Reigate they are (in order to save a few hundred yards length of road) cutting through a hill. They have lowered a little hill on the London side of Sutton. Thus is the money of the country actually thrown away: the produce of labour is taken from the industrious, and given to the idlers. Mark the process; the town of Brighton, in Sussex, 50 miles from the Wen, is on the seaside, and is thought by the stock-jobbers to afford a *salubrious air*. It is so situated that a coach which leaves it not very early in the morning reaches London by noon; and, starting to go back in two hours and a half afterwards, reaches Brighton not very late at night. Great parcels of stock-jobbers stay at Brighton with the women and children. They skip backward and forward on the coaches, and actually carry on stock-jobbing, in 'Change Alley, though they reside at Brighton. This place is, besides, a place of great resort with

the *whiskered* gentry. There are not less than about twenty coaches that leave the Wen every day for this place; and there being three or four different roads, there is a great rivalship for the custom. This sets the people to work to shorten and to level the roads; and here you see hundreds of men and horses constantly at work to make pleasant and quick travelling for the Jews and jobbers. The Jews and jobbers pay the turnpikes to be sure; but they get the money from

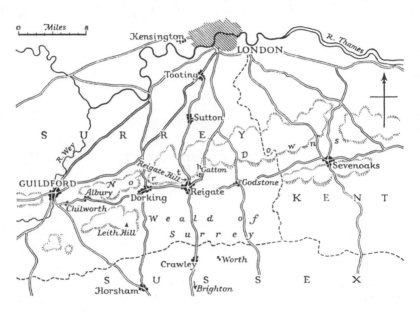

the land and the labourer. They drain these, from John-a'-Groats House to the Land's End, and they lay out some of the money on the Brighton roads! 'Vast *improvements*, ma'am!' as Mrs Scrip said to Mrs *Omnium*, in speaking of the new enclosures on the villainous heaths of Bagshot and Windsor.

Now, some will say, 'Well, it is only a change from hand to hand.' Very true, and if Daddy Coke of Norfolk like the change, I know why I should dislike it. More and more new houses are building as you leave the Wen to come on this road. *Whence come* the means of building these new houses and keeping the inhabitants? Do they come out of *trade* and *commerce*? Oh, no! they come from *the land*; but if Daddy Coke like this, what has any one else to do with it? Daddy Coke and Lord Milton like 'national faith'; it would be a pity to disappoint their liking. The best of this is, it will bring *down to the very dirt*; it will bring down their faces to the very earth, and fill their mouths full of sand; it will thus pull down a set of the basest lick-spittles of power and the most intolerable tyrants towards their inferiors in wealth, that the sun ever shone on. It is time that these degenerate dogs were swept away at any rate. The blackthorns are in full bloom, and make a grand show. When you quit Reigate to go towards Crawley you enter on what is called the *Weald of Surrey*. It is a level country, and the soil a very, very strong loam, with clay beneath to a great depth. The fields are small, and about a third of the land covered with oak-woods and coppice-woods. This is a country of wheat and beans; the latter of which are about three inches high, the former about seven, and both looking very well. I did not see a field of bad-looking wheat from Reigate Hill foot to Crawley, nor from Crawley across to this place, where, though the whole country is but poorish, the wheat looks very well; and if this weather hold about twelve days, we shall recover the lost time. They have been stripping trees (taking the bark off) about five or six days. The nightingales sing very much, which is a sign of warm weather. The house-martins and the swallows are come in abundance; and they seldom do come until the weather be set in for mild.

Wednesday, 7 May.

The weather is very fine and warm; the leaves of the *Oaks* are coming out very fast: some of the trees are nearly in half-leaf. The *Birches* are out in leaf. I do not think that I ever saw the wheat look, take it all together, so well as it does at this time. I see, in the stiff land, no signs of worm or slug. The winter, which destroyed so many turnips, must, at any rate, have destroyed these mischievous things. The oats look well. The barley is very young; but I do not see any-thing amiss with regard to it.

The land between this place and Reigate is stiff. How the corn may be, in other places, I know not; but, in coming down, I met with a farmer of Bedfordshire, who said that the wheat looked very well in that county; which is not a county of clay, like the Weald of Surrey. I saw a Southdown farmer, who told me that the wheat is good there, and that is a fine corn-country. The bloom of the fruit trees is the finest I ever saw in England. The pear-bloom is, at a distance, like that of the *Gueldre Rose*; so large and bold are the bunches. The plum is equally fine; and even the blackthorn (which is the hedge-plum) has a bloom finer than I ever saw it have before. It is rather *early* to offer any opinion as to the crop of corn; but if I were compelled to bet upon it, I would bet upon a good crop. Frosts frequently come after this time; and if they come in May they cause 'things to come about' very fast. But if we have no more frosts: in short, if we have, after this, a good summer, we shall have a fine laugh at the Quakers' and the Jews' press. Fifteen days' sun will bring *things about* in reality. The wages of labour, in the country, have taken a rise, and the poor-rates an increase, since the first of March . . .

[*Rural Rides* 1, 160–2]

[ii] *From Dover to Canterbury*

Dover, Wednesday, 3 Sept. 1823 (evening). On Monday I was balancing in my own mind whether I should go to France or not. Today I have decided the question in the negative, and shall set off this evening for the Isle of Thanet, that spot so famous for corn.

I broke off without giving an account of the country between Folkestone and Dover, which is a very interesting one in itself, and was peculiarly interesting to me on many accounts. I have often mentioned, in describing the parts of the country over which I have travelled; I have often mentioned the *chalk-ridge* and also the *sand-ridge*, which I had traced, running parallel with each other from about Farnham, in Surrey, to Sevenoaks, in Kent. The reader must remember how particular I have been to observe that, in going up from Chilworth, and Albury, through Dorking, Reigate, Godstone, and so on, the two chains, or ridges, approach so near to each other, that in many places you actually have a chalk-bank to your right and a sand-bank to your left, at not more than forty yards from each other. In some places, these chains of hills run off from each other to a great distance, even to a distance of twenty miles. They then approach again towards each other, and so they go on. I was always desirous to ascertain whether these chains, or ridges, continued on thus *to the sea*. I have now found that they do. And if you go out into the channel, at Folkestone, there you see a sand cliff and a chalk cliff. Folkestone stands upon the sand, in a little dell about seven or eight hundred yards from the very termination of the ridge. All the way along, the chalk ridge is the most lofty, until you come to Leith Hill and Hindhead; and here, at Folkestone, the sand-ridge tapers off in a sort of flat towards the sea. The land is like what it is at Reigate, a very steep hill; a hill of full a mile high, and bending exactly in the same manner as the hill at Reigate does. The turnpike-road winds up it and goes over it in exactly the same manner as that at Reigate. The land to the south of the hill begins a poor, thin, white loam upon the chalk; soon gets to be a very fine rich loam upon the chalk; goes on till it mingles the chalky loam with the sandy loam; and thus it goes on down to the sea-beach, or to the edge of the cliff. It is a beautiful bed of earth here, resembling in extent that on the south side of Portsdown Hill rather than that of Reigate. The crops here are always good if they are good anywhere. A large part of this fine tract of land, as well as the little town of Sandgate (which is a beautiful little place upon the beach itself), and also great part of the town of Folkestone belong, they tell me, to Lord Radnor, who takes his title of viscount from Folkestone. Upon the hill begins, and continues on for some miles, that stiff red loam, approaching to a clay, which I have several times described as forming the soil at the top of this chalk-ridge. I spoke of it in the *Register* of the 16th of August last . . . and I then said that it was like the land on the top of this very ridge at Ashmansworth in the north of Hampshire. At Reigate you find precisely the same soil upon the top of the hill, a very red, clayey sort of loam, with big yellow flint stones in it. Everywhere the soil is the same upon the top of the high part of this ridge. I have now found it to be the same, on the edge of the sea, that I found it on the north-east corner of Hampshire.

From the hill, you keep descending all the way to Dover, a distance of about six miles, and it is absolutely six miles of down hill. On your right, you have the lofty land which forms a series of chalk cliffs, from the top of which you look into the sea; on your left, you have ground that goes rising up from you in the same sort of way. The turnpike-road goes down the middle of a valley, each side of which, as far as you can see, may be about a mile and a half. It is six miles long, you will remember; and here, therefore, with very little interruption, very few chasms, there are *eighteen square miles of corn*. It is a patch such as you very seldom see, and especially of corn so good as it is here. I should think that the wheat all along here would average pretty nearly four quarters to the acre. A few oats are sown. A great deal of barley, and that a very fine crop.

The town of Dover is like other sea-port towns; but really much more clean, and with less blackguard people in it than I ever observed in any sea-port before. It is a most picturesque place, to be sure. On one side of it rises, upon the top of a very steep hill, the Old Castle, with all its fortifications. On the other side of it there is another chalk hill, the side of which is pretty nearly perpendicular, and rises up from sixty to a hundred feet higher than the tops of the houses, which stand pretty nearly close to the foot of the hill.

I got into Dover rather late. It was dusk when I was going down the street towards the quay. I happened to look up, and was quite astonished to perceive cows grazing upon a spot apparently fifty feet above the tops of the houses, and measuring horizontally not, perhaps, more than ten or twenty feet from a line which would have formed a continuation into the air. I went up to the same spot, the next day, myself; and you actually look down upon the houses, as you look out of a window upon people in the street. The valley that runs down from Folkestone is, when it gets to Dover, crossed by another valley that runs down from Canterbury, or, at least, from the Canterbury direction. It is in the gorge of this cross valley that Dover is built. The two chalk hills jut out into the sea, and the water that comes up between them forms a harbour for this ancient, most interesting, and beautiful place. On the hill to the north stands the castle of Dover, which is fortified in the ancient manner, except on the sea side, where it has the steep *Cliff* for a fortification. On the south side of the town the hill is, I believe, rather more lofty than that on the north side; and here is the cliff which is described by Shakespeare in the play of *King Lear*. It is fearfully steep, certainly. Very nearly perpendicular for a considerable distance. The grass grows well, to the very tip of the cliff; and you see cows and sheep grazing there with as much unconcern as if grazing in the bottom of a valley.

It was not, however, these natural curiosities that took me over *this* hill; I went to see, with my own eyes, something of the sorts of means that had been made use of to squander away countless millions of money. Here is a hill containing, probably, a couple of square miles or more, hollowed like a honeycomb. Here are line upon line, trench upon trench, cavern upon cavern, bomb-proof upon bomb-proof; in short the very sight of the thing convinces you that either madness the most humiliating, or profligacy the most scandalous must have been at work here for years. The question that every man of sense asks is: What reason had you to suppose that the *French would ever come to this hill* to attack it, while the rest of the country was so much more easy to assail? However, let any man of good plain understanding go and look at the works that have here been performed and that are now all tumbling into ruin. Let him ask what this cavern was for; what that ditch was for; what this tank was for; and why all these horrible holes and hiding places at an expense of millions upon millions? Let this scene be brought and placed under the eyes of the people of England, and let them be told that Pitt and Dundas and Perceval had these things done to prevent the country from being conquered; with voice unanimous the nation would instantly exclaim: Let the French or let the devil take us, rather than let us resort to means of defence like these. This is, perhaps, the only set of fortifications in the world ever framed for mere *hiding*. There is no appearance of any intention to annoy an enemy. It is a parcel of holes made in a hill, to hide Englishmen from Frenchmen. Just as if Frenchmen would come to this hill! Just as if they would not go (if they came at all) and land in Romney Marsh, or on Pevensey Level, or anywhere else, rather than come to this hill; rather than crawl up Shakespeare's Cliff. All the way along the coast, from this very hill to Portsmouth, or pretty nearly all the way, is a flat. What the devil should they come to this hill for, then? And when you ask this question, they tell you that it is to have an army here *behind* the French, after they had marched into the country! And for a purpose like this; for a purpose so stupid, so senseless, so mad as this, and withal, so scandalously disgraceful, more brick and stone have been buried in this hill than would go to build a neat new cottage for every labouring man in the counties of Kent and of Sussex!

Dreadful is the scourge of such ministers. However those who supported them will now have to suffer. The money must have been squandered purposely, and for the worst ends. Fool as Pitt was; unfit as an old hack of a lawyer, like Dundas, was to judge of the means of defending their country, stupid as both these fellows were, and as their brother lawyer, Perceval, was too: unfit as these lawyers were to judge in any such a case, they must have known that this was an useless expenditure of money. They must have known that; and, therefore, their general folly, their general ignorance, is no apology for their conduct. What they wanted was to prevent the landing, not of Frenchmen, but of French principles; that is to say, to prevent the example of the French from being alluring to the people of England. The devil a bit did they care for the Bourbons. They rejoiced at the killing of the king. They rejoiced at the atheistical decree. They rejoiced at everything calculated to alarm the timid and to excite horror in the people of England in general. They wanted to keep out of England those principles which had a natural tendency to destroy boroughmongering, and to put an end to peculation and plunder. No matter whether by means of martello towers, making a great chalk hill a honeycomb, cutting a canal thirty feet wide to stop the march of the armies of the Danube and the Rhine: no matter how they squandered the money, so that it silenced some and made others bawl to answer their great purpose of preventing French example from having an influence in England. Simply their object was this: to make the French people miserable; to force back the Bourbons upon them as a *means* of making them miserable; to degrade France, to make the people wretched; and then to have to say to the people of England, Look there: *see what they have got by their attempts to obtain liberty*! This was their object. They did not want martello towers and honeycombed chalkhills and mad canals: they did not want these to keep out the French armies. The boroughmongers and the parsons cared nothing about the French armies. It was the French example that the lawyers, boroughmongers and parsons wished to keep out. And what have they done? It is impossible to be upon this honeycombed hill, upon this enormous mass of anti-Jacobin expenditure, without seeing the chalk cliffs of Calais and the cornfields of France. At this season it is impossible to see those fields without knowing that the farmers are getting in their corn there as well as here; and it is impossible to think of that fact without reflecting, at the same time, on the example which the farmers of France hold out to the farmers of England. Looking down from this very anti-Jacobin hill, this day, I saw the parsons' shocks of wheat and barley, left in the field after the farmer had taken his away. Turning my head, and looking across the Channel, 'There,' said I, pointing to France, 'there the spirited and sensible people have ridded themselves of this burden, of which our farmers so bitterly complain.' It is impossible not to recollect here, that, in numerous petitions, sent up, too, by the *loyal*, complaints have been made that the English farmer has to carry on a competition against the French farmer, who has *no tithes to pay*! Well, *loyal gentlemen*, why do not you petition, then, to be relieved from tithes? What do you mean else? Do you mean to call upon our big gentlemen at Whitehall for them to compel the French to pay tithes? Oh, you loyal fools! Better hold your tongues about the French not paying tithes. Better do that, at any rate; for never will they pay tithes again.

Here is a large tract of *land* upon these hills at Dover, which is the property of the public, having been purchased at an enormous expense. This is now let out as pasture land to the people of the town. I dare say that the letting of this land is a curious affair. If there were a member for Dover who would do what he ought to do he would soon get before the public a list of the tenants, and of the

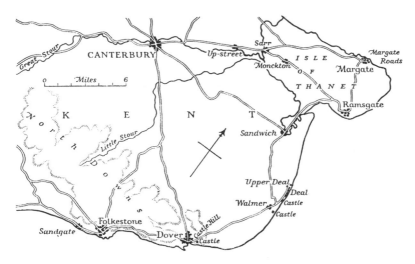

rents paid by them. I should like very much to see such list. Butterworth, the bookseller in Fleet Street, he who is a sort of metropolitan of the Methodists, is one of the members for Dover. The other is, I believe, that Wilbraham or Bootle or Bootle Wilbraham, or some such name, that is a Lancashire magistrate. So that Dover is prettily set up. However, there is nothing of this sort that can, in the present state of things, be deemed to be of any real consequence. As long as the people at Whitehall can go on paying the interest on the debt in full, so long will there be no change worth the attention of any rational man. In the meanwhile, the French nation will be going on rising over us; and our ministers will be cringing and crawling to every nation upon earth who is known to possess a cannon or a barrel of powder.

This very day I have read Mr Canning's speech at Liverpool, with a Yankee consul sitting on his right hand. Not a word now about the bits of bunting and the fir frigates; but now America is the lovely daughter, who in a moment of excessive love has gone off with a lover (to wit, the French) and left the tender mother to mourn! What a fop! And this is the man that talked so big and so bold. This is the clever, the profound, the blustering, too, and above all things, 'the high spirited' Mr Canning. However, more of this hereafter. I must from this Dover, as fast as I can.

Sandwich, Wednesday, 3 Sept., Night.

I got to this place about half an hour after the ringing of the eight o'clock bell, or curfew, which I heard at about two miles distance from the place. From the town of Dover you come up the Castle Hill, and have a most beautiful view from the top of it. You have the sea, the chalk cliffs of Calais, the high land at Boulogne, the town of Dover just under you, the valley towards Folkestone, and the much more beautiful valley towards Canterbury; and going on a little further, you have the Downs and the Essex or Suffolk coast in full view, with a most beautiful corn country to ride along through. The corn was chiefly cut between Dover and Walmer. The barley almost all cut and tied up in sheaf. Nothing but the beans seemed to remain standing along here. They are not quite so good as the rest of the corn; but they are by no means bad. When I came to the village of Walmer, I inquired for the castle; that famous place, where Pitt, Dundas, Perceval, and all the whole tribe of plotters against the French Revolution had carried on their plots. After coming through the village of Walmer, you see the entrance of the castle away to the right. It is situated pretty nearly on the water's edge, and at the bottom of a little dell, about a furlong or so from the turnpike-road. This is now the habitation of our great minister, Robert Bankes Jenkinson, son of Charles of that name. When I was told, by a girl who was leasing in a field by the road side, that that was Walmer Castle, I stopped short, pulled my horse round, looked steadfastly at the gateway, and could not help exclaiming: 'Oh, thou who inhabitest that famous dwelling; thou, who hast always been in place, let who might be out of place! Oh, thou everlasting placeman! thou sage of "over-production", do but cast thine eyes upon this barley field, where, if I am not greatly deceived, there are from seven to eight quarters upon the acre! Oh, thou whose *Courier* newspaper has just informed its readers that wheat will be seventy shillings the quarter in the month of November: oh, thou wise man, I pray thee come forth from thy castle, and tell me what thou wilt do if wheat should happen to be, at the appointed time, thirty-five shillings, instead of seventy shillings, the quarter. Sage of over-production, farewell. If thou hast life, thou wilt be minister as long as thou canst pay the interest of the debt in full, but not one moment longer. The moment thou ceasest to be able to squeeze from the Normans a sufficiency to count down to the Jews their full tale, that moment, thou great stern-path-of-duty man, thou wilt begin to be taught the true meaning of the words *Ministerial Responsibility.*'

Deal is a most villainous place. It is full of filthy-looking people. Great desolation of abomination has been going on here; tremendous barracks, partly pulled down and partly tumbling down, and partly occupied by soldiers. Everything seems upon the perish. I was glad to hurry along through it, and to leave its inns and public-houses to be occupied by the tarred, and trowsered, and blue-and-buff crew whose very vicinage I always detest. From Deal you come along to Upper Deal, which, it seems, was the original village; thence upon a beautiful road to Sandwich, which is a rotten borough. Rottenness, putridity is excellent for land, but bad for boroughs. This place, which is as villainous a hole as one would wish to see, is surrounded by some of the finest land in the world. Along on one side of it lies a marsh. On the other sides of it is land which they tell me bears *seven quarters* of wheat to an acre. It is certainly very fine; for I saw large pieces of radish-seed on the roadside; this seed is grown for the seedsmen in London; and it will grow on none but rich land. All the corn is carried here except some beans and some barley.

Canterbury, Thursday Afternoon, 4 Sept.
In quitting Sandwich, you immediately cross a river up which vessels bring coals from the sea. This marsh is about a couple of miles wide. It begins at the sea-beach, opposite the Downs, to my right hand, coming from Sandwich, and it wheels round to my left and ends at the sea-beach, opposite Margate roads. This marsh was formerly covered with the sea, very likely; and hence the land within this sort of semicircle, the name of which is Thanet, was called an *Isle.* It is, in fact, an island now, for the same reason that Portsea is an island, and that New York is an island; for there certainly is the water in this river that goes round and connects one part of the sea with the other. I had to cross this river, and to cross the marsh, before I got into the famous Isle of Thanet, which it was my intention

to cross. Soon after crossing the river, I passed by a place for making salt, and could not help recollecting that there are no excise men in these salt-making places in France, that, before the Revolution, the French were most cruelly oppressed by the duties on salt, that they had to endure, on that account, the most horrid tyranny that ever was known, except, perhaps, that practised in an *Exchequer* that shall here be nameless; that thousands and thousands of men and women were every year sent to the galleys for what was called smuggling salt; that the fathers and even the mothers were imprisoned or whipped if the children were detected in smuggling salt: I could not help reflecting, with delight, as I looked at these salt-pans in the Isle of Thanet; I could not help reflecting that, in spite of Pitt, Dundas, Perceval, and the rest of the crew, in spite of the caverns of Dover and the martello towers in Romney Marsh: in spite of all the spies and all the bayonets, and the six hundred millions of debt and the hundred and fifty millions of dead-weight, and the two hundred millions of poor-rates that are now squeezing the boroughmongers, squeezing the farmers, puzzling the fellows at Whitehall and making Mark Lane a scene of greater interest than the Chamber of the Privy Council; with delight as I jogged along under the first beams of the sun, I reflected that, in spite of all the malignant measures that had brought so much misery upon England, the gallant French people had ridded themselves of the tyranny which sent them to the galleys for endeavouring to use without tax the salt which God sent upon their shores. Can any man tell why we should still be paying five, or six, or seven shillings a bushel for salt, instead of one? We did pay fifteen shillings a bushel, tax. And why is two shillings a bushel kept on? Because, if they were taken off, the salt-tax-gathering crew must be discharged! This tax of two shillings a bushel causes the consumer to pay five, at the least, more than he would if there were no tax at all! When, great God! when shall we be allowed to enjoy God's gifts in freedom, as the people of France enjoy them?

On the marsh I found the same sort of sheep as on Romney Marsh; but the cattle here are chiefly Welsh; black, and called runts. They are nice hardy cattle; and, I am told, that this is the description of cattle that they fat all the way up on this north side of Kent.

When I got upon the corn land in the Isle of Thanet, I got into a garden indeed. There is hardly any fallow; comparatively few turnips. It is a country of corn. Most of the harvest is in; but there are some fields of wheat and of barley not yet housed. A great many pieces of lucerne, and all of them very fine. I left Ramsgate to my right about three miles, and went right across the island to Margate; but that place is so thickly settled with stock-jobbing cuckolds, at this time of the year, that, having no fancy to get their horns stuck into me, I turned away to my left when I got within about half a mile of the town. I got to a little hamlet, where I breakfasted; but could get no corn for my horse, and no bacon for myself! All was corn around me. Barns, I should think, two hundred feet long; ricks of enormous size and most numerous; crops of wheat, five quarters to an acre, on the average; and a public-house without either bacon or corn! The labourers' houses, all along through this island, beggarly in the extreme. The people dirty, poor-looking; ragged, but particularly *dirty*. The men and boys with dirty faces, and dirty smock-frocks, and dirty shirts; and, good God! what a difference between the wife of a labouring man here, and the wife of a labouring man in the forests and woodlands of Hampshire and Sussex! Invariably have I observed that the richer the soil, the more destitute of woods; that is to say, the more purely a corn country, the more miserable the labourers. The cause is this, the great, the big bull frog grasps all. In this beautiful island every inch of land is appropriated by the rich. No hedges, no ditches, no commons, no grassy lanes; a country divided into great farms; a few trees surround the great farm-house. All the rest is bare of trees; and the wretched labourer has not a stick of wood, and has no place for a pig or cow to graze, or even to lie down upon. The rabbit countries are the countries for labouring men. There the ground is not so valuable. There it is not so easily appropriated by the few. Here, in this island, the work is almost all done by the horses. The horses plough the ground; they sow the ground; they hoe the ground; they carry the corn home; they thresh it out; and they carry it to market: nay, in this island, they *rake* the ground; they rake up the straggling straws and ears; so that they do the whole, except the reaping and the mowing. It is impossible to have an idea of anything more miserable than the state of the labourers in this part of the country.

After coming by Margate, I passed a village called Monckton, and another called Sarr. At Sarr there is a bridge, over which you come out of the island, as you go into it over the bridge at Sandwich. At Monckton they had *seventeen men working on the roads*, though the harvest was not quite in, and though, of course, it had all to be threshed out; but, at Monckton, they had *four threshing machines*; and they have three threshing machines at Sarr, though there, also, they have several men upon the roads! This is a shocking state of things; and in spite of everything that the Jenkinsons and the Scots can do, this state of things must be changed.

At Sarr, or a little way further back, I saw a man who had just begun to reap a field of canary seed. The plants were too far advanced to be cut in order to be bleached for the making of plat; but I got the reaper to select me a few green stalks that grew near a bush that stood on the outside of the piece. These I have brought on with me, in order to give them a trial. At Sarr I began to cross the marsh, and had, after this, to come through the village of Up-street, and another village called Steady, before I got to Canterbury. At Up-street I was struck with the words written upon a board which was fastened upon a pole, which pole was standing in a garden near a neat little box of a house. The words were these. 'PARADISE PLACE. *Spring guns and steel traps are set here.*' A pretty idea it must give us of Paradise to know that spring guns and steel traps are set in it! This is doubtless some stock-jobber's place; for, in the first place, the name is likely to have been selected by one of that crew; and, in the next place, whenever any of them go to the country, they look upon it that they are to begin a sort of warfare against everything around them. They invariably look upon every labourer as a thief.

As you approach Canterbury, from the Isle of Thanet, you have another instance of the squanderings of the lawyer ministers. Nothing equals the ditches, the caverns, the holes, the tanks, and hiding-places of the hill at Dover; but, considerable as the city of Canterbury is, that city, within its gates, stands upon less ground than those horrible erections, the barracks of Pitt, Dundas, and Perceval. They are perfectly enormous; but thanks be unto God, they begin to crumble down. They have a sickly hue: all is lassitude about them: endless are their lawns, their gravel walks, and their ornaments; but their lawns are unshaven, their gravel walks grassy, and their ornaments putting on the garments of ugliness. You see the grass growing opposite the doorways. A hole in the window strikes you here and there. Lamp posts there are, but no lamps. Here are horse-barracks, foot-barracks, artillery-barracks, engineer-barracks: a whole country of barracks; but only here and there a soldier. The thing is actually perishing. It is typical of the state of the great Thing of things. It gave me inexpressible pleasure to perceive the gloom that seemed to hang over these barracks, which once swarmed with soldiers and their blithe companions, as a hive swarms with bees. These barracks now look like the environs of a hive in winter. Westminster Abbey Church is not the place for the monument of Pitt; the statue of the great snorting bawler ought to be stuck up here, just in the midst of this hundred or two of acres covered with barracks. These barracks, too, were erected in order to compel the French to return to the payment of tithes; in order to bring their necks again under the yoke of the lords and the clergy. That has not been accomplished. The French, as Mr Hoggart assures us, have neither tithes, taxes, nor rates; and the people of Canterbury know that they have a *hop-duty* to pay, while Mr Hoggart, of Broad Street, tells them that he has farms to let, in France, where there are hop-gardens and where there is no hop-duty. They have lately had races at Canterbury; and the mayor and aldermen, in order to get the Prince Leopold to attend them, presented him with the Freedom of the City; but it rained all the time and he did not come! The mayor and aldermen do not understand things half so well as this German gentleman, who has managed his matters as well, I think as any one that I ever heard of.

This fine old town, or rather city, is remarkable for cleanliness and niceness, notwithstanding it has a cathedral in it. The country round it is very rich, and this year, while the hops are so bad in most other parts, they are not so very bad just about Canterbury.

[*Rural Rides* 1, 239–50]

[iii] *From Chilworth, in Surrey, to Winchester*

Thursley, Four Miles from Godalming, Surrey,
Sunday Evening, 23 October, 1825.

We set out from Chilworth to-day about noon. This is a little hamlet, lying under the south side of St Martha's Hill; and on the other side of that hill, a little to the north-west, is the town of Guildford, which (taken with its environs) I, who have seen so many, many towns, think the prettiest, and, taken all together, the most agreeable and most happy-looking that I ever saw in my life. Here are hill and dell in endless variety. Here are the chalk and the sand, vieing with each other in making beautiful scenes. Here is a navigable river and fine meadows. Here are woods and downs. Here is something of everything but *fat marshes* and their skeleton-making *agues*. The vale, all the way down to Chilworth from Reigate, is very delightful.

We did not go to Guildford, nor did we cross the *River Wey*, to come through Godalming; but bore away to our left, and came through the village of Hambleton, going first to Hascomb to show Richard* the South Downs from that high land, which looks southward over the *Wealds* of Surrey and Sussex, with all their fine and innumerable oak-trees. Those that travel on turnpike-roads know nothing of England. From Hascomb to Thursley almost the whole way is across fields, or commons, or along narrow lands. Here we see the people without any disguise or affectation. Against a *great road* things are made for *show*. Here we see them *without any show*. And here we gain real knowledge as to their situation. We crossed to-day three turnpike-roads, that from Guildford to Horsham, that from Godalming to Worthing, I believe, and that from Godalming to Chichester.

Thursley, Wednesday, 26 Oct.

The weather has been beautiful ever since last Thursday morning; but there has been a white frost every morning, and the days have been coldish. *Here*, however, I am quite at home in a room where there is one of my *American fireplaces*, bought by my host of Mr Judson, of Kensington, who has made many a score of families comfortable instead of sitting shivering in the cold. At the house of the gentleman whose house I am now in, there is a good deal of *fuel-wood*; and here I see in the parlours those fine and cheerful fires that make a great part of the happiness of the Americans. But these fires are to be had only in this sort of fireplace. Ten times the fuel; nay, no quantity, would effect the same object, in any other fireplace. It is equally good for coal as for wood; but, for *pleasure*, a wood-fire is the thing. There is round about almost every gentleman's or great farmer's house more wood suffered to rot every year, in one shape or another, than would make (with this fireplace) a couple of rooms constantly warm, from October to June. *Here*, peat, turf, saw-dust, and wood, are burnt in these fireplaces. My present host has three of the fireplaces.

Being out a-coursing to-day, I saw a queer-looking building upon one of the thousands of hills that nature has tossed up in endless variety of form round the skirts of the lofty Hindhead. This building, is, it seems, called a *Semaphore*, or *Semiphare*, or something of that sort. What this word may have been hatched out of I cannot say; but

* Cobbett's youngest son.

it means a *job*, I am sure. To call it an *alarm-post* would not have been so convenient; for people not endued with Scotch *intellect* might have wondered why the devil we should have to pay for alarm-posts; and might have thought that, with all our 'glorious victories', we had 'brought our hogs to a fine market' if our dread of the enemy were such as to induce us to have alarm-posts all over the country! Such unintellectual people might have thought that we had 'conquered France by the immortal Wellington' to little purpose, if we were still in such fear as to build alarm-posts; and they might, in addition, have observed that for many hundred of years England stood in need of neither signal-posts nor standing army of mercenaries; but relied safely on the courage and public spirit of the people themselves. By calling the thing by an outlandish name, these reflections amongst the unintellectual are obviated. *Alarm-post* would be a nasty name; and it would puzzle people exceedingly, when they saw one of these at a place like Ashe, a little village on the north side of the chalk-ridge (called the Hog's Back) going from Guildford to Farnham! What can this be *for*? Why are these expensive things put up all over the country? Respecting the movements of *whom* is wanted this *alarm-system*? Will no member ask this in Parliament? Not one; not a man: and yet it is a thing to ask about. Ah! it is in vain, THING, that you thus are *making your preparations*; in vain that you are setting your trammels! The debt, the blessed debt, that best ally of the people, will break them all; will snap them, as the hornet does the cobweb; and even these very 'Semaphores' contribute towards the force of that ever-blessed debt. Curious to see how things *work*! The 'Glorious Revolution', which was made for the avowed purpose of maintaining the Protestant ascendancy, and which was followed by such terrible persecution of the Catholics; that 'glorious' affair, which set aside a race of kings because they were Catholics, served as the *precedent* for the American Revolution, also called 'glorious', and this second revolution compelled the successors of the makers of the first to begin to cease their persecutions of the Catholics! Then again, the debt was made to raise and keep armies on foot to prevent reform of Parliament, because, as it was feared by the aristocracy, reform would have humbled them; and this debt, created for this purpose, is fast sweeping the aristocracy out of their estates, as a clown, with his foot, kicks field-mice out of their nests. There was a hope that the debt could have been reduced by stealth, as it were; that the aristocracy could have been saved in this way. That hope now no longer exists. In all likelihood the funds will keep going down. What is to prevent this, if the interest of Exchequer Bills be raised, as the broadsheet tells us it is to be? What! the funds fall in time of peace; and the French funds not fall in time of peace! However, it will all happen just as it ought to happen. Even the next session of Parliament will bring out matters of some interest. The thing is now working in the surest possible way.

The great business of life, in the country, appertains, in some way or other, to the *game*, and especially at this time of the year. If it were not for the game, a country life would be like an *everlasting honeymoon*, which would, in about half a century, put an end to the human race. In towns, or large villages, people make a shift to find the means of rubbing the rust off from each other by a vast variety of sources of contest. A couple of wives meeting in the street, and giving each other a wry look, or a look not quite civil enough, will, if the parties be hard pushed for a ground of contention, do pretty well. But in the country there is, alas! no such resources. Here are no walls for people to take of each other. Here they are so placed as to prevent the possibility of such lucky local contact. Here is more than room of every sort, elbow, leg, horse, or carriage, for them all. Even at *church* (most of the people being in the meeting-houses) the pews are surprisingly too large. Here, therefore, where all circumstances seem calculated to cause never-ceasing concord with its accompanying dullness, there would be no relief at all, were it not for the *game*. This, happily, supplies the place of all other sources of alternate dispute and reconciliation; it keeps all in life and motion, from the lord down to the hedger. When I see two men, whether in a market-room, by the way-side, in a parlour, in a church-yard, or even in the church itself, engaged in a manifestly deep and most momentous discourse, I will, if it be any time between September and February, bet ten to one that it is, in some way or other, about *the game*. The wives and daughters hear so much of it that they inevitably get engaged in the disputes; and thus all are kept in a state of vivid animation. I should like very much to be able to take a spot, a circle of 12 miles in diameter, and take an exact account of all the *time* spent by each individual, above the age of ten (that is the age they begin at), in talking, during the game season of one year, about the game and about sporting exploits. I verily believe that it would amount, upon an average, to six times as much as all the other talk put together; and, as to the anger, the satisfaction, the scolding, the commendation, the chagrin, the exultation, the envy, the emulation, where are there any of these in the country unconnected with *the game*?

There is, however, an important distinction to be made between *hunters* (including coursers) and *shooters*. The latter are, as far as relates to their exploits, a disagreeable class compared with the former; and the reason of this is, their doings are almost wholly their own; while, in the case of the others, the achievements are the property of the dogs. Nobody likes to hear another talk *much* in praise of his own acts, unless those acts have a manifest tendency to produce some good to the hearer; and shooters do talk *much* of their own exploits, and those exploits rather tend to *humiliate* the hearer. Then a *greater shooter* will, nine times out of ten, go so far as almost to *lie a little*; and though people do not tell him of it, they do not like him the better for it; and he but too frequently discovers that they do not believe him: whereas, hunters are mere followers of the dogs, as mere spectators; their praises, if any are called for, are bestowed on the greyhounds, the hounds, the fox, the hare, or the horses. There is a little rivalship in the riding, or in the behaviour of the horses; but this has so little to do with the personal merit of the sportsmen, that it never produces a want of good fellowship in the evening of the day. A shooter who has been *missing* all day, must have an uncommon good share of good sense not to feel mortified while the slaughterers are relating the adventures of that day; and this is what cannot exist in the case of the hunters. Bring me into a room, with a dozen men in it, who have been sporting all day; or rather let me be in an adjoining room, where I can hear the sound of their voices, without being able to distinguish the words, and I will bet ten to one that I tell whether they be hunters or shooters.

I was once acquainted with a *famous shooter* whose name was William Ewing. He was a barrister of Philadelphia, but became far more renowned by his gun than by his law cases. We spent scores of days together a-shooting, and were extremely well matched, I having excellent dogs and caring little about my reputation as a shot, his dogs being good for nothing, and he caring more about his reputation as a shot than as a lawyer. The fact which I am going to relate respecting this gentleman ought to be a warning to young men how they become enamoured of this species of vanity. We had gone about ten miles from our home, to shoot where partridges were said to be very plentiful. We found them so. In the course of a November day, he had, just before dark, shot, and sent to the farm-house, or kept in his bag, *ninety-nine* partridges. He made some few *double shots*, and he might have a *miss* or two, for he sometimes shot when out of my sight, on account of the woods. However, he said that he killed at every shot; and as he had counted the birds, when he went to dinner at the farm-house and when he cleaned his gun, he, just before sunset, knew that he had killed *ninety-nine* partridges, every one upon the wing, and a great part of them in woods very thickly set with largish trees. It was a grand achievement; but, unfortunately, he wanted to make it *a hundred*. The sun was setting, and, in that country, darkness comes almost at once; it is more like the going out of a candle than that of a fire; and I wanted to be off, as we had a very bad road to go, and as he, being under strict petticoat government, to which he most loyally and dutifully submitted, was compelled to get home that night, taking me with him, the vehicle (horse and gig) being mine. I, therefore, pressed him to come away, and moved on myself towards the house (that of old John Brown, in Bucks county, grandfather of that General Brown, who gave some of our whiskered heroes such a rough handling last war, which was waged for the purpose of 'deposing James Madison'), at which house I would have stayed all night, but from which I was compelled to go by that watchful government, under which he had the good fortune to live. Therefore, I was in haste to be off. No: he would kill the *hundredth* bird! In vain did I talk of the bad road and its many dangers for want of moon. The poor partridges, which we had scattered about, were *calling* all around us; and, just at this moment, up got one under his feet, in a field in which the wheat was three or four inches high. He shot and *missed*. 'That's it,' said he, running as if to *pick up* the bird. 'What!' said I, 'you don't think you *killed*, do you? Why there is the bird now, not only alive, but *calling* in that wood'; which was at about a hundred yards' distance. He, in that *form of words* usually employed in such cases, asserted that he shot the bird and saw it fall; and I, in much about the same form of words, asserted that he had *missed*, and that I, with my own eyes, saw the bird fly into the wood. This was too much! To *miss* once out of a hundred times! To lose such a chance of immortality! He was a good-humoured man; I liked him very much; and I could not help feeling for him, when he said, 'Well, *sir*, I killed the bird; and if you choose to go away and take your dog away, so as to prevent me from *finding* it, you must do it; the dog is yours, to be sure.' 'The *dog*,' said I, in a very mild tone, 'why, Ewing, there is the spot; and could we not see it, upon this smooth green surface, if it were there?' However, he began to *look about*; and I called the dog, and affected to join him in the search. Pity for his weakness got the better of my dread of the bad road. After walking backward and forward many times upon about twenty yards square with our eyes to the ground, looking for what both of us knew was not there, I had passed him (he going one way and I the other), and I happened to be turning round just after I had passed him, when I saw him, putting his hand behind him, *take a partridge out of his bag and let it fall upon the ground*! I felt no temptation to detect him, but turned away my head, and kept looking about. Presently he, having returned to the spot where the bird was, called out to me, in a most triumphant tone, '*Here! Here!* Come here!' I went up to him, and he, pointing with his finger down to the bird, and looking hard in my face at the same time, said, 'There, Cobbett; I hope that will be a *warning* to you never to be obstinate again!' 'Well,' said I, 'come along'; and away we went as merry as larks. When we got to Brown's, he told them the story, triumphed over me most clamorously; and though he often repeated the story to my face, I never had the heart to let him know that I knew of the imposition, which puerile vanity had induced so sensible and honourable a man to be mean enough to practise.

A *professed shot* is, almost always, a very disagreeable brother sportsman. He must, in the first place, have a head rather of the emptiest to *pride himself* upon so poor a talent. Then he is always out of temper, if the game fail or if he miss it. He never participates in that great delight which all sensible men enjoy at beholding the beautiful action, the docility, the zeal, the wonderful sagacity of the pointer and the setter. He is always thinking about *himself*: always anxious to surpass his companions. I remember that, once, Ewing and I had lost our dog. We were in a wood, and the dog had gone out and found a covey in a wheat stubble joining the wood. We had been whistling and calling for him for, perhaps, half an hour or more. When we came out of the wood we saw him pointing, with one foot up; and soon after, he, keeping his foot and body unmoved, gently turned round his head towards the spot where he heard us, as if to bid us come on, and when he saw that we saw him, turned his head back again. I was so delighted that I stopped to look with admiration. Ewing, astonished at my want of alacrity, pushed on, shot one of the partridges, and thought no more about the conduct of the dog than if the sagacious creature had had nothing at all to do with the matter.

When I left America in 1800 I gave this dog to Lord Henry Stuart, who was, when he came home a year or two afterwards, about to bring him to astonish the sportsmen even in England; but those of Pennsylvania were resolved not to part with him, and therefore they *stole* him the night before his lordship came away. Lord Henry had plenty of pointers after his return, and he *saw* hundreds; but always declared that he never saw anything approaching in excellence this American dog. For the information of sportsmen I ought to say that this was a small-headed and sharp-nosed pointer, hair as fine as that of a greyhound, little and short ears, very light in the body, very long legged, and swift as a good lurcher. I had him a puppy, and he never had any *breaking*, but he pointed staunchly at once; and I am of opinion that this sort is, in all respects, better than the heavy breed . . .

I am quite satisfied that there are as many *sorts* of men as there are of dogs . . . But is the *sort* the same? It cannot be *education* alone that makes the amazing difference that we see. Besides, we see men of the very same rank and riches and education differing as widely as the pointer does from the pug. The name, *man*, is common to all the sorts, and hence arises very great mischief. What confusion must there be in rural affairs, if there were no names whereby to distinguish hounds, greyhounds, pointers, spaniels, terriers, and sheepdogs, from each other! And what pretty work if, without regard to the sorts of dogs, men were to attempt to *employ them*! Yet this is done in the case of *men*! A man is always *a man*; and without the least regard as to sort, they are promiscuously placed in all kinds of situations. Now, if Mr Brougham, Doctors Birkbeck, Macculloch and Black, and that profound personage, Lord John Russell, will, in their forthcoming 'London University', teach us how to divide men *into sorts*, instead of teaching us to 'augment the capital of the nation' by making paper-money, they will render us a real service. That will be *feelosofy* worth attending to. What would be said of the 'squire who should take a fox-hound out to find partridges for him to shoot at? Yet would this be *more* absurd than to set a man to law-making who was manifestly formed for the express purpose of sweeping the streets or digging out sewers?

Farnham, Surrey, Thursday, 27 Oct.
We came over the heath from Thursley, this morning, on our way to Winchester. Mr Wyndham's fox-hounds are coming to

Thursley on Saturday. More than three-fourths of all the interesting talk in that neighbourhood, for some days past, had been about this anxiously looked-for event. I have seen no man, or boy, who did not talk about it. There had been false report about it; the hounds did *not come*; and the anger of the disappointed people was very great. At last, however, the *authentic* intelligence came, and I left them all as happy as if all were young and all just going to be married. An abatement of my pleasure, however, on this joyous occasion, was that I brought away with me *one*, who was eager as the best of them,

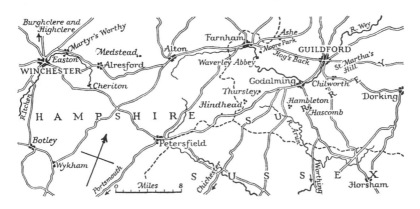

Richard, though now only 11 years and 6 months old, had, it seems, one fox-hunt, in Herefordshire, last winter; and he actually has begun to talk rather *contemptuously* of hare hunting. To show me that he is in no *danger*, he has been leaping his horse over banks and ditches by the road side, all our way across the country from Reigate; and he joined with such glee in talking of the expected arrival of the fox-hounds that I felt some little pain at bringing him away. My engagement at Winchester is for Saturday; but if it had not been so, the deep and hidden ruts in the heath, in a wood in the midst of which the hounds are sure to find, and the immense concourse of horsemen that is sure to be assembled, would have made me bring him away. Upon the high, hard and open countries I should not be afraid for him, but here the danger would have been greater than it would have been right for me to suffer him to run.

We came hither by way of Waverley Abbey and Moore Park. On the commons I showed Richard some of my old hunting scenes, when I was of his age, or younger, reminding him that I was obliged to hunt on foot. We got leave to go and see the grounds at Waverley where all the old monks' garden walls are totally gone, and where the spot is become a sort of lawn. I showed him the spot where the strawberry garden was, and where I, when sent to gather *hautboys*, used to eat every remarkably fine one, instead of letting it go to be eaten by Sir Robert Rich. I showed him a tree, close by the ruins of the Abbey, from a limb of which I once fell into the river, in an attempt to take the nest of a *crow*, which had artfully placed it upon a branch so far from the trunk as not to be able to bear the weight of a boy eight years old. I showed him an old elm-tree, which was hollow even then, into which I, when a very little boy, once saw a cat go, that was as big as a middle-sized spaniel dog, for relating which I got a great scolding, for standing to which I, at last, got a beating; but stand to which I still did. I have since many times repeated it; and I would take my oath of it to this day. When in New Brunswick I saw the great wild grey cat, which is there called a *Lucifee*; and it seemed to me to be just such a cat as I had seen at Waverley. I found the ruins not very greatly diminished; but it is strange how small the mansion, and ground, and everything but the trees, appeared to me. They were all great to my mind when I saw them last; and that early impression had remained, whenever I had talked or thought of the spot; so that, when I came to see them again, after seeing the sea and so many other immense things, it seemed as if they had all been made small. This was not the case with regard to the trees, which are nearly as big here as they are any where else; and the old cat-elm, for instance, which Richard measured with his whip, is about 16 or 17 feet round.

From Waverley we went to Moore Park, once the seat of Sir William Temple, and when I was a very little boy, the seat of a lady, or a Mrs Temple. Here I showed Richard Mother Ludlum's Hole; but, alas! it is not the enchanting place that I knew it, nor that which Grose describes in his Antiquities! The semicircular paling is gone; the basins, to catch the never-ceasing little stream, are gone; the iron cups, fastened by chains, for people to drink out of, are gone; the pavement all broken to pieces; the seats for people to sit on, on both sides of the cave, torn up and gone; the stream that ran down a clean paved channel now making a dirty gutter; and the ground opposite, which was a grove, chiefly of laurels, intersected by closely mowed grass-walks, now become a poor, ragged-looking alder-coppice. Near the mansion, I showed Richard the hill upon which Dean Swift tells us he used to run for exercise, while he was pursuing his studies here; and I would have showed him the garden-seat, under which Sir William Temple's heart was buried, agreeably to his will; but the seat was gone, also the wall at the back of it; and the exquisitely beautiful little lawn in which the seat stood was turned into a parcel of divers-shaped cockney-clumps, planted according to the strictest rules of artificial and refined vulgarity.

At Waverley, Mr Thompson, a merchant of some sort, has succeeded (after the monks) the Orby Hunters and Sir Robert Rich. At Moore Park, a Mr Laing, a West India planter or merchant, has succeeded the Temples; and at the castle of Farnham, which you see from Moore Park, Bishop Prettyman Tomline has, at last, after perfectly regular and due gradations, succeeded William of Wykham! In coming up from Moore Park to Farnham town, I stopped opposite the door of a little old house, where there appeared to be a great parcel of children. 'There, Dick,' said I, 'when I was just such a little creature as that whom you see in the door-way, I lived in this very house with my grandmother Cobbett.' He pulled up his horse, and looked *very hard at it*, but said nothing, and on we came.

Winchester, Sunday Noon, 30 Oct.

We came away from Farnham about noon on Friday, promising Bishop Prettyman to notice him and his way of living more fully on our return. At Alton we got some bread and cheese at a friend's, and then came to Alresford by Medstead, in order to have fine turf to ride on, and to see on this lofty land that which is, perhaps, the finest *beech-wood* in all England. These high down countries are not garden plats, like Kent; but they have, from my first seeing them, when I was about *ten*, always been my delight. Large sweeping downs, and deep dells here and there, with villages amongst lofty trees, are my great delight. When we got to Alresford it was nearly dark, and not being able to find a room to our liking, we resolved to go, though in the dark, to Easton, a village about six miles from Alresford down by the side of the Hichen River.

Coming from Easton yesterday, I learned that Sir Charles Ogle, the eldest son and successor of Sir Chaloner Ogle, had sold, to some general, his mansion and estate at Martyr's Worthy, a village on the north side of the Hichen, just opposite Easton. The Ogles had been here for *a couple of centuries*, perhaps. They are *gone off now*, 'for good and all', as the country people call it. Well, what I have to say to Sir Charles Ogle upon this occasion is this: 'It was *you*, who moved at the county meeting in 1817, that *Address to the Regent*, which you brought ready engrossed upon parchment, which Fleming, the sheriff, declared to have been carried, though a word of it never was heard by the meeting; which address *applauded the power of imprisonment bill, just then passed*; and the like of which address you will not in all human probability ever again move in Hampshire, and, I hope, nowhere else. So, you see, Sir Charles, there is one consolation, at any rate.'

I learned too that Greame, a famously loyal 'squire and justice, whose son was, a few years ago, made a distributor of stamps in this county, was become so modest as to exchange his big and ancient mansion at Cheriton, or somewhere there, for a very moderate-sized house in the town of Alresford! I saw his household goods advertised in the Hampshire newspaper, a little while ago, to be sold by public auction. I rubbed my eyes, or, rather, my spectacles, and looked again and again; for I remembered the loyal 'squire; and I, with singular satisfaction, record this change in his scale of existence, which has, no doubt, proceeded solely from that prevalence of mind over matter which the Scotch *feelosofers* have taken such pains to inculcate, and which makes him flee from greatness as from that which diminishes the quantity of 'intellectual enjoyment'; and so now he,

'Wondering man can want the larger pile,
Exults, and owns his cottage with a smile.'

And they really tell me that his present house is not much bigger than that of my dear, good old grandmother Cobbett. But (and it may not be wholly useless for the 'squire to know it) she never burnt *candles*; but *rushes* dipped in grease, as I have described them in my *Cottage Economy*; and this was one of the means that she made use of in order to secure a bit of good bacon and good bread to eat, and that made her never give me potatoes, cold or hot. No bad hint for the 'squire, father of the distributor of stamps. Good bacon is a very nice thing, I can assure him; and if the quantity be small, it is all the sweeter; provided, however, it be not *too small* . . .

This being Sunday, I heard, about 7 o'clock in the morning, a sort of jangling, made by a bell or two in the *cathedral*. We were getting ready to be off, to cross the country to Burghclere, which lies under the lofty hills at Highclere, about 22 miles from this city; but hearing the bells of the cathedral, I took Richard to show him the tomb of that famous bishop of Winchester, William of Wykham; who was the chancellor and the minister of the great and glorious king, Edward III; who sprang from poor parents in the little village of Wykham, three miles from Botley; and who, amongst other great and most munificent deeds, founded the famous college or school of Winchester, and also one of the colleges of Oxford. I told Richard about this as we went from the inn down to the cathedral; and when I *showed him the tomb*, where the bishop lies on his back, in his Catholic robes, with his mitre on his head, his shepherd's crook by his side, with little children at his feet, their hands put together in a praying attitude, he looked with a degree of inquisitive earnestness that pleased me very much. I took him as far as I could about the cathedral. The 'service' was now begun. There is a *dean*, and God knows how many *prebends* belonging to this immensely rich bishopric and chapter: and there were, at this 'service', *two or three men* and *five or six boys* in white surplices, with a congregation of *fifteen women* and *four men*! Gracious God! If William of Wykham could, at that moment, have been raised from his tomb! If Saint Swithin, whose name the cathedral bears, or Alfred the Great, to whom St Swithin was tutor: if either of these could have come, and had been told that *that* was *now* what was carried on by men, who talked of the 'damnable errors' of those who founded that very church! But it beggars one's feelings to attempt to find words whereby to express them upon such a subject and such an occasion. How, then, am I to describe what I felt when I yesterday saw in Hyde Meadow a *county bridewell* standing on the very spot where stood the abbey which was founded and endowed by Alfred, which contained the bones of that maker of the English name, and also those of the learned monk, St Grimbald, whom Alfred brought to England *to begin the teaching at Oxford*!

After we came out of the cathedral Richard said, 'Why, papa, nobody can build such places *now*, can they?' 'No, my dear,' said I. 'That building was made when there were no poor wretches in England called *paupers*; when there were no *poor-rates*; when every labouring man was clothed in good woollen cloth; and when all had a plenty of meat and bread and beer.' This talk lasted us to the inn, where, just as we were going to set off, it most curiously happened that a parcel which had come from Kensington by the night coach was put into my hands, containing, amongst other things, a pamphlet, sent to me from Rome, being an Italian translation of No I of the *Protestant Reformation* . . .

[*Rural Rides* I, 278–90]

[iv] *From Petersfield to Kensington*

Petworth, Saturday, 12 November 1825.
I was at this town in the summer of 1823, when I crossed Sussex from Worth to Huntingdon, in my way to Titchfield in Hampshire. We came this morning to Petersfield, with an intention to cross to Horsham, and go thence to Worth, and then into Kent; but Richard's horse seemed not to be fit for so strong a bout, and therefore we resolved to bend our course homewards, and first of all to fall back upon our resources at Thursley, which we intend to reach tomorrow, going through North Chapel, Chiddingfold, and Brook.

At about four miles from Petersfield we passed through a village called Rogate. Just before we came to it, I asked a man who was hedging on the side of the road how much he got a day. He said, 1*s.* 6*d.*: and he told me that the *allowed* wage was 7*d.* a day for the man *and a gallon loaf a week for the rest of his family*; that is to say, one pound and two and a quarter ounces of bread for each of them and nothing more! And this, observe, is one-third short of the bread allowance of gaols, to say nothing of the meat and clothing and lodging of the inhabitants of gaols. If the man have full work; if he get his eighteen pence a day, the whole nine shillings does not pur-chase a gallon loaf each for his wife and three children, and two gallon loaves for himself. In the gaols, the convicted felons have a pound and a half each of bread a day to begin with: they have some meat generally, and it has been found absolutely necessary to allow them meat when they work at the tread-mill. It is impossible to make them work at the tread-mill without it. However, let us take the bare allowance of bread allowed in gaols. This allowance is, for five people, fifty-two pounds and a half in the week; whereas, the man's nine shillings will buy but fifty-two pounds of bread; and this, observe, is a vast deal better than the state of things in the north of Hampshire, where the day-labourer gets but eight shillings a week. I asked this man how much a day they gave to a young able man who had no family, and who was compelled to come to the parish-officers for work. Observe that there are a great many young men in this situation, because the farmers will not employ single men *at full wages*, these full wages being wanted for the married man's family, just to keep them alive according to the calculation that we have just seen. About the borders of the north of Hampshire they give to these single men two gallon loaves a week, or, in money, two shillings and eightpence, and nothing more. Here, in this part of Sussex, they give the single man sevenpence a day, that is to say, enough to buy two pounds and a quarter of bread for six days in the week, and as he does not work on the Sunday, there is no sevenpence allowed for the Sunday, and of course nothing to eat: and this is the allowance, settled by the magistrates, for a young, hearty, labouring man; and that, too, in the part of England where, I believe, they live better than in any other part of it. The poor creature here has sevenpence a day for six days in the week to find him food, clothes, washing, and lodging! It is just sevenpence, less than one half of what the meanest foot soldier in the standing army receives; besides that the latter has clothing, candle, fire, and lodging into the bargain! Well may we call our happy state of things the 'envy of surrounding nations, and the admiration of the world'! We hear of the efforts of Mrs Fry, Mr Buxton, and numerous other persons to improve the situation of felons in the gaols; but never, no never, do we catch them ejaculating one single pious sigh for these innumerable sufferers, who are doomed to become felons or to waste away their bodies by hunger.

When we came into the village of Rogate, I saw a little group of persons standing before a blacksmith's shop. The church-yard was on the other side of the road, surrounded by a low wall. The earth of the church-yard was about four feet and a half higher than the common level of the ground round about it; and you may see, by the nearness of the church windows to the ground, that this bed of earth has been made by the innumerable burials that have taken place in it. The group, consisting of the blacksmith, the wheelwright, perhaps, and three or four others, appeared to me to be in a delibera-tive mood. So I said, looking significantly at the churchyard, 'It has taken a pretty many thousands of your forefathers to raise that ground up so high.' 'Yes, sir,' said one of them. 'And,' I said, 'for about nine hundred years those who built that church thought about religion very differently from what we do.' 'Yes,' said another. 'And,' I said, 'do you think that all those who made that heap there are gone to the devil?' I got no answer to this. 'At any rate,' added I, 'they never worked for a pound and a half of bread a day.' They looked hard at me, and then looked hard at one another; and I, having trotted off, looked round at the first turning, and saw them looking after us still. I should suppose that the church was built about seven or eight hundred years ago, that is to say, the present church for the first church built upon this spot was, I dare say, erected more than a thousand years ago. If I had had time, I should have told this group that, before the Protestant Reformation, the labourers of Rogate received fourpence a day from Michaelmas to Lady-day; fivepence a day from Lady-day to Michaelmas except in harvest and grass-mowing time, when able labourers had sevenpence a day; and that, at this time, bacon was *not so much as a halfpenny a pound*; and, moreover, that the parson of the parish maintained out of the tithes all those persons in the parish that were reduced to indigence by means of old age or other cause of inability to labour. I should have told them this, and, in all probability, a great deal more, but I had not time; and, besides, they will have an opportunity of reading all about it in my little book called the *History of the Protestant Reformation*.

From Rogate we came on to Trotten, where a Mr Twyford is the squire, and where there is a very fine and ancient church close by the squire's house. I saw the squire looking at some poor devils who were making 'wauste improvements, ma'am', on the road which passes by the squire's door. He looked uncommonly hard at me. It was a scrutinizing sort of look, mixed, as I thought, with a little surprise, if not of jealousy, as much as to say, 'I wonder who the devil you can be?' My look at the squire was with the head a little on one side, and with the cheek drawn up from the left corner of the mouth, expressive of anything rather than a sense of inferiority to the squire, of whom, however, I had never heard speak before. Seeing the good and commodious and capacious church, I could not help reflecting on the intolerable baseness of this description of men, who have remained mute as fishes, while they have been taxed to build churches for the convenience of the cotton-lords and the stock-jobbers. First, their estates have been taxed to pay interest of debts contracted with these stock-jobbers, and to make wars for the sale of the goods of the cotton-lords. This drain upon their estates has collected the people into great masses, and now the same estates are taxed to build churches for them in these masses. And yet the tame fellows remain as silent as if they had been born deaf and dumb and blind . . .

From Trotten we came to Midhurst, and, having baited our horses, went into Cowdry Park to see the ruins of that once noble mansion, from which the Countess of Salisbury (the last of the Plantagenets) was brought by the tyrant Henry VIII to be cruelly murdered, in revenge for the integrity and other great virtues of her son, Cardinal Pole, as we have seen in . . . the *History of the Protestant Reformation* . . . It was . . . Lord Montague, I believe, who had this ancient and noble mansion completely repaired and fitted up as a place of residence: and a few days, or a very few weeks, at any rate, after the work was completed, the house was set on fire (by accident, I suppose), and left nearly in the state in which it now stands, except that the ivy has grown up about it, and partly hidden the stones from our sight. You may see, however, the hour of the day or night at which the fire took place; for there still remains the brass of the face of the clock and the hand pointing to the hour. Close by this mansion there runs a little river which runs winding away through the valleys, and at last falls into the Arron. After viewing the ruins, we had to return to the turn-pike road, and then enter another part of the park, which we crossed in order to go to Petworth. When you are in a part of this road through the park, you look down and see the house in the middle of a very fine valley, the distant boundary of which, to the south and south-west, is the South Down Hills. Some of the trees here are very fine, particularly some most magnificent rows of the Spanish chestnut. . . . The land is very good about here. It is fine rich loam at top, with clay further down. It is good for all sorts of trees, and they seem to grow here very fast.

We got to Petworth pretty early in the day. On entering it you see the house of Lord Egremont, which is close up against the park-wall, and which wall bounds this little vale on two sides. There is a sort of town-hall here, and on one side of it there is the bust of Charles II, I should have thought; but they tell me it is that of Sir William Wyndham, from whom Lord Egremont is descended. But there is *another building*, much more capacious and magnificent than the town-hall; namely, the Bridewell, which, from the modernness of its structure, appears to be one of those 'wauste improvements, ma'am', which distinguish this *enlightened* age. This structure vies, in point of magnitude, with the house of Lord Egremont itself, though that is one of the largest mansions in the whole kingdom. The Bridewell has a wall round it that I should suppose to be twenty feet high. This place was not wanted when the labourer got twice as much instead of half as much as the common standing soldier. Here you see the true cause why the young labouring man is 'content' to exist upon 7*d*. a day for six days a week, and nothing for Sunday. Oh! we are a most free and enlightened people; our happy constitution in church and state has supplanted Popery and slavery; but we go to a Bridewell unless we quietly exist and work upon 7*d.* a day!

Thursley, Sunday, 13 Nov.

To our great delight we found Richard's horse quite well this morning and off we set for this place. The first part of our road, for about three miles and a half, was through Lord Egremont's park. The morning was very fine; the sun shining; a sharp frost after a foggy

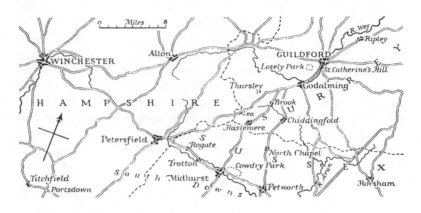

evening; the grass all white, the twigs of the trees white, the ponds frozen over; and everything looking exceedingly beautiful. The spot itself being one of the very finest in the world, not excepting, I dare say, that of the father of Saxe Cobourg itself, who has, doubtless, many such fine palaces.

In a very fine pond, not far from the house and close by the road, there are some little artificial islands, upon one of which I observed an arbutus loaded with its beautiful fruit (quite ripe) even more thickly than any one I ever saw even in America. There were, on the side of the pond, a most numerous and beautiful collection of waterfowl, foreign as well as domestic. I never saw so great a variety of water-fowl collected together in my life. They had been ejected from the water by the frost, and were sitting apparently in a state of great dejection; but this circumstance had brought them into a comparatively small compass; and we facing our horses about, sat and looked at them, at the pond, at the grass, at the house, till we were tired of admiring. Everything here is in the neatest and most beautiful state. Endless herds of deer, of all the varieties of colours; and what adds greatly to your pleasure in such a case, you see comfortable retreats prepared for them in different parts of the woods. When we came to what we thought the end of the park, the gate-keeper told us that we should find other walls to pass through. We now entered upon woods, we then came to another wall, and there we entered upon farms to our right and to our left. At last we came to a third wall, and the gate in that let us out into the turnpike-road. The gate-keeper here told us that the whole enclosure was *nine miles round*; and this, after all, forms, probably, not a quarter part of what this nobleman possesses. And is it wrong that one man should possess so much? By no means; but in my opinion it is wrong that a system should exist which compels this man to have his estate taken away from him unless he throw the junior branches of his family for maintenance upon the public.

Lord Egremont bears an excellent character. Everything that I have ever heard of him makes me believe that he is worthy of this princely estate. But I cannot forget that his two brothers, who are now very old men, have had, from their infancy, enormous revenues in sinecure places in the West Indies, while the general property and labour of England is taxed to maintain those West Indies in their state of dependence upon England; and I cannot forget that the burden of these sinecures are amongst the grievances of which the West Indians justly complain. True, the taxing system has taken from the family of Wyndham, during the lives of these two gentlemen, as much, and even more, than what that family has gained by those sinecures; but then let it be recollected that it is not the helpless people of England who have been the cause of this system. It is not the fault of those who receive 7*d*. a day. It is the fault of the family of Wyndham and of such persons; and if they have chosen to suffer the Jews and jobbers to take away so large a part of their income, it is not fair for them to come to the people at large to make up for the loss . . .

North Chapel is a little town in the Weald of Sussex where there were formerly post-chaises kept; but where there are none kept now. And here is another complete revolution. In almost every country town the post-chaise houses have been lessened in number, and those that remain have become comparatively solitary and mean. The guests at inns are not now gentlemen, but *bumpers*, who, from being called (at the inns) 'riders' became 'travellers', and are now 'commercial gentlemen', who go about in *gigs*, instead of on horseback, and who are in such numbers as to occupy a great part of the room in all the inns in every part of the country. There are, probably, twenty thousand of them always out, who may perhaps have, on an average throughout the year, three or four thousand 'ladies' travelling, with them. The expense of this can be little short of fifteen millions a year, all to be paid by the country people who consume the goods, and a large part of it to be drawn up to the Wen.

From North Chapel we came to Chiddingfold, which is in the Weald of Surrey; that is to say, the country of oak-timber. Between these two places there are a couple of pieces of that famous commodity called 'government property'. It seems that these places, which have extensive buildings on them, were for the purpose of making gunpowder. Like most other of these enterprises, they have been given up, after a time, and so the ground and all the buildings, and the monstrous fences, erected at enormous expense, have been sold. They were sold, it seems, some time ago, in lots, with the intention of being pulled down and carried away, though they are now nearly new, and built in the most solid, substantial, and expensive manner; brick walls eighteen inches through, and the buildings covered with lead and slate. It appears that they have been purchased by a Mr Stovell, a Sussex banker; but for some reason or other, though the purchase was made long ago, 'government' still holds the possession; and, what is more, it keeps people there to take care of the premises. It would be curious to have a complete history of these pretty establishments at Chiddingfold; but this is a sort of history that we shall never be treated with until there be somebody in Parliament to rummage things to the bottom. It would be very easy to call for a specific account of the cost of these establishments, and also of the quantity of powder made at them. I should not be at all surprised if the concern, all taken together, brought the powder to a hundred times the price at which similar powder could have been purchased.

When we came through Chiddingfold the people were just going to church; and we saw a carriage and pair conveying an old gentleman and some ladies to the churchyard steps. Upon inquiry, we found that this was Lord Winterton, whose name, they told us, was Turnour. I thought I had heard of all the lords, first or last; but if I had ever heard of this one before, I had forgotten him. He lives down in the Weald, between the gunpowder establishments and

Horsham, and has the reputation of being a harmless, good sort of man, and that being the case I was sorry to see that he appeared to be greatly afflicted with the gout, being obliged to be helped up the steps by a stout man. However, it is as broad, perhaps, as it is long: a man is not to have all the enjoyments of making the gout, and the enjoyments of abstinence, too: that would not be fair play; and I dare say that Lord Winterton is just enough to be content with the consequences of his enjoyments.

This Chiddingfold is a very pretty place. There is a very pretty and extensive green opposite the church; and we were at the proper time of the day to perceive that the modern system of education had by no means overlooked this little village. We saw *the schools* marching towards the church in military order. Two of them passed us on our road. The boys looked very hard at us, and I saluted them with, 'There's brave boys, you'll all be parsons or lawyers or doctors.' Another school seemed to be in a less happy state. The scholars were too much in uniform to have had their clothes purchased by their parents; and they looked, besides, as if a little more victuals and a little less education would have done as well. There were about twenty of them without one single tinge of red in their whole twenty faces. In short I never saw more deplorable looking objects since I was born. And can it be of any use to expend money in this sort of way upon poor creatures that have not half a bellyfull of food? We had not breakfasted when we passed them. We felt, at that moment, what hunger was. We had some bits of bread and meat in our pockets, however; and these, which were merely intended as stay-stomachs, amounted, I dare say, to the allowance of any half dozen of these poor boys for the day. I could, with all my heart, have pulled the victuals out of my pocket and given them to them; but I did not like to do that which would have interrupted the march, and might have been construed into a sort of insult. To quiet my conscience, however, I gave a poor man that I met soon afterwards sixpence, under the pretence of rewarding him for telling me the way to Thursley, which I knew as well as he, and which I had determined, in my own mind, not to follow.

We had now come on the turnpike-road from my Lord Egremont's park to Chiddingfold. I had made two or three attempts to get out of it, and to bear away to the north-west, to get through the oak-woods to Thursley; but I was constantly prevented by being told that the road which I wished to take would lead me to Haslemere. If you talk to ostlers, or landlords, or post-boys; or, indeed, to almost anybody else, they mean by a *road* a *turnpike-road*; and they positively will not talk to you about any other. Now, just after quitting Chiddingfold, Thursley lies over fine woods and coppices, in a north-west direction, or thereabouts; and the turnpike-road, which goes from Petworth to Godalming, goes in a north-north-east direction. I was resolved, be the consequences what they might, not to follow the turnpike-road one single inch further; for I had not above three miles or thereabouts to get to Thursley, through the woods; and I had, perhaps, six miles at least to get to it the other way; but the great thing was to see the interior of these woods; to see the stems of the trees, as well as the tops of them. I saw a lane opening the right direction; I saw indeed that my horses must go up to their knees in clay; but I resolved to enter and go along that lane, and long before the end of my journey I found myself most amply compensated for the toil that I was about to encounter. But talk of toil! It was the horse that had the toil; and I had nothing to do but to sit upon his back, turn my head from side to side and admire the fine trees in every direction. Little bits of fields and meadows here and there, shaded all over, or nearly all over, by the surrounding trees. Here and there a labourer's house buried in the woods. We had drawn out our luncheons and eaten them while the horses took us through the clay; but I stopped at a little house and asked the woman, who looked very clean and nice, whether she would let us dine with her. She said 'Yes' with all her heart, but that she had no place to put our horses in, and that her dinner would not be ready for an hour, when she expected her husband home from church. She said they had a bit of bacon and a pudding and some cabbage; but that she had not much bread in the house. She had only one child, and that was not very old, so we left her, quite convinced that my old observation is true, that people in the woodland counties are best off, and that it is absolutely impossible to reduce them to that state of starvation in which they are in the corn-growing part of the kingdom. Here is that great blessing, abundance of fuel at all times of the year, and particularly in the winter.

We came on for about a mile further in these clayey lanes, when we renewed our inquiries as to our course, as our road now seemed to point towards Godalming again. I asked a man how I should get to Thursley? He pointed to some fir-trees upon a hill, told me I must go by them, and that there was no other way. 'Where then,' said I, 'is Thursley?' He pointed with his hand and said, 'Right over those woods; but there is no road there, and it is impossible for you to get through those woods.' 'Thank you,' said I; 'but through those woods we mean to go.' Just at the border of the woods I saw a cottage. There must be some way to that cottage; and we soon found a gate that let us into a field, across which we went to this cottage. We there found an old man and a young one. Upon inquiry we found that it was *possible* to get through these woods. Richard gave the old man threepence to buy a pint of beer, and I gave the young one a shilling to pilot us through the woods. These were oak-woods with under-wood beneath; and there was a little stream of water running down the middle of the woods, the annual and long overflowings of which has formed a meadow sometimes a rod wide, and sometimes twenty rods wide, while the bed of the stream itself was the most serpentine that can possibly be imagined, describing, in many places, nearly a complete circle, going round for many rods together, and coming within a rod or two of a point that it had passed before. I stopped the man several times to sit and admire this beautiful spot, shaded in great part by lofty and widespreading oak-trees. We had to cross this brook several times, over bridges that the owner had erected for the convenience of fox-hunters. At last, we came into an ash-coppice, which had been planted in regular rows, at about four feet distances, which had been once cut, and which was now in a state of six years' growth. A road through it, made for the fox-hunters, was as straight as a line, and of so great a length that, on entering it, the further end appeared not to be a foot wide. Upon seeing this, I asked the man whom these coppices belonged to, and he told me to Squire Leech, at Lea. My surprise ceased, but my admiration did not.

A piece of ordinary coppice ground, close adjoining this, and with no timber in it, and upon just the same soil (if there had been such a piece), would, at ten years' growth, be worth, at present prices, from five to seven pounds the acre. This coppice, at ten years' growth, will be worth twenty pounds the acre; and, at the next cutting, when the stems will send out so many more shoots, it will be worth thirty pounds the acre. I did not ask the question when I afterwards saw Mr Leech, but, I dare say, the ground was trenched before it was planted; but what is that expense when compared with the great, the permanent profit of such an undertaking! And, above all things, what a convenient species of property does a man here create. Here are no tenants' rack, no anxiety about crops and seasons; the rust and the mildew never come here; a man knows what he has got, and he knows that nothing short of an earthquake can take it from him, unless, indeed, by attempting to vie with the stock-jobber in the expense of living, he enable the stock-jobber to come and perform the office of the earthquake. Mr Leech's father planted, I think it was forty acres of such coppice in the same manner; and, at the same time, he *sowed the ground with acorns*. The acorns have become oak-trees, and have begun and made great progress in diminishing the value of the ash, which have now to contend against the shade and the roots of the oak. For present profit, and, indeed, for permanent profit, it would be judicious to grub up the oak; but the owner has determined otherwise. He cannot endure the idea of destroying an oak wood . . .

We got to Thursley after our beautiful ride through Mr Leech's coppices, and the weather being pretty cold, we found ourselves most happily situated here by the side of an *American fireplace*, making extremely comfortable a room which was formerly amongst the most uncomfortable in the world. This is another of what the malignant parsons call Cobbett's Quackeries. But my real opinion is that the whole body of them, all put together, have never, since they were born, conferred so much benefit upon the country as I have conferred upon it by introducing this fireplace . . .

Kensington, Sunday, 20 Nov.
Coming to Godalming on Friday, where business kept us that night, we had to experience at the inn the want of our American fireplace. A large and long room to sit in, with a miserable thing called a screen to keep the wind from our backs, with a smoke in the room half an hour after the fire was lighted, we, consuming a full bushel of coals in order to keep us warm, were not half so well off as we should have been in the same room, and without any screen, and with two gallons of coals, if we had our American fireplace. I gave the landlord my advice upon the subject . . .

It looked like rain on Saturday morning, we therefore sent our horses on from Godalming to Ripley, and took a post-chaise to convey us after them. Being shut up in the post-chaise did not prevent me from taking a look at a little snug house stuck under the hill on the roadside, just opposite the old chapel on St Catherine's Hill, which house was not there when I was a boy. I found that this house is now occupied by the family Molyneux, for ages the owners of Losely Park, on the outskirts of which estate this house stands. The house at Losely is of great antiquity, and had, or perhaps has, attached to it the great manors of Godalming and Chiddingfold. I believe that Sir Thomas More lived at Losely, or, at any rate, that the Molyneuxes are, in some degree, descended from him . . .

When we got to Ripley, we found the day very fine, and we got upon our horses and rode home to dinner, after an absence of just one month, agreeably to our original intention, having seen a great deal of the country, having had a great deal of sport, and having, I trust, laid in a stock of health for the winter, sufficient to enable us to withstand the suffocation of this smoking and stinking Wen.

But Richard and I have done something else besides ride, and hunt, and course, and stare about us, during this month. He was eleven years old last March, and it was now time for him to begin to know something about letters and figures. He has learned to work in the garden, and having been a good deal in the country, knows a great deal about farming affairs. He can ride anything of a horse, and over anything that a horse will go over. So expert at hunting, that his first teacher, Mr Budd, gave the hounds up to his management in the field; but now he begins to talk about nothing but *fox hunting*! That is a dangerous thing. When he and I went from home, I had business in Reigate. It was a very wet morning, and we went off long before daylight in a post-chaise, intending to have our horses brought after us. He began to talk in anticipation of the sport he was going to have, and was very inquisitive as to the probability of our meeting with fox-hounds, which gave me occasion to address him thus: 'Fox-hunting is a very fine thing, and very proper for people to be engaged in, and it is very desirable to be able to ride well and to be in at the death; but that is not ALL; that is not everything. Any fool can ride a horse and draw a cover; any groom or any stable-fellow, who is as ignorant as the horse, can do these things; but all gentlemen that go a-fox-hunting' (I hope God will forgive me for the lie) 'are scholars, Richard. It is not the riding, nor the scarlet coats, that make them gentlemen, it is their scholarship.' What he thought I do not know; for he sat as mute as a fish, and I could not see his countenance. 'So,' said I, 'you must now begin to learn something, and you must begin with arithmetic.' He had learned from mere play to read, being first set to work of his own accord . . . That had induced us to give him *Robinson Crusoe*; and that had made him a passable reader. Then he had scrawled down letters and words upon paper, and had written letters to me in the strangest way imaginable. His knowledge of figures he had acquired from the necessity of knowing the several numbers upon the barrels of seeds brought from America, and the numbers upon the doors of houses. So that I had pretty nearly a blank sheet of paper to begin upon; and I have always held it to be stupidity to the last degree to attempt to put book-learning into children who are too young to reason with.

I began with a pretty long lecture on the utility of arithmetic; the absolute necessity of it, in order for us to make out our accounts of the trees and seeds that we should have to sell in the winter, and the utter impossibility of our getting paid for our pains unless we were able to make out our accounts, which accounts could not be made out unless we understood something about arithmetic. Having thus made him understand the utility of the thing, and given him a very strong instance in the case of our nursery affairs, I proceeded to explain to him the meaning of the word arithmetic, the power of figures, according to the place they occupied. I then, for it was still dark, taught him to add a few figures together, I naming the figures one after another, while he, at the mention of each new figure, said the amount, and if incorrectly, he was corrected by me. When we had got a sum of about 24, I said now there is another line of figures on the left of this, and therefore you are to put down the 4 and carry 2. 'What is *carrying*?' said he. I then explained to him the *why* and the *wherefore* of this, and he perfectly understood me at once. We then did several other little sums; and by the time we got to Sutton, it becoming daylight, I took a pencil and set him a little sum on paper, which, after making a mistake or two, he did very well. By the time we got to Reigate he had done several more, and at last a pretty long one, with very few errors. We had business all day, and thought no more of our scholarship until we went to bed, and then we did, in our postchaise fashion, a great many lines in arithmetic before we went to sleep. Thus we went on mixing our riding and hunting with our arithmetic, until we quitted Godalming, when he did a sum very nicely in *multiplication of money*, falling a little short of what I had laid out, which was to make him learn the four rules in whole numbers first, and then in money, before I got home.

Friends' houses are not so good as inns for executing a project like this; because you cannot very well be by yourself; and we slept but four nights at inns during our absence. So that we have actually stolen the time to accomplish this job, and Richard's journal records that he was more than fifteen days out of the thirty-one coursing or hunting. Nothing struck me more than the facility, the perfect readiness with which he at once performed addition of money. There is a *pence table* which boys usually learn, and during the learning of which they usually get no small number of thumps. This table I found it wholly unnecessary to set him. I had written it for him in one of the leaves of his journal book. But upon looking at it, he said, 'I don't want this, because, you know, I have nothing to do but *divide by twelve*.' That is right, said I, you are a clever fellow, Dick; and I shut up the book.

Now when there is so much talk about education, let me ask how many pounds it generally costs parents to have a boy taught this much of arithmetic; how much time it costs also; and, which is a far more serious consideration, how much mortification, and very often how much loss of health, it costs the poor scolded broken-hearted child, who becomes dunder-headed and dull for all his life-time, merely because that has been imposed upon him as a task which he ought to regard as an object of pleasant pursuit. I never even once desired him to stay a moment from any other thing that he had a mind to go at. I just wrote the sums down upon paper, laid them upon the table, and left him to tackle them when he pleased. In the case of the multiplication table, the learning of which is something of a job, and which it is absolutely necessary to learn perfectly, I advised him to go up into his bedroom and read it twenty times over out loud every morning before he went a-hunting, and ten times over every night after he came back, till it all came as pat upon his lips as the names of the persons he knew. He did this, and at the end of about a week he was ready to set on upon multiplication. It is the irksomeness of the thing which is the great bar to learning of every sort. I took care not to suffer irksomeness to seize his mind for a moment, and the consequence was that which I have described. I wish clearly to be understood as ascribing nothing to extraordinary *natural* ability. There are, as I have often said, as many *sorts* of men as there are of dogs; but I do not pretend to be of any peculiarly excellent sort, and I have never discovered any indications of it. There are, to be sure, sorts that are naturally stupid; but the generality of men are not so; and I believe that every boy of the same age, equally healthy, and brought up in the same manner, would (unless of one of the stupid kinds) learn in just the same sort of way; but not if begun to be thumped at five or six years old, when the poor little things have no idea of the utility of anything; who are hardly sensible beings, and have but just understanding enough to know that it will hurt them if they jump down a chalk pit. I am sure, from thousands of instances that have come under my own eyes, that to begin to teach children book-learning before they are capable of reasoning is the sure and certain way to enfeeble their minds for life; and if they have natural genius, to cramp, if not totally to destroy, that genius . . .

I look upon my boy as being like other boys in general. Their fathers can teach arithmetic as well as I; and if they have not a mind to pursue my method, they must pursue their own. Let them apply to the outside of the head and to the back, if they like; let them bargain for thumps and the birch rod; it is their affair and not mine. I never yet saw in my house a child that was *afraid*; that was in any fear whatever; that was ever for a moment under any sort of apprehension, on account of the learning of anything; and I never in my life gave a command, an order, a request, or even advice, to look into any book; and I am quite satisfied that the way to make children dunces, to make them detest books, and justify that detestation, is to tease them and bother them upon the subject.

As to the age at which children ought to begin to be taught, it is very curious that, while I was at a friend's house during my ride, I looked into, by mere accident, a little child's abridgement of the History of England: a little thing about twice as big as a crown-piece. Even into this abridgement the historian had introduced the circumstance of Alfred's father, who, 'through a *mistaken notion* of kindness to his son, had suffered him to live to the age of twelve years without any attempt being made to give him education'. How came this writer to know that it was a *mistaken notion*? Ought he not rather, when he looked at the result, when he considered the astonishing knowledge and great deeds of Alfred, ought he not to have hesitated before he thus criticised the notions of his father? It appears from the result that the notions of the father were perfectly correct; and I am satisfied that if they had begun to thump the head of Alfred when he was a child, we should not at this day have heard talk of Alfred the Great.

[*Rural Rides* 11, 1–23]

[v] *Northern Tour*

Sheffield, 31 January 1830.

On the 26th instant I gave my third lecture at Leeds. I should in vain endeavour to give an adequate description of the pleasure which I felt at my reception, and at the effect which I produced in that fine and opulent capital of this great county of York; for the *capital* it is in fact, though not in name. On the first evening, the playhouse, which is pretty spacious, was not completely filled in all its parts; but on the second and the third it was filled brim full, boxes, pit and gallery; besides a dozen or two of gentlemen who were accommodated with seats on the stage. Owing to a cold which I took at Huddersfield . . . I was, as the players call it, not in very good *voice*; but the audience made allowance for that, and very wisely preferred sense to sound. I never was more delighted than with my audience at Leeds; and what I set the highest value on is, that I find I produced a prodigious effect in that important town.

There had been a meeting at Doncaster a few days before I went to Leeds from Ripley, where one of the speakers, a Mr Becket Denison, had said, speaking of the taxes, that there must be an application of the *pruning hook* or of the *sponge*. This gentleman is a banker, I believe: he is one of the Beckets connected with the Lowthers; and he is a brother, or very near relation, of that Sir John Becket, who is judge advocate general. So that, at last, others can talk of the pruning hook and the sponge as well as I.

From Leeds I proceeded on to this place, not being able to stop at either Wakefield or Barnsley, except merely to change horses. The people in those towns were apprized of the time that I should pass through them; and, at each place, great numbers assembled to see me, to shake me by the hand, and to request me to stop. I was so hoarse as not to be able to make the post-boy hear me when I called to him; and, therefore, it would have been useless to stop; yet I promised to go back if my time and my voice would allow me. They do not; and I have written to the gentlemen of those places to inform them that when I go to Scotland in the spring I will not fail to stop in those towns, in order to express my gratitude to them. All the way along from Leeds to Sheffield it is coal and iron, and iron and coal. It was dark before we reached Sheffield; so that we saw the iron furnaces in all the horrible splendour of their everlasting blaze.

Nothing can be conceived more grand or more terrific than the yellow waves of fire that incessantly issue from the top of these furnaces, some of which are close by the way-side. Nature has placed the beds of iron and the beds of coal alongside of each other, and art has taught man to make one operate upon the other, as to turn the iron-stone into liquid matter, which is drained off from the bottom of the furnace, and afterwards moulded into blocks and bars, and all

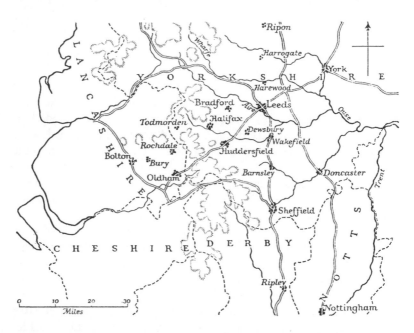

sorts of things. The combustibles are put into the top of the furnace, which stands thirty, forty or fifty feet up in the air, and the ever-blazing mouth of which is kept supplied with coal and coke and iron-stone from little iron waggons forced up by steam, and brought down again to be refilled. It is a surprising thing to behold; and it is impossible to behold it without being convinced that, whatever other nations may do with cotton and with wool, they will never equal England with regard to things made of iron and steel. This Sheffield, and the land all about it, is one bed of iron and coal. They call it black Sheffield, and black enough it is; but from this one town and its environs go nine-tenths of the knives that are used in the whole world; there being, I understand, no knives made at Birmingham;

the manufacture of which place consists of the larger sort of implements, of locks of all sorts, and guns and swords, and of all the endless articles of hardware which go to the furnishing of a house. As to the land, viewed in the way of agriculture, it really does appear to be very little worth. I have not seen, except at Harewood and Ripley, a stack of wheat since I came into Yorkshire; and even there, the whole I saw; and all that I have seen since I came into Yorkshire; and all that I saw during a ride of six miles that I took into Derbyshire the day before yesterday; all put together would not make the one-half of what I have many times seen in one single rick-yard of the vales of Wiltshire. But this is all very proper: these coal-diggers, and iron-melters, and knife-makers, compel us to send the food to them, which, indeed, we do very cheerfully, in exchange for the produce of their rocks, and the wondrous works of their hands.

The trade of Sheffield has fallen off less in proportion than that of the other manufacturing districts. North America, and particularly the United States, where the people have so much victuals to cut, form a great branch of the custom of this town. If the people of Sheffield could only receive a tenth part of what their knives sell for by retail in America, Sheffield might pave its streets with silver. A gross of knives and forks is sold to the Americans for less than three knives and forks can be bought at retail in a country store in America. No fear of rivalship in this trade. The Americans may lay on their tariff, and double it and triple it; but as long as they continue to cut their victuals from Sheffield they must have the things to cut it with.

The ragged hills all round about this town are bespangled with groups of houses inhabited by the working cutlers. They have not suffered like the working weavers; for to make knives there must be the hand of man. Therefore, machinery cannot come to destroy the wages of the labourer. The home demand has been very much diminished; but still the depression has here not been what it has been, and what it is where the machinery can be brought into play. We are here just upon the borders of Derbyshire, a nook of which runs up and separates Yorkshire from Nottinghamshire. I went to a village, the day before yesterday, called Mosborough, the whole of the people of which are employed in the making of sickles and scythes; and where, as I was told, they are very well off even in these times. A prodigious quantity of these things go to the United States of America. In short, there are about twelve millions of people there continually consuming these things; and the hardware merchants here have their agents and their stores in the great towns of America; which country, as far as relates to this branch of business, is still a part of old England.

Upon my arriving here on Wednesday night, the 27th instant, I by no means intended to lecture until I should be a little recovered from my cold; but, to my great mortification, I found that the lecture had been advertised, and that great numbers of persons had actually assembled. To send them out again, and give back the money, was a thing not to be attempted. I, therefore, went to the music hall, the place which had been taken for the purpose, gave them a specimen of the state of my voice, asked them whether I should proceed, and they answering in the affirmative, on I went. I then rested until yesterday, and shall conclude my labours here tomorrow, and then proceed to 'fair Nottingham' as we used to sing when I was a boy, in celebrating the glorious exploits of 'Robin Hood and Little John'. By the by, as we went from Huddersfield to Dewsbury, we passed by a hill which is celebrated as being the burial-place of the famed Robin Hood, of whom the people in this country talk to this day.

At Nottingham they have advertised for my lecturing at the playhouse for the 3rd, 4th, and 5th of February, and for a public breakfast to be given to me on the first of those days, I having declined a dinner agreeably to my original notification, and my friends insisting upon something or other in that sort of way. It is very curious that I have always had a very great desire to see Nottingham. This desire certainly originated in the great interest I used to take, and that all country boys took, in the history of Robin Hood, in the record of whose achievements, which were so well calculated to excite admiration in the country boys, this Nottingham, with the word 'fair' always before it, was so often mentioned. The word *fair*, as used by our forefathers, meant fine; for we frequently read in old descriptions of parts of the country of such a district or such a parish containing a *fair* mansion and the like; so that this town appears to have been celebrated as a very fine place, even in ancient times; but within the last thirty years Nottingham has stood high in my estimation from the conduct of its people; from their public spirit; from their excellent sense as to public matters; from the noble struggle which they have made from the beginning of the French war to the present hour; if only forty towns in England equal in size to Nottingham had followed its bright example, there would have been no French war against liberty; the debt would have been now nearly paid off, and we should have known nothing of those manifold miseries which now afflict, and those greater miseries which now menace, the country. The French would not have been in Cadiz; the Russians would not have been at Constantinople; the Americans would not have been in the Floridas; we should not have had to dread the combined fleets of America, France, and Russia; and, which is the worst of all, we should not have seen Englishmen reduced to such a state of misery as for the honest labouring man to be fed worse than the felons in the gaols.

[Rural Rides II, 216–19]

[vi] *Ipswich and Bury St Edmunds*

I know of no town to be compared with Ipswich, except it be Nottingham; and there is this difference in the two; that Nottingham stands high, and, on one side, looks over a very fine country; whereas Ipswich is in a dell, meadows running up above it, and a beautiful arm of the sea below it. The town itself is substantially built, well paved, everything good and solid, and no wretched dwellings to be seen on its outskirts. From the town itself you can see nothing; but you can, in no direction, go from it a quarter of a mile without finding views that a painter might crave, and then the country round about it so well cultivated; the land in such a beautiful state, the farmhouses all white and so much alike; the barns, and everything about the homesteads so snug; the stocks of turnips so abundant everywhere; the sheep and cattle in such fine order; the wheat all drilled; the ploughman so expert; the furrows, if a quarter of a mile long, as straight as a line, and laid as truly as if with a level: in short, here is everything to delight the eye, and to make the people proud of their country; and this is the case throughout the whole of this county. I have always found Suffolk farmers great boasters of their superiority over others; and I must say that it is not without reason.

But observe this has been a very *highly-favoured county*: it has had poured into it millions upon millions of money, drawn from Wiltshire and other inland counties. I should suppose that Wiltshire alone has, within the last forty years, had two or three millions of money drawn from it, *to be given to Essex and Suffolk*. At one time there were not less than sixty thousand men kept on foot in these counties. The increase of London, too, the swelling of the immortal Wen, have assisted to heap wealth upon these counties; but, in spite of all this, the distress pervades all ranks and all degrees, except those who live on the taxes. At Eye, butter used to sell for eightpence a pound: now it sells for ninepence halfpenny, though the grass has not yet begun to spring; and eggs were sold at thirty for a shilling. Fine times for me whose principal food is eggs and whose sole drink is milk, but very bad times for those who sell me the food and the drink.

Coming from Ipswich to Bury St Edmunds, you pass through Needham Market and Stowmarket, two very pretty market towns; and, like all the other towns in Suffolk, free from the drawback of shabby and beggarly houses on the outskirts. I remarked that I did not see in the whole county one single instance of paper or rags supplying the place of glass in any window, and did not see one miserable hovel in which a labourer resided. The county, however, is *flat*: with the exception of the environs of Ipswich, there is none of that beautiful variety of hill and dale and hanging woods that you see at every town in Hampshire, Sussex and Kent. It is curious, too, that though the people, I mean the poorer classes of people, are extremely neat in their houses, and though I found all their gardens dug up and prepared for cropping, you do not see about their cottages (and it is just the same in Norfolk) that ornamental gardening; the walks, and the flower borders, and the honeysuckles and roses trained over the doors or over arched sticks, that you see in Hampshire, Sussex, and Kent, that I have many a time sitten upon my horse to look at so long and so often, as greatly to retard me on my journey. Nor is this done for show or for ostentation. If you find a cottage in those counties, by the side of a by *lane*, or in the midst of a forest, you find just the same care about the garden and the flowers. In those counties, too, there is great taste with regard to *trees* of every description, from the hazel to the oak. In Suffolk it appears to be just the contrary: here is the great dissight of all these three eastern counties. Almost every bank of every field is studded with *pollards*, that is to say, trees that have been beheaded, at from six to twelve feet from the ground, than which nothing in nature can be more ugly. They send out shoots from the head, which are lopped off once in ten or a dozen years for fuel, or other purposes. To add to the deformity, the ivy is suffered to grow on them which, at the same time, checks the growth of the shoots. These pollards become hollow very soon and, as timber, are fit for nothing but gateposts, even before they be hollow. Upon a farm of a hundred acres these pollards, by root and shade, spoil at least six acres of the ground, besides being most destructive to the fences. Why not plant six acres of the ground with timber and underwood? Half an acre a year would most amply supply the farm with poles and brush, and with everything wanted in the way of fuel; and why not plant hedges to be unbroken by these pollards? I have scarcely seen a single farm of a hundred acres without pollards sufficient to find the farm-house in fuel, without any assistance from coals, for several years.

However, the great number of farm-houses in Suffolk, the neatness of those houses, the moderation in point of extent which you generally see, and the great store of the food in the turnips, and the admirable management of the whole, form a pretty good compensation for the want of beauties. The land is generally as clean as a garden ought to be; and though it varies a good deal as to lightness and stiffness, they make it all bear prodigious quantities of swedish turnips; and on them pigs, sheep, and cattle all equally thrive. I did not observe a single poor miserable animal in the whole county.

To conclude an account of Suffolk and not to sing the praises of Bury St Edmund's would offend every creature of Suffolk birth; even at Ipswich, when I was praising that place, the very people of that town asked me if I did not think Bury St Edmund's the nicest town in the world. Meet them wherever you will, they have all the same boast; and indeed, as a town *in itself*, it is the neatest place that ever was seen. It is airy, it has several fine open places in it, and it has the remains of the famous abbey walls and the abbey gate entire; and it is so clean and so neat that nothing can equal it in that respect. It was a favourite spot in ancient times; greatly endowed with monasteries and hospitals. Besides the famous Benedictine Abbey, there was once a college and a friary; and as to the abbey itself, it was one of the greatest in the kingdom; and was so ancient as to have been founded only about forty years after the landing of St Austin in Kent. The land all round about it is good; and the soil is of that nature as not to produce much dirt at any time of the year; but the country about it is *flat*, and not of that beautiful variety that we find at Ipswich.

After all, what is the reflection now called for? It is that this fine county, for which nature has done all that she can do, soil, climate, sea-ports, people; everything that can be done, and an internal government, civil and ecclesiastical, the most complete in the world,

wanting nothing but to *be let alone*, to make every soul in it as happy
as people can be upon earth; the peace provided for by the county
rates; property protected by the law of the land; the poor provided for
by the poor-rates; religion provided for by the tithes and the church-
rates; easy and safe conveyance provided for by the highway-rates;
extraordinary danger provided against by the militia-rates; a complete government in itself; *but having to pay a portion of sixty millions*

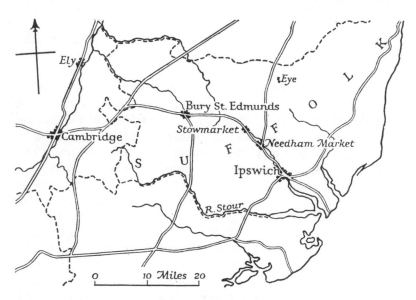

*a year in taxes over and above all this; and that, too, on account of
wars carried on, not for the defence of England; not for the upholding
of English liberty and happiness, but for the purpose of crushing
liberty and happiness in other countries; and all this because, and
only because, a septennial Parliament has deprived the people of
their rights.*

That which we *admire* most is not always that which would be
our choice. One might imagine that after all that I have said about
this fine country, I should certainly prefer it as a place of residence.
I should not, however: my choice has been always very much divided
between the woods of Sussex and the downs of Wiltshire. I should
not like to be compelled to decide: but if I were compelled, I do
believe that I should fix on some vale in Wiltshire. Water meadows
at the bottom, corn-land going up towards the hills, those hills being

down land, and a farm-house, in a clump of trees, in some little cross vale between the hills, sheltered on every side but the south . . .

[*Rural Rides* 11, 225–8] [MARCH 1830]

[vii] *Ely Cathedral*

I knew that Ely was a small place, but I was determined to go to see the spot where the militia-men were flogged, and also determined to find some opportunity or other of relating that story as publicly as I could . . . Arrived at Ely, I first walked round the beautiful cathedral, that honour to our Catholic forefathers, and that standing disgrace to our Protestant selves. It is impossible to look at that magnificent pile without *feeling* that we are a fallen race of men. The cathedral would, leaving out the palace of the bishop and the houses of the dean, canons and prebendaries, weigh more, if it were put into a scale, than all the houses in the town, and all the houses for a mile round the neighbourhood if you exclude the remains of the ancient monasteries. You have only to open your eyes to be convinced that England must have been a far greater and more wealthy country in those days than it is in these days. The hundreds of thousands of loads of stone, of which this cathedral and the monasteries in the neighbourhood were built, must all have been brought by sea from distant parts of the kingdom. These foundations were laid more than a thousand years ago; and yet there are vagabonds who have the impudence to say that it is the Protestant religion that has made England a great country.

Ely is what one may call a miserable little town: very prettily situated, but poor and mean. Everything seems to be on the decline, as, indeed, is the case everywhere, where the clergy are the masters. They say that this bishop has an income of £18,000 a year. He and the dean and chapter are the owners of all the land and tithes for a great distance round about in this beautiful and most productive part of the country; and yet this famous building, the cathedral, is in a state of disgraceful irrepair and disfigurement. The great and magnificent windows to the east have been shortened at the bottom, and the space plastered up with brick and mortar, in a very slovenly manner, for the purpose of saving the expense of keeping the glass in repair. Great numbers of the windows in the upper part of the build-ing have been partly closed up in the same manner, and others quite closed up. One door-way, which apparently had stood in need of repair, has been rebuilt in modern style, because it was cheaper; and the churchyard contained a flock of sheep acting as vergers for those who live upon the immense income, not a penny of which ought to be expended upon themselves while any part of this beautiful building is in a state of irrepair. This cathedral was erected 'to the honour of God and the Holy Church'. My daughters went to the service in the afternoon, in the choir of which they saw God honoured by the presence of *two old men*, forming the whole of the congregation. I dare say that in Catholic times five thousand people at a time have been assembled in this church. The cathedral and town stand upon a little hill, about three miles in circumference, raised up, as it were, for the purpose, amidst the rich fen land by which the hill is surrounded, and I dare say that the town formerly consisted of houses built over a great part of this hill, and of probably from fifty to a hundred thousand people. The people do not now exceed above four thousand, including the bed-ridden and the babies.

[*Rural Rides* 11, 229–30] [MARCH 1830]

[viii] *Progress in the North*

Newcastle upon Tyne, 23 September 1832. From Bolton, in Lancashire, I came through Bury and Rochdale to Todmorden, on the evening of Tuesday, the 18th September. I have formerly described the valley of Todmorden as the most curious and romantic that was ever seen, and where the water and the coal seemed to be engaged in a struggle for getting foremost in point of utility to man. On the 19th I stayed all day at Todmorden to write and to sleep. On the 20th I set off for Leeds by the stage coach, through Halifax and Bradford; and as to *agriculture*, certainly the poorest country that I have ever set my eyes on, except that miserable Nova Scotia . . . This country, from Todmorden to Leeds, is, however, covered over with population, and the two towns of Halifax and Bradford are exceedingly populous. There appears to be nothing produced by the earth but the natural grass of the country, which, however, is not bad. The soil is a sort of yellow-looking, stiffish stuff, lying about a foot thick, upon a bed of rocky stone, lying upon solid rock beneath. The grass does not seem to burn here; nor is it bad in quality; and all the grass appears to be wanted to rear milk for this immense population that absolutely covers the whole face of the country. The only grain crops that I saw were those of very miserable oats; some of which were cut and carried; some standing in *shock*, the sheaves not being more than about a foot and a half long; some still standing, and some yet *nearly green*. The land is very high from Halifax to Bradford, and proportionably cold. Here are some of those 'Yorkshire Hills' that they see from Lancashire and Cheshire.

I got to Leeds about four o'clock, and went to bed at eight precisely. At five in the morning of the 21st I came off by the coach to Newcastle, through Harrogate, Ripon, Darlington, and Durham. As I never was in this part of the country before, and can, therefore, never have described it upon any former occasion, I shall say rather more about it now than I otherwise should do. Having heard and read so much about the 'Northern Harvest', about the 'Durham Ploughs' and the 'Northumberland system of husbandry', what was my surprise at finding, which I verily believe to be the fact, that there is not as much corn grown in the North Riding of Yorkshire, which begins at Ripon, and in the whole county of Durham, as is grown in the Isle of Wight alone. A very small part, comparatively speaking, is *arable* land; and all the outward appearances show that that which is arable was formerly pasture. Between Durham and Newcastle there is a pretty general division of the land into grass fields and corn fields; but even here the absence of *homesteads*, the absence of barns, and of labourers' cottages, clearly show that agriculture is a sort of novelty; and that nearly all was pasturage not many years ago, or, at any rate, only so much of the land was cultivated as was necessary to furnish straw for the horses kept for other purposes than those of agriculture, and oats for those horses, and bread corn sufficient for the graziers and their people. All along the road from Leeds to Durham I saw hardly any wheat at all, or any wheat stubble, no barley, the chief crops being oats and beans mixed with peas. These everywhere appeared to be what we should deem most miserable crops. The oats, tied up in sheaves, or yet uncut, were scarcely ever more than two feet and a half long, the beans were about the same height, and in both cases the land so full of grass as to appear to be *a pasture*, after the oats and the beans were cut.

The land appears to be divided into very extensive farms. The corn, when cut, you see put up into little stacks of a circular form, each containing about *three* of our southern waggon-loads of sheaves, which stacks are put up round about the stone house and the buildings of the farmer. How they thrash them out I do not know, for I could see nothing resembling a barn or a barn's door. By the corn being put into such small stacks, I should suppose the thrashing places to be very small, and capable of holding only one stack at a time. I have many times seen one single rick containing a greater quantity of sheaves than fifteen or twenty of these stacks; and I have seen more than twenty stacks, each containing a number of sheaves equal to at least fifteen of these stacks; I have seen more than twenty of these large stacks standing at one and the same time in one single homestead in Wiltshire . . .

But this by no means implies that these are beggarly counties, even exclusive of their waters, coals, and mines. They are not agricultural counties; they are not counties for the producing of bread, but they are counties made for the express purpose of producing meat; in which respect they excel the southern counties in a degree beyond all comparison. I have just spoken of the *beds of grass* that are everywhere seen after the oats and the beans have been cut. Grass is the natural produce of this land, which seems to have been made on purpose to produce it; and we are not to call land poor because it will produce nothing but meat. The size and shape of the fields, the sort of fences, the absence of all homesteads and labourers' cottages, the thinness of the country churches, everything shows that this was always a country purely of pasturage. It is curious that, belonging to every farm, there appears to be a large quantity of turnips. They are sowed in drills, cultivated between, beautifully clean, very large in the bulb even now, and apparently having been sowed early in June, if not in May. They are generally the white globe turnip, here and there a field of the Swedish kind. These turnips are not fed off by sheep and followed by crops of barley and clover, as in the south, but are raised, I suppose, for the purpose of being carried in and used in the feeding of oxen, which have come off the grass lands in October and November. These turnip lands seem to take all the manure of the farm; and as the reader will perceive, they are merely an adjunct to the pasturage, serving during the winter instead of hay, wherewith to feed the cattle of various descriptions.

This, then, is not a country of farmers, but a country of graziers; a country of pasture, and not a country of the plough; and those who formerly managed the land here were not husbandmen, but herdsmen . . . The cattle here are the most beautiful by far that I ever saw. The sheep are very handsome; but the horned cattle are the prettiest creatures that my eyes ever beheld. My sons will recollect that when they were little boys I took them to see the 'Durham Ox', of which they drew the picture, I dare say, a hundred times. That was upon a large scale, to be sure, the model of all these beautiful cattle: short horns, straight back, a taper neck, very small in proportion where it joins on the small and handsome head, deep dewlap, small-boned in the legs, hoop-ribbed, square-hipped, tail slender. A great part of them are white, or are approaching very nearly to white: they all appear to be half fat, cows and oxen and all; and the meat from them is said to be, and I believe it, as fine as that from Lincolnshire, Herefordshire, Romney Marsh, or Pevensey Level, and I am ready, at any time, to swear, if need be, that one pound of it fed upon this grass is worth more, to me at least, than any ten pounds or twenty pounds fed upon oil-cake, or the stinking stuff of distilleries; aye, or even upon turnips. This is all *grass-land*, even from Staffordshire to this point. In its very nature it produces grass that fattens . . .

These Yorkshire and Durham cows are to be seen in great numbers in and about London, where they are used for the purpose of giving milk, of which I suppose they give great quantities; but it is always an observation that, if you have these cows, you must *keep them exceedingly well*; and this is very true; for upon the food which does very well for the common cows of Hampshire and Surrey they would dwindle away directly and be good for nothing at all; and these sheep, which are as beautiful as even imagination could make them, so round and so loaded with flesh, would actually perish upon those downs and in those folds where our innumerable flocks not only live but fatten so well, and with such facility are made to produce us such quantities of fine mutton and such bales of fine wool. There seems to be something in the soil and climate, and particularly in the soil, to create everywhere a sort of cattle and of sheep fitted to it . . .

I looked with particular care on the sides of the road all the way through Yorkshire and Durham. The distance, altogether, from Oldham in Lancashire to Newcastle upon Tyne, is about a hundred and fifty miles; and, leaving out the *great* towns, I did not see so many churches as are to be seen in any twenty miles of any of the valleys of Wiltshire. All these things prove that these are by nature counties of pasturage, and that they were formerly used solely for that purpose. It is curious that there are none of those lands here which we call 'meadows'. The rivers run in *deep beds*, and have generally very steep sides; no little rivulets and occasional overflowings that make the meadows in the south, which are so very beautiful, but the grass in which is not of the rich nature that the grass is in these counties in the north; it will produce milk enough, but it will not produce beef. It is hard to say which part of the country is the

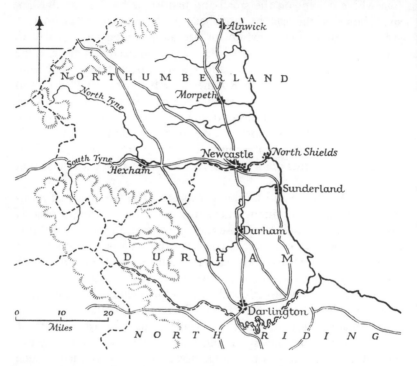

most valuable gift of God; but everyone must see how perverse and injurious it is to endeavour to produce in the one that which nature has intended to confine to the other. After all the unnatural efforts that have been made here to ape the farming of Norfolk and Suffolk, it is only *playing at farming*, as stupid and 'loyal' parents used to set their children *to play at soldiers during the last war* . . .

Hexham, 1 Oct. 1832.

I left Morpeth this morning pretty early to come to this town, which lies on the banks of the Tyne, at thirty-four miles distant from Morpeth, and at twenty distant from Newcastle. Morpeth is a great market-town, for cattle especially. It is a solid old town; but it has the disgrace of seeing an enormous new gaol rising up in it. From cathedrals and monasteries we are come to be proud of our gaols, which are built in the grandest style, and seemingly as if to imitate the Gothic architecture.

From Morpeth to within about four miles of Hexham the land is but very indifferent; the farms of an enormous extent. I saw in one place more than a hundred corn-stacks in one yard, each having from six to seven Surrey wagon-loads of sheaves in a stack; and not another house to be seen within a mile or two of the farm-house. There appears to be no such thing as barns, but merely a place to take in a stack at a time, and thrash it out by a machine. The country seems to be almost wholly destitute of people. Immense tracks of corn-land, but neither cottages nor churches. There is here and there a spot of good land, just as in the deep valleys that I crossed; but, generally speaking, the country is poor; and its bleakness is proved by the almost total absence of the oak-tree, of which we see scarcely one all the way from Morpeth to Hexham. Very few trees of any sort, except in the bottom of the warm valleys; what there are, are chiefly the *ash*, which is a very hardy tree, and will live and thrive where the *oak* will not grow at all, which is very curious, seeeing that it comes out into leaf so late in the spring, and sheds its foliage so early in the fall. The trees which stand next in point of hardiness are the *sycamore*, the *beech*, and the *birch*, which are all seen here; but none of them fine. The *ash* is the most common tree, and even it flinches upon the hills, which it never does in the south. It has generally become yellow in the leaf already; and many of the trees are now bare of leaf before any frost has made its appearance.

The cattle all along here are of a coarse kind; the cows sway-backed and badly shaped; Kiloe oxen, except in the dips of good land by the sides of the bourns which I crossed. Nevertheless, even here, the fields of turnips of both sorts are very fine. Great pains seem to be taken in raising the crops of these turnips: they are cultivated in rows, are kept exceedingly clean, and they are carried in as winter food for all the animals of the farm, the horses excepted.

As I approached Hexham, which, as the reader knows, was formerly the seat of a famous abbey, and the scene of a not less famous battle,* and was indeed at one time the *see* of a bishop, and which has now churches of great antiquity and cathedral-like architecture; as I approached this town, along a valley down which runs a small river that soon after empties itself into the Tyne, the land

* The Battle of Hexham, fought in 1464, was a victory for the Yorkists over the Lancastrians during the Wars of the Roses.

became good, the ash-trees more lofty, and green as in June; the other trees proportionably large and fine; and when I got down into the vale of Hexham itself, there I found the *oak-tree*, certain proof of a milder atmosphere; for the *oak*, though amongst the hardest *woods*, is amongst the tenderest of plants known as the natives of our country. Here everything assumes a different appearance. The Tyne, the southern and northern branches of which meet a few miles above Hexham, runs close by this ancient and celebrated town, all round which the ground rises gradually away towards the hills, crowned here and there with the remains of those castles which were formerly found necessary for the defence of this rich and valuable valley, which, from tip of hill to tip of hill, varies, perhaps, from four to seven miles wide, and which contains as fine corn-fields as those of Wiltshire, and fields of turnips, of both kinds, the largest, finest, and best cultivated that my eyes ever beheld. As a proof of the goodness of the land and the mildness of the climate here, there is, in the grounds of the gentleman who had the kindness to receive and to entertain me (and that in a manner which will prevent me from ever forgetting either him or his most amiable wife); there is, standing in his ground, *about an acre of my corn*, which will ripen perfectly well; and in the same grounds, which, together with the kitchen-garden and all the appurtenances belonging to a house, and the house itself, are laid out, arranged and contrived in a manner so judicious, and to me so original, as to render them objects of great interest, though in general I set very little value on the things which appertain merely to the enjoyments of the rich . . .

North Shields, 2 Oct. 1832.

These sides of the Tyne are very fine: corn-fields, woods, pastures, villages; a church every four miles, or thereabouts; cows and sheep beautiful; oak-trees, though none very large; and, in short, a fertile and beautiful country, wanting only the gardens and the vine-covered cottages that so beautify the counties in the south and the west. All the buildings are of stone. Here are coal-works and railways every now and then. The working people seem to be very well off; their dwellings solid and clean, and their furniture good; but the little gardens and orchards are wanting. The farms are all large; and the people who work on them either live in the farm-house, or in build-ings appertaining to the farm-house; and they are all well fed, and have no temptation to acts like those which sprang up out of the ill-treatment of the labourers in the south. Besides, the mere country people are so few in number, the state of society is altogether so different, that a man that has lived here all his life-time can form no judgement at all with regard to the situation, the wants, and the treatment of the working people in the counties of the south.

They have begun to make a railway from Carlisle to Newcastle; and I saw them at work at it as I came along . . .

Alnwick, 7 Oct. 1832.

From Sunderland I came early in the morning of the 5th of October once more (and I hope not for the last time) to Newcastle, there to lecture on the paper-money, which I did in the evening . . .

From Newcastle to Morpeth the country is what I before described it to be. From Morpeth to this place (Alnwick), the country, generally speaking, is very poor as to land, scarcely any trees at all; the farms enormously extensive; only two churches, I think, in the whole of twenty miles; scarcely anything worthy of the name of a tree, and not one single dwelling having the appearance of a labourer's house. Here appears neither hedging nor ditching; no such thing as a sheep-fold or a hurdle to be seen; the cattle and sheep very few in number; the farm servants living in the farm-houses, and very few of them; the thrashing done by machinery and horses; a country without people. This is a pretty country to take a minister from to govern the south of England! A pretty country to take a Lord Chancellor from to prattle about *Poor Laws* and about *surplus population*! My Lord Grey has, in fact, spent his life here, and Brougham has spent his life in the Inns of Court, or in the botheration of speculative books. How should either of them know anything about the eastern, southern, or western counties? . . .

They tell me that Lord Howick,* who is just married by the by, made a speech here the other day, during which he said, 'that the Reform was only the means to an end; and that the end was cheap government'. Good! stand to that, my lord, and, as you are now married, pray let the country fellows and girls marry too: let us have *cheap government*, and I warrant you that there will be room for us all, and plenty for us to eat and drink. It is the drones, and not the bees, that are too numerous; it is the vermin who live upon the taxes, and not those who work to raise them, that we want to get rid of. We are keeping fifty thousand tax-gatherers to breed gentlemen and

* The son and heir to Lord Grey, the Whig Prime Minister.

ladies for the industrious and laborious to keep. These are the opinions which I promulgate; and whatever your flatterers may say to the contrary, and whatever *feelosofical* stuff Brougham and his rabble of writers may put forth, these opinions of mine will finally prevail. I repeat my anxious wish (I would call it a hope if I could), that your father's resolution may be equal to his sense, and that he will do that which is demanded by the right which the people have to insist upon measures to restore the greatness and happiness of the country; and, if he show a disposition to do this, I should deem myself the most criminal of all mankind, if I were to make use of any influence that I possess to render his undertaking more difficult than it naturally must be; but if he show not that disposition, it will be my bounden duty to endeavour to drive him from the possession of power; for, be the consequences to individuals what they may, the greatness, the freedom, and the happiness of England must be restored.

[*Rural Rides* II, 277–98]

The Life of WILLIAM-COBBETT, — written by himself —
—" Now you lying Varlets you shall see how a plain Tale will put you down!"

1st Plate.

Father kept the sign of the Jolly-Farmer at Farnham. I was his Pot-Boy and thought an Ornament to the profession, — at Seven Years Old my natural genius began to expand and display'd itself in a taste for Plunder and oppresion. — I robbed Orchards, set Father's Bull-Dog at the Cats. — quarelled with all the Poor-Boys, and beat all the little Girls of the Town. — to the great admiration of the inhabitants; — who prophecied that my talents (unless the Devil was in it,) would one day elevate me to a Post in some publick-situation. —

Vide My own Memoirs
in the Political Register of 1809.

London Pub.d Sep.r 29, 1809. by H. Humphrey St James's Street.

The Life of WILLIAM·COBBETT. _written by himself._

London Published Sept 29 1809 by H. Humphrey 27 St James's

2ᵈ Plate.

as I shot up into a hobble-dehoy, I took to driving the Plow for the benefit of mankind, which was always my prime object; — hearing that the Church-Wardens were after me, I determined to become a Hero, and secretly quitting my agricultural pursuits, and Sukey Stubbs, — Volunteered as a Private-Soldier, into the 51st Regiment, commanded by that tried Patriot and Martyre Lord Edwᵈ Fitzgerald, — and embarked for the Plantations.

Vide my own Memoires
in the Political Register for 18..

The Life of WILLIAM-COBBETT, — written by himself.

London Publish'd September 9, by H. Humphrey 27 S.t James's Street.

3.d Plate.

arrived in safety (according to the proverb), being a Scholard, (for all
the world knows that I can Read and Write,) I was promoted to the
rank of a Corporal, and soon after appointed to teach the Officers
their duty — found them all so damnably stupid, that 'though I
took the pains to draw up my instructions on Cards, I could not
with all my Caning and Kicking, drive one manual movement
into their thick heads!

_ NB: These Cards were so much admired by Gen.l Dundas, that he made them the foundation
of his New Military Systemn.

_ Vide: my Own Memoirs
in the Political Register of 1809 _

The Life of WILLIAM·COBBETT, —written by himself.

London. Published Sept 29.1809. by H. Humphrey 27 St James's Street.

4th. Plate.

— I was now made Sarjeant-Major and Clerk to the Regiment, and there being only One Man in it, besides myself, who could read, or keep himself sober, (viz — poor little Corporal-Bestland) I constituted him my Deputy; — being intrusted with the care of the Regimental-Books, the Corporal and myself (tho' both of us blastedly afraid of a pair of Bloody Shoulders,) — purloined, and Copied by night such Documents as promised to be serviceable in the great National Object which I had in view; — namely, to Disorganize the Army, preparatory to the Revolutionizing it altogether! ——

—— Vide — my Own Memoirs in the Political Register of 1809.

The Life of WILLIAM COBBETT,... written by himself.

London Published Sept.r 29.th 1809 by H. Humphrey 27 St James's Street

5.th Plate ——

—— my next step was to procure a Discharge from my ever lamented associate the Lord Edw.d Fitzgerald: with this I returned to England, and directly set about writing "the Soldier's Friend", which I nightly dropt about the Horse Guards; and drank "Damnation to the House of Brunswick!" more over I wrote 27 Letters to my Royal Master, to Mr Pitt and the Judge Advocate, against my Officers, 23 of which Letters were stolen by the public-Robbers, and never came to hand, — so that I had no means of obtaining Credit for my Charges, & procuring a Court Martial but by solemnly Pledging my precious Soul to the Devil in the presence of Judge Gould for the Truth of my alegations, and my ability to support them by evidence !!! ——

Vide my own Memoirs in the Political Register 1809 ——

N.º 6.

Tell William Cobbett, to come into Court, to make good his charge

William Cobbett! William Cobbett!

The Life of WILLIAM COBBETT ... written by himself.

Plate 6.ᵗʰ

— the Court-Martial was assembled at Chelsea as I requested, and
Captⁿ Powell and the other accused Persons were placed at the Bar: —
— when — blast-my-Eyes! — I saw, the whole of that damnd 51ˢᵗ Regiment
Drummers, Fifers and all, marching boldly into the Hall to bear Testi-
-mony against Me!! — on this, I instantly ran to a boat which I had
Providentially secured, and crossed the Thames. ————
— damnd infernal-Ideots! — did the Judge Advocate and his Gang
of Publick Robbers think that I would stay to witness my own
Exposure and condemnation?

— Vide, my own Memoirs
in the Political Register — 1809

"Gillray inv! & fec!" The Life of WILLIAM·COBBETT, _ written by himself.

London Published Sept 27 1809 by H. Humphrey 27 St James's Street

Plate 7.th

I did not look behind me till I got to S.t Omers _ & thence fl. to America; here, I offerd to become a Spy for the English Government, which was scornfully rejected; _ I then turned to Plunder & Libel the Yankees, for which I was Fined 5000 Dollars & kicked out of the Country! _ I came back to England, after absconding for Seven years, & set up the Crown & Mitre, to establish my Loyalty; accepted from the Doctor £4000, to print & disperse a pamflet against 'the Hell fire yell of Reform' _ but applied the Money to purchase an estate at Botley, & left y.e Doctor to pay the Paper & Printing! _ being now Lord of the Manor, I began by sowing the Seeds of discontent through Hampshire, I opposed the Poor, sent the Aged to Hell, & damn'd the Eyes of my Parish Apprentices before they were open'd in the morning! _ & being now supported by a band of Reformers, I renewed my old favourite Toast of 'Damnation to the House of Brunswick!' & exalted by the sale of 10000 Political Registers every week, I find myself the greatest Man in the World! _ except that Idol of all my Adorations, his Royal & Imperial Majesty, NAPOLEONE!

See my own Memoires in my Political Register 1809

The Life of WILLIAM·COBBETT, written by himself.

London Printed by G. Humphrey, Sep.ʳ 14 1809 – N.º 27 S.ᵗ James's Street

Plate 8.ᵗʰ

*but alas, in the midst of my towering prospects, while I was yet hesitating between
a Radical Reform and a Revolution, & doubtful whether to assume the Character of Old-Noll or
Jack Cade, — down came my Political Register, & the shriek of my visionary greatness vanished.
my Schemes for my Country's good perish'd by the blaze of my own Candles! — The Ghost! —
— slid! ? — Lord forgive me for swearing! — the Ghost of Cap.ᵗ Powell utter'd a scream of Joy —
little Jesse's brandy-faced-bitch of a Mother — Lord pardon me! — called out for Justice! —
the Bats and Harpies of Revolution hid their heads in the gloom of night, — and to compleat
the horrible Scene, the rigid Paumbroker of Hell, Old-Beelzebub, enter'd and demanded his
property, the Forfiet Soul, which I had pledged! — Lord have mercy upon me! —
— Our Father! — to the Truth of my accusation's! — oh Loh! — oh! — Hell-Flames.*

——— Vide My own Memoirs
in the Political Register 1809